THE NEW KEY TO
COSTA RICA

Beatrice Blake
Anne Becher

Publications in English S.A.
San José, Costa Rica

Updated, revised and expanded 9th edition, copyright 1990 by Beatrice Blake

Cover and illustrations: Deirdre Hyde
Maps: Huberth Monge
Drawings, p. 83-85: Anabel Maffioli
Proofreading: Lucinda Tosi

Published and distributed by:

Publications in English
Apdo. 7-1230, 1000 San José, Costa Rica
Tel: (506) 34-3789, fax: (506) 34-0978

Distributed outside Costa Rica by:

Bookpeople
Berkeley, CA, USA
(800) 277-1516
(800) 624-4466 in CA

Inland Book Company
East Haven, CT, USA
(800) 243-0138
(203) 468-0589 in CT or Canada

ITMB Publishing, Ltd.
Vancouver, BC, Canada
(604) 687-3320
Fax: (604) 687-5925

Distributions Ulysse
Montreal, QC, Canada
(514) 843-9447

Bradt Publications
Chalfont St. Peter, Bucks., England
02407 3478, fax: 734 509262

For
peace with justice
in harmony with nature

ACKNOWLEDGEMENTS

Each year brings many changes to tourism in Costa Rica. Interesting new projects develop, but at the same time the dilemmas involved become more challenging. I want to thank all the people who are thinking and working hard to make sure that tourism does not run rampant over the very environment and native cultures which attract people to Costa Rica in the first place. My dear friends Paula Palmer, Bob Mack and Sergio León are constantly involved in this struggle, as well as Juanita Sánchez and Gloria Mayorga of the Cocles Reserve, Francisco Sotocruz, Anabel Maffioli and Carlos Coles of Arbofilia, Rita Alfaro of the Fundación Neotrópica, and the members of the Monteverde Conservation League, to name just a few. The ecological and social awareness of Anne Becher set the course for this book when we rewrote it together three years ago. Even though life has taken her and her husband Joe Richie all the way from Costa Rica to Maine to Argentina and back to Colorado, her thoughts and suggestions are still a vital part of the *Key*.

Deirdre Hyde is another fighter for environmental issues and uses her wonderful artistic talent to bring those issues to life. We are proud and happy to have her delightful cover and illustrations. Jerry Ruhlow is just as avid about saving Costa Rica's sportfishing resources, and we are honored to have his contribution to the fishing section. Hubert Monge's beautiful maps again grace our book. Many thanks to Sara Blanchette for her patient and generous advice about word-processing, to Rafa Vargas for his expert computer typesetting, to Lucinda Tosi for her alert proofreading and, as always, to Alvaro Gómez for his direction in all the details of production.

I am always grateful to readers who take the time to write with suggestions, recommendations and new information, so here's an official thank you to Marguerite and Horace Godshall of Pennsylvania, Bob Murdoch of Florida, Prof. Bruce Loeffler of Colorado College, and Prof. Mark A. Davis of Macalester College in Minnesota. And many thanks to all the people who have helped me get to know their areas better--José Miguel García of Turrialba, Anita Myketuk and Don Melton of Manuel Antonio, Alvaro Wiessel and Randall García of Guanacaste, Leona Wellington of Sarapiquí, and Dr. Luís Diego Gómez of Wilson Gardens near San Vito.

None of my research would have been possible without the partnership of my husband, Dennis Moran, and the sweetness of our son, Danny. Essential also are the constant, loving support of my assistant, Adita Molina, and our dear neighbors, Martina Alvarez Gutiérrez and family.

And deepest love and gratitude go to the strong, generous and joyful spirit of my mother, Jean Wallace, who started the original version of the *Key* in 1978, in honor of this special little country in which she finally found her home.

Beatrice Blake
September 1989

TABLE OF CONTENTS

COSTA RICA
DISARMED DEMOCRACY

Costa Ricans are increasingly aware of the importance of their way of life in a world that is racked by violence and fear. They are intensely proud of their democracy and of their tradition of non-violence. Even former combatants in the 1948 civil war are not regarded as heroes, and do not speak of the glory of war.

Historically, Costa Rica has almost always remained uninvolved in the conflicts that have shaken her sister republics. John L. Stephens, a North American archaeologist who visited in 1840, mentioned even then that Costa Rica was in island of tranquility compared to the rest of Central America. Although the national character tends to ignore or imagine itself above the problems of Central America, Costa Rica's new leadership had taken a decisive and responsible role in waging peace.

Costa Rica acted progressively long before that was the general trend. The early abolition of slavery during the colonial period, the establishment of free, obligatory, tax-financed education in the constitution of 1869, the elimination of the death penalty in 1882, and the abolition of the army in 1948, all testify to Costa Rica's unique character and vision, and all laid the groundwork for the present social order.

Indigenous peoples here never allowed themselves to be dominated by the Spanish colonizers, so Costa Rica didn't develop the class divisions that exist to this day in other Latin American countries. Its poverty and isolation, plus the predominance of the small farmer, led to independence of spirit and

11

thought. The development of the educational and electoral systems during the late 1800's provided the basis for a participatory democracy. By the end of the 19th century, political violence began to decrease and the budget of the police force began to exceed that of the army. When the victorious forces of the 1948 civil war decided to constitutionally abolish the army, a *de facto* situation that had been developing from the beginning of the century was legally ratified.

Costa Ricans see the abolition of the army as having several functions: it impedes the formation of a professional military group capable of gaining autonomy; it makes it possible for public funds to be used for development; it legitimizes the electoral path as the only route to power; it establishes Costa Rica's neutrality in the region--a country which is militarily weak cannot be attacked without provoking international condemnation of the aggressor; it shows the illegitimacy of any armed opposition to a state which has openly renounced the use of force.

Costa Ricans view the military as an encumbrance to their political and social life as well as to the public budget. They prefer to be free to dedicate their energies to creating social justice, which they see as the foundation of internal and international peace. Thus they channel 27% of their national resources to education and culture. Because of their nationalized medical and social security systems, Costa Rican health is on a par with that of industrialized nations. The Interamerican Human Rights Court and the United Nations University for Peace both have their headquarters here. In an attempt to ensure the well-being of future generations, 27% of Costa Rica's territory is legally set aside as national parks, biological reserves, forest reserves and buffer zones, wildlife refuges and Indian reserves. Having the budget to actually guarantee the protection of these areas is another matter.

At the same time that Costa Rica pursues her goals of social justice and ecological balance, she is fighting an uphill battle against her tremendous foreign debt. The International Monetary Fund demands austerity from a government whose bureaucracy employs 20% of the workforce. The developed countries pump in millions of dollars of aid, but much of it has to be used to service the same foreign debt. Even though Costa Rica is economically dependent on the United States, she is clear about maintaining her own point of view and her close relationships with European and Latin American social democracies. She recognizes the US as the dominant superpower of the region, and an important ally and friend. The United States has a positive image for most Costa Ricans, but that does not mean that they will let the US change their way of doing things.

Costa Ricans have seen a 1000% devaluation of their currency since 1980. A respectable middle-range salary is still under US$300 per month, and the national average is about $175 per month. Doctors, teachers and other government workers demand higher salaries and pensions from a budget that is stretched to its limits.

Despite all this, Ticos, rich and poor, actively support their democracy. On election day they honk horns, wave party flags, dress up in party colors, and proudly display their index fingers dipped in purple indelible ink to show they have voted. Whether or not their candidate wins, they will tell you, "The most important thing is that we voted, and that our elections were free and fair". The Communist parties, which have played an important role in Costa Rican history, won less than 3% of the vote in the last election.

Even with the enthusiasm that turns their election day into a national fiesta, Costa Ricans are skeptical about politics and politicians. Their roots are still in the soil and in the unity of their families. Babies are the acknowledged rulers of the household. Rarely does one see a crying child or a screaming parent. Young men and women often walk with a loving arm around their mothers. Mothers' Day is one of the biggest national holidays. Grandparents, too, are often part of the family group. The strong family that made it possible for early poverty-stricken farmers to survive is perhaps still the real basis of Costa Rican stability.

At the same time, women are a solid 50% of the workforce, and are rapidly increasing their numbers as doctors, lawyers and government officials. Dr. Victoria Garrón became the first woman Vice-President of the Republic in 1986, and Dr. Rosemary Karpinski the first woman president of the Legislative Assembly.

Costa Ricans' love for the beauty and freedom of their country is almost palpable. At 6:00 pm each September 14, the eve of their Independence Day, everyone drops what they are doing to sing the national anthem. People get out of their cars in the middle of the street, busloads of people stand up and sing, and in corner stores and homes across the country, everyone joins in. It's a rousing hymn in tribute to peace, hard work, and the generosity of the earth, but it also warns that if these things are threatened, Costa Ricans will "convert their rough farming tools into arms", as they did when William Walker tried to invade in the 19th century.

Despite this last part of the national anthem, Costa Rica's commitment to peace is very real. Watching their valiant struggle to preserve their ideals on a planet still accustomed to violence is inspiring. After having lived through a generation without an army, they can confidently declare to the world that armed self-defense is not the only way to resolve conflicts. As President Oscar Arias said when he learned he had become a Nobel Laureate, "The prize is for Costa Rica."

This country's incredible natural beauty is matched by her spirit. We hope that this book will enable to enjoy and appreciate both.

Beatrice Blake
Anne Becher
September, 1989

HISTORY

PRECOLUMBIAN COSTA RICA

The largest and most developed precolumbian population in Costa Rica was that of the Chorotegas, whose ancestors had migrated from Southern Mexico to the Nicoya Peninsula, probably in the thirteenth century. They were running away from enemies who wanted to enslave them; their name translates as "fleeing people."

Much of the information we have about the Chorotegas was collected by Gonzalo Fernández de Oviedo, a Spanish explorer who lived with them for a short period in 1529.

Outstanding farmers, they obtained three harvests of corn per year. They also grew cotton, beans, fruits, and cacao, which they introduced to Costa Rica. They used cacao seeds as currency. Land was communally owned and the harvest was divided according to need, so that old people and widows with children could be cared for. They lived in cities of up to 20,000 people. The towns had central plazas with a marketplace and a religious center; only women could enter the market. Women wore skirts, the length of which depended upon their social level. Men could go naked but often wore a large cloth or a woven and dyed sleeveless cotton shirt.

Women worked in ceramics, producing vessels painted in black and red, decorated with plumed serpents (the symbol for unity of matter and spirit), jaguars, monkeys, and crocodiles. They carved stylized jade figures in human and animal shapes. The figures could have been used in fertility ceremonies or to bring good luck in the hunt. They wrote books on deerskin parchment, and used a ritual calendar.

War was institutionalized. There was a permanent military organization that fought to obtain land and slaves. Slaves were used as human sacrifices. Eating someone who had been sacrificed to the gods was a purification rite. The Chorotegas would also sacrifice virgins by throwing them into volcano craters.

The Chibcha Indians from Colombia migrated to the South Pacific part of Costa Rica. They lived in permanent, well-fortified towns. Their concern with security could have arisen from their possession of gold--they fashioned it into human and animal figures (especially turtles, armadillos and sharks). Both women and men fought for the best lands and for prisoners, whom they used as slaves or human sacrifices. They believed in life after death; vultures eating corpses performed a vital role in transporting people to the other world.

These people probably made the granite spheres that lie in linear formations in the valley of the Río Térraba and on the Isla del Caño off the coast of the Península de Osa. They range in diameter from 7.5 centimeters (the size of an orange) to 1.8 meters. Their almost perfect sphericity and careful placement make their meaning one of Costa Rica's precolumbian mysteries.

Indians from the jungles of Brazil and Ecuador migrated to the lowland jungles of the Costa Rican Atlantic Coast. They lived semi-nomadically, hunting, fishing and cultivating *yuca, pejibaye,* pumpkin and squash. Their chief's nobility was hereditary, passed down through the female line of the family.

Social prestige was gained by good warriors. Apparently, decapitated heads of enemies were war trophies. Their stone figurines represent warriors with a knife in one hand and a head in the other.

They worshipped the sun, the moon and the bones of their ancestors. All things had souls. During religious festivals there was a ritual inebriation with a fermented *chicha* made from *yuca* or *pejibaye.* The burial mounds of these people have yielded the greatest number of precolumbian artifacts in the country.

COLONIAL COSTA RICA

On September 18, 1502, during his fourth and last voyage to the New World, Christopher Columbus anchored in the Bay of Cariari (now Limón), after a violent tempest wrecked his ships. During the 17 days that he and his crew were resting and making repairs, they visited a few coastal Indian villages. The

Indians treated them well and they left with the impression that *Veragua* (a name that Columbus used for the Caribbean Coast between Honduras and Panamá) was a land rich in gold, whose gentle and friendly Indians could be easily conquered.

A few years later, in 1506, King Ferdinand of Spain sent a governor to colonize Veragua. Governor Diego de Nicuesa and his colonizers received a different welcome. First, their ship went aground on the coast of Panamá, and they had to walk up the Atlantic shore. Food shortages and tropical diseases reduced the group by half. Then they met the Indians, who burned crops rather than feed the invaders. The Spanish realized that their task was not going to be easy. There was no centralized Indian empire to conquer and sack, and the scattered tribes were at home in a climate and terrain that the explorers found devastating. This first attempt at colonization was a miserable failure.

After Vásco Núñez de Balboa discovered the Pacific Ocean in 1513, the Spaniards started exploring the west coast of Veragua. In 1522, an exploratory land expedition set out from northern Panamá. Despite sickness, starvation and tropical weather, the survivors of the long, hazardous trip called it a success: they had obtained gold and pearls and their priest claimed he had converted over 30,000 Indians to Catholicism between Panamá and Nicaragua.

More explorers and would-be colonizers arrived. There were attempted settlements on both coasts, but they ended in tragedy for the settlers who died of hunger, were driven out by the Indians or fought among themselves and dissolved their communities.

Juan Vásquez de Coronado arrived as Governor in 1562. He found a group of Spaniards and Spanish-Indian *mestizos* living inland from the Pacific coast. Coronado explored Costa Rica, treating the Indians he met more humanely than had his predecessors. He decided that the highlands were more suitable for settlement, so he moved the settlers to the Cartago Valley where the climate was pleasant and the soils were rich from the lava deposited by Volcán Irazú. In 1563, Cartago was established as the capital of Costa Rica.

In contrast to the pattern in most Spanish colonies, there was no large exploitable workforce in Costa Rica. The Indian population was decimated early on by war and disease. At one point even the governor was forced to work his own small plot of land to survive.

Costa Rica's Spanish population remained small and their lifestyle humble through the seventeenth century. In 1709, Spanish money became so scarce that settlers used *cacao* beans as currency, just like the Chorotegas. Women wore goat hair skirts; soldiers had no uniforms. Volcán Irazú erupted in 1723, almost destroying Cartago. Nevertheless, they survived, and the area settled by Spaniards actually grew through the 1700's. Three new cities were founded in the Meseta Central: Cubujuquí (Heredia) in 1706, Villanueva de la Boca del Monte (San José) in 1737 and Villa Hermosa (Alajuela) in 1782.

Costa Rica had no riches and was difficult to reach from Guatemala, the seat of Spain's Central American empire, so it was left free from foreign intrusion into its affairs. Forgotten by its "mother country", Costa Rica was almost self-sufficient in its poverty.

INDEPENDENCE

In October 1821, word arrived from Guatemala that on September 15, Spain had granted independence to its American colonies. It had taken the news one month to travel through the mountains and valleys to Costa Rica. After a period of internal strife, Costa Rica declared itself a state in the short-lived Federal Republic of Central America.

The first president of Free Costa Rica, Juan Mora Fernández, built roads, schools, and gave land grants to anyone who would plant coffee. By the mid-1800's, coffee was Costa Rica's principal export, and coffee growers were a powerful and wealthy elite.

A society of coffee growers built a road to transport coffee from the Meseta Central to Costa Rica's port, Puntarenas. They exported first to Chile, then later to Germany and England. By mid-century, European money was entering the pockets of Costa Rican coffee-growers, and Europeans were arriving en masse on this tropical frontier. Costa Rica was becoming cosmopolitan. A university had been founded in 1844 to disseminate European thinking. Costa Rican politicians sported European liberal ideologies.

By 1848 the coffee elite was influential enough to elect its own representative for President. Juan Rafael Mora was a self-made man who had become one of the most powerful coffee growers in the country. He was charismatic, astute, and respected by the coffee elite and the *campesinos* alike. He became a veritable national hero by leading an "army" of Costa Ricans to defend his country when it was invaded by one of the most detested figures in Central American history, the North American William Walker.

THE SAGA OF WILLIAM WALKER

A study of William Walker's early life gives one little indication of how this man came to be the scourge of Central America. Walker was graduated from the University of Nashville at the age of 14, and by the time he was 19, he held both a law and a medical degree from the University of Pennsylvania. He followed this memorable academic record with two years of post-graduate study in Paris and Heidelberg.

His success stopped there, however. Returning from Europe, Walker quickly failed as a doctor, lawyer and journalist. He had in ill-fated courtship with a beautiful deaf-mute New Orleans socialite, then in 1849 turned up as a gold miner in California. He didn't fare well in this occupation either, and soon started working as a hack writer in several California cities.

At this point, something happened in the mind of William Walker, and he launched himself into a career as a soldier of fortune. From then on, he succeeded in creating chaos wherever he took his five-foot, three-inch, one-hundred-pound frame.

In the early 1850's, Walker sailed with several hundred men on a "liberating expedition" to the Baja California peninsula and Mexico. The expedition was financed by the Knights of the Golden Circle, a movement bent on promoting the "benefits" of slavery. Walker spent a year in Mexico during which time he awarded himself the military title of Colonel and proclaimed himself "President of Sonora and Baja California."

Back in the United States after several encounters with the Mexican army, he was arrested for breaking the Neutrality Act of 1818. His acquittal of the charge gained him fame and willing followers. His next expedition was to Nicaragua.

Walker went with two main goals. One was to convert Central America into slave territory and annex it to the southern USA, the other was to conquer Nicaragua and ready it for the construction of a trans-isthmic canal. The new riches that were being discovered in California attracted a lot of Easterners, but crossing the United States by land was slow and difficult.

Walker had made contacts with a group of economically power-ful North Americans who thought that a sea route could be more efficient and profitable. Southern Nicaragua would be a perfect site for the isthmus crossing; ships could sail up the San Juan River that formed the Nicaragua-Costa Rica border, cross Lake Nicaragua, and then pass through a to-be-built 18-mile canal from the lake to the Pacific.

His contacts arranged for an invitation to Walker from the Liberal Party of Nicaragua, which was embattled with the Con-servatives. In June, 1855, he landed in Nicaragua with 58 men. After losing his first encounter with the Conservatives, Walker held out until several hundred reinforcements arrived from Cali-fornia, bringing new model carbines and six-shooters. They soon overpowered the Conservatives, and after an "open" election, Walker became "President of the Republic of Nicaragua".

Central Americans from throughout the isthmus rose to fight Walker and his band of *filibusteros*. In February, 1856, Presi-dent Juan Rafael Mora of Costa Rica declared war on Walker, but not on Nicaragua. Mora raised an army of 9000 in less than a week. This "army", led by the President and his brother-in-law José María Cañas, was composed of *campesinos,* merchants and government bureaucrats ill-dressed for combat, armed with farm tools, *machetes* and old rifles. They marched for two weeks to Guanacaste. Three hundred filibusters were resting at the Santa Rosa hacienda (now a national monument in Santa Rosa National Park), after they had invaded Costa Rica, prepar-ing to conquer San José. The Costa Rican army, by then di-minished to 2500 men, attacked the filibusters, who fled back to Nicaragua after 14 minutes of battle.

Two thousand Costa Ricans followed Walker up to Nicara-gua and, in a generally masterful campaign, fought him to a standstill. The turning point was in Rivas, Nicaragua. Walker and his band were barricaded in a large wood building from which they could not be dislodged. Juan Santamaría, a drummer boy, volunteered to set fire to the building and succeeded in forcing Walker's retreat. In his action, Juan lost his life, and became Costa Rica's national hero.

Walker's attempt to convert Nicaragua and the rest of Cen-tral America into slave territory was backed by US President James Buchanan, and his failure angered the President. When Walker confiscated the trans-isthmic transportation concession that US financier Cornelius Vanderbilt had already started in-

La Casona, scene of Walker's defeat

stalling, Vanderbilt began to finance some of Walker's enemies. This was the beginning of the end of Walker's career.

After another engagement in late 1856 on Lake Nicaragua where the Costa Rican army brilliantly cut Walker off from his support troops, the rag-tag *filibustero* forces were near defeat. The first of May, 1857, Walker surrendered to a US warship.

The adventurer traveled to Nicaragua again in late 1857, but he was taken prisoner before he could wreak any havoc. When he was released in 1860, he sailed to Honduras, where upon landing he seized the custom house. This brought a British warship to the scene, on board of which Walker, pursued by the Hondurans, eventually took refuge. Offered safe conduct into US hands by the British commander, Walker insisted he was the rightful president of Honduras. The British therefore put him ashore again, and Walker was taken by the Hondurans and promptly shot.

The net result of Walker's Central American marauding was the death of some 20,000 men. The inscription on William Walker's tombstone reads, "Glory to the patriots who freed Central America of such a bloody pirate! Curses to those who brought him and to those who helped him."

Juan Rafael Mora is now acclaimed for having saved Central America from Walker and the imperialist interests he represented, but he wasn't so popular when he returned from battle. People accused Mora of having been too ambitious and blamed him for an epidemic of cholera that infected Costa Rican soldiers in Nicaragua and spread to kill almost 10 percent of the Costa Rican population.

Mora manipulated the 1859 election to win over massive opposition. In August 1859, his enemies overthrew him. A year later, Mora led a coup d'etat against the new president, also a

21

member of the coffee elite. His attempt failed; he was shot by a firing squad in 1860--an inglorious end for a man who is now a national hero. Through the 1860's quarrels among the coffee growers put presidents in power and later deposed them. Nevertheless, most presidents during these years were civilians with liberal and intellectual characters. Despite the political instability of the decade, the country established a well-based educational system. New schools were founded, European professors were brought to design academic programs, and the first bookstores in San José opened their doors.

THE ATLANTIC RAILROAD AND UNITED FRUIT

By the mid-1800's, Costa Rica realized it needed an Atlantic Port to facilitate coffee export to Europe. When Tomás Guardia declared himself Chief of State in 1871, he decided to build a railway to Limón. He contracted Henry Meiggs, a North American who had built railways in Chile and Perú. Meiggs went to England to secure loans for the project. He obtained 3,400,000 sterling pounds, of which only 1,000,000 actually arrived. These loans caused the first foreign debt in Costa Rica's history.

Costa Rica's population wasn't large enough to provide the project with the necessary labor force, so thousands of Jamaican, Italian, and Chinese workers were recruited. After an optimistic start, it soon became evident that it was going to be a slow, dangerous, and costly process. Construction of the railroad claimed some 4000 workers' lives, cost the equivalent of eight million dollars, and lasted 19 years. The jungle proved itself a formidable and deadly barrier.

Meiggs' nephew, Minor C. Keith, became the director a few years after the project started. The railroad he inherited was constantly beleaguered by severe shortages of funds, so he started experimenting with banana production and exportation as a way to help finance the project. When he realized that the banana business could yield very profitable results, Keith made a deal with the new president, Bernardo Soto, in 1884. In return for a grant from the Costa Rican government of 800,000 acres of untilled land along the tracks, tax-free for 20 years, and a 99-year lease on the railroad, Keith would renegotiate the project's pending debts to England, and complete construction at his own expense.

By 1886, Keith had settled the financial problems with England. He spent the next four years laying the last 52 miles of track that climbed through the steep, treacherous valley of the Reventazón river. Relations between Keith and the labor force weren't good. In 1888 Italian workers organized the first strike in Costa Rica's history, demanding prompt payments. and sanitary working and living conditions.

The railroad was completed in 1890. Until 1970 it was the only route from the Meseta Central to Limón. And it is still the only major means of transportation for many people who live in the tiny towns it passes. Children take the train to school; it serves as an ambulance for the sick and as a hearse for the dead.

After they finished the railway, many Italian workers settled in Costa Rica's highlands. Chinese workers settled in various parts of the country. The Jamaicans stayed on the Atlantic Coast and started working on the banana plantations which Minor Keith established on his 800,000 free acres. The development of banana plantations where there had been jungles forced the Indians to move up into the mountains.

In 1899, Keith and a partner founded the United Fruit Company. *La Yunai,* as it was called, quickly became a legendary social, economic, political and agricultural force in many Latin American countries. Costa Rican author Carlos Luis Fallas describes work conditions on the steamy plantations in his book *Mamita Yunai,* and Gabriel García Márquez tells what it did to the imaginary town of Macondo in *One Hundred Years of Solitude.* Although Costa Rica was the smallest country where United worked, United possessed more land here than in any other country. Costa Rica became the world's leading banana producer.

The year 1907 was United's peak year in Costa Rica, but by 1913 it was facing serious problems. Panamá disease had infected banana trees; United's employees began protesting unfair working conditions. A 1913 strike was broken by the Costa Rican government--two strike leaders were chased into the plantations and killed.

The Company initiated a new policy: it would lease company land to independent growers and buy bananas from them. Tensions with workers grew; a 1934 strike led by two young San José communists, Manuel Mora and Jaime Cerdas, finally brought better working and living conditions. They maintained

23

the original demands of 1913, and added to the list regular payment of salaries, free housing, medical clinics on plantations and accident insurance. United wouldn't talk with the strikers, but the planters leasing land from United did, and convinced United to sign an agreement.

In the late 30's a new disease, Sigatoka, infected banana trees up and down the coast. In 1938 United started to pick up and move west to the Pacific lowlands.

United lasted as long as it did on the Atlantic Coast only because it possessed so much land. Banana trees deplete soil of its humus and nitrogen. The clay soils of rainforest areas compact easily when the jungle is cut and they are cultivated. Since the soil could last only five to eight years, United used a plot of land until it didn't produce anymore, and then would move on to virgin land.

Minor Keith ended up a very wealthy man who married the daughter of one of the presidents of Costa Rica. Most profits from the banana industry went to the foreign owners of the production, shipping and distribution networks that made export possible.

LIBERALISM ARRIVES IN COSTA RICA

The 1880's saw an increasing split between a traditional, conservative church and a liberalizing state. The bishop of Costa Rica criticized the European ideas that were becoming popular with the elite and the politicians. The bishop was expelled from the country in 1884, and in 1885 there was an official denouncement of an earlier church-state concord that declared Catholicism the state religion. Public outcry at the government's treatment of the church was minimal.

The first truly democratic election characterized by real public participation was in 1889. Liberals saw it as the fruit of their efforts to educate and raise democratic consciousness in the people. In fact, their efforts worked so well that the public gave their overwhelming support to the liberals' opposition. Supporters of the liberals threatened not to recognize the new president, so 10,000 armed opposition members flooded the streets of San José. The liberals then demonstrated their firm commitment to democracy by recognizing the new, rightfully elected president.

Costa Rica's democratic tradition has endured until today with only a few exceptions. One was in 1917, when the Minister of War and the Navy, Federico Tinoco, overthrew an unpopular president. Tinoco's brutal and repressive dictatorship lasted through 30 months of widespread opposition. Finally Tinoco fled the country. A provisional president held office for a year until normality was reached, and Costa Rica resumed its democratic tradition with a fair presidential election.

ROOTS OF THE 1948 CIVIL WAR

Rafael Angel Calderón Guardia was the legally-elected president between 1940-44. A profoundly religious Catholic, Calderón's political ideology was Social Christian. One of his first actions was to reinstate religious education in public schools. Another was to found the University of Costa Rica. He initiated many social reforms which still exist today, including social security, workers' rights to organize, land reform, guaranteed minimum wage and collective bargaining. These reforms earned Calderón the adoration of the poor and the opposition of the upper classes.

Calderón ran a puppet candidate, Teodoro Picado, in the 1944 election. Picado won, but the election was widely criticized as fraudulent. Young, middle-class intellectuals, as well as traditionally anti-communist Costa Ricans distrustful of church-state involvement resented Calderón's grasping for power and criticized the odd alliance he had made with Catholic Archbishop Monseñor Víctor Sanabria and Manuel Mora of the Communist Party.

Farmers, businessmen, *campesinos,* liberal labor unions, and young intellectuals organized against Calderón. Calderón's allies were the government, the Church, the communist labor unions and the army.

In the 1948 election, Calderón ran against Otilio Ulate, who represented the unified opposition. Ulate won the election by a small margin, but the government demanded a recount. Disagreement was complicated by a fire that destroyed half the ballots the day after the election. Government forces refused to yield the power to Ulate. Teodoro Picado remained in power.

Pepe Figueres, a coffee grower and outspoken opponent of Calderón who had been exiled in Mexico, had returned to Costa

Rica before the elections. On March 12, 1948, he and his men captured the airport at San Isidro de El General. Foreign arms were airlifted in quickly, due to Figueres' advance planning. Armed groups, trained by Guatemalan military advisors, were formed throughout the country. President Picado declared a state of siege, using borrowed Nicaraguan soldiers and mobilized banana workers from the communist unions. They were unaccustomed to the cool climate of San José, and wore blankets over their shoulders, Mexican style, to keep warm. For this reason, Calderón supporters were called *mariachis*. After 40 days of civil war, during which more than 2000 people died, a negotiated treaty was signed. Picado stepped down and Figueres took over as provisional president.

Figueres governed for 18 months, long enough to draft a new constitution. Prohibition of presidential re-election, illegalization of communist parties and labor unions, abolition of the army, the right to vote for women and blacks, and the establishment of a neutral body that would oversee elections, were some of the new constitutional laws. Banks and insurance companies were nationalized, and 10 percent of all bank funds were seized for reconstruction. All of Calderón's social reforms were maintained. In 1949, Figueres turned the country over to Ulate, the rightful president.

Costa Rica elected Figueres president twice, in 1954 and 1970. "Don Pepe" remains one of Costa Rica's most beloved elder statesmen. In recent years of international tension, his wise voice has been strong in calling for tolerance and peace.

SINCE 1948

The 1948 revolutionaries formed the National Liberation Party (PLN). Almost without fail, Costa Ricans have alternated their presidents--one from the PLN, the next from the opposition. There have been only two exceptions to this pattern, both when a PLN candidate succeeded a very popular PLN president.

The opposition is an odd coalition of wealthy business owners who see the PLN's social democratic direction as harmful to their interests, and poor people who generally side with the party that is out of power. The poor still remember the name of Rafael Angel Calderón Guardia, and have an undying faith that if his son, Rafael Angel Calderón Fournier, becomes president, their situation will improve. This faith is the Costa

Rican equivalent of *caudillismo*, a Latin American tradition of almost religious belief in a strong leader, exemplified by Argentina's Perón. For this reason, even though he has lost twice in a row, Rafael Angel Calderón (known to his opponents as "Junior") is leading the ticket of the opposition Unidad party for the third time, hoping to win the elections in February 1990.

Nicaragua has been an important political issue in Costa Rica during the past several years. In 1978 and 1979, under President Rodrigo Carazo, northern Costa Rica served as a virtual base for Sandinista operations. The Sandinista's goals of democracy and social justice reminded Costa Ricans of their own 1948 "revolution". The Sandinista arms build-up and East Bloc aid to Nicaragua have since disillusioned many Costa Ricans, which led them to lend tacit support to the *contras* while they were operating out of Costa Rica, despite their government's official neutrality policy under PLN President Luís Alberto Monge.

Costa Rica elected a president in February 1986 from the younger generation of the PLN. Oscar Arias is an economist, lawyer and author of several books on the Costa Rican economy and power structure. His main campaign promise was to work for peace in Central America. The first part of his task was to enforce Costa Rica's declared neutrality policy, and to stand up to the United States and the politicians within his own party who were supporting contra activity within Costa Rica, such as the secret airstrip that figured in the Iran-Contra scandal.

As the world knows by now, Arias' untiring efforts to fulfill his promise won him the 1987 Nobel Peace Prize. While the peace process has met with skepticism and even ennui in the first world press, for many Central Americans it signifies a coming of age--a chance to unite and shape their future in a new way. Even though the process has been slower than scheduled, much more communication has taken place between warring factions than ever before, and bloodshed has lessened. The economic and social problems at the root of Central America's conflicts are deep, and require not just talk, but concerted action. Arias insists that this action can only occur in an atmosphere of peace. The world's eyes are on Central America as it tries to solve its problems through the Costa Rican example.

BIBLIOGRAPHY

American University, Foreign Area Studies. *Costa Rica. A Country Study*. Washington, DC, U.S. Government, 1981.

Casey Gasper, Jeffrey. *Limón 1880-1940*. San José, Editorial Costa Rica, 1979.

Jones, Clarence and Morrison, Paul. "Evolution of the Banana Industry in Costa Rica" in *Economic Geography,* January, 1952.

May, Stacy and Plaza, Galo. *The United Fruit Company in Latin America*. New York, National Planning Association, 1958.

Meléndez, Carlos. *Historia de Costa Rica*. San José, Editorial Universidad Estatal a Distancia, 1981.

Rodríguez Vega, Eugenio. *Biografía de Costa Rica*. San José, Editorial Costa Rica, 1980.

THE ECOLOGICAL PICTURE

Costa Rica is part of a land bridge between North and South America. Her geographical and climatic conditions make it possible for flora and fauna characteristic of both continents as well as the Antilles to co-exist, thus creating incredibly diverse ecosystems.

Costa Rica measures only 300 km (185 miles) across at her widest point, but four mountain ranges divide her like a backbone. Mount Chirripó, at 3820 m (12,500 feet), is the highest point in southern Central America. It is part of Costa Rica's oldest and southernmost mountain range, the Cordillera de Talamanca, which extends into Panamá. The Central Volcanic Range is made up of volcanoes Turrialba, Irazú, Barva and Poás. Over half of Costa Rica's 2,940,690 inhabitants live in the Central Valley, whose fertile soil was created by the activity of these volcanoes over the last two million years. To the northwest is the non-volcanic Tilarán range which reaches 1700 m (5500 feet) at Monteverde. Farthest northwest, towards the Nicaraguan border, is the Guanacaste Range which contains five active volcanoes including Rincón de la Vieja, Miravalles (now being used to generate geothermal energy), and Volcán Arenal. The most ancient rocks in the area, over 100 million years old, occur in the "Nicoya complex", low mountains which outcrop here and there along the Pacific.

Climate

Given its location between 8 and 12 degrees north of the Equator, day length and temperature do not change drastically with the seasons. The sun rises around 5 am and sets around 6 pm year-round. One experiences temperature difference by changing altitude. The misty highlands are in the 10-13°C (50-55°F) range, while the Central Valley, at 1200 m (3800 feet), averages 22°C (72°F). Sea level temperature is 26°C (80°F) tempered by sea breezes on the coast. Slight variations occur in December, January and February due to cold winds from the North American winter. These cooler temperatures bring on the dry season or "summer", as Central Americans call it, which lasts from December through April. Temperatures rise as the sun approaches a perpendicular position over Costa Rica. This causes increased evaporation and brings on the rainy season, or "winter", which lasts from May through November, except for a 2-week dry season, the *veranillo,* sometime in July (see p. 39).

The Atlantic coast is an exception to this rule. Tradewinds laden with moisture from the Caribbean approach Costa Rica from the northeast. As the moisture rises to the chilly heights of the Cordilleras, it condenses into rain on their eastern slopes. For this reason, there is no definite dry season in the Atlantic zone, but the beaches tend to be sunnier than the mountains. A similar phenomenon makes for heavier rainfall in the Osa Península area. Tradewinds from the southeast discharge their moisture against the mountains that separate the Osa from the rest of the country. The Atlantic plains and the Osa both receive 4000-7000 mm (150 to 300") of rain a year, compared to an average of 2500 mm (100") in the Central Valley.

Ecological zones

Costa Rica's 20,000 square-mile territory offers a great diversity of ecological zones, from sub-alpine dwarfed vegetation to rich rain forest, to beautiful tropical beaches. Cloud forests like the one at Monteverde are filled with plants which are specifically adapted to gather water and promote condensation and precipitation. These high, misty forests are responsible for Costa Rica's rich water resources. Augmenting the water-gathering function of the trees themselves are epiphytes, plants which live on trees in order to have growing space or to better reach the light. Unlike para-sites, epiphytes filter their own food from water, dust particles and organic matter accumulated around their roots. They add to the diversity of the forest by adapting themselves to conditions that are impossible for other plants. Costa Rica has 1100 different species of orchids, 95 percent of which are epiphytes. The 200 species of bromeliads, much

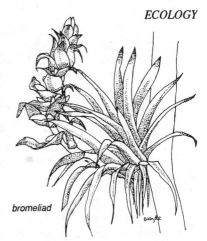

bromeliad

more commonly seen than orchids, are also epiphytes. Epiphytes, vines and the treetops create a canopy which maintains the humidity inside the forest and provides a home for many small animals which never touch the ground.

The dry tropical forests of Guanacaste like those in Santa Rosa National Park feature huge deciduous trees that burst into bloom at the beginning of the dry season. The scarlet *poró* tree, the orange-red flame-of-the-forest, the purple *jacaranda,* the pink and white meadow oak and the yellow *corteza amarilla* are like huge bouquets on the landscape. Other plants flower during the rainy season, thus keeping active a large number of different pollinating insects and birds.

Six species of mangroves exist in Costa Rica's Pacific salt-water swamps, forming a complex community with marine animals and plants.

The rain forests of the Pacific, like Corcovado National Park on the Osa Península, are some of the most complex ecological systems on the planet. They maintain similar species to those found in the Atlantic rain forests, and because of a short dry season, they also shelter some species common to dry forests.

Diversity and interrelationship

Its 850 bird species, more than there are in the entire North American continent, make this tiny country a birdwatchers' paradise. Keep your eyes open on a walk through any of Costa Rica's wild places, and you'll see the wonderful ways birds,

31

insects, frogs and reptiles have evolved to protect themselves. Some imitate leaves, flowers, and stems of plants; others are indistinguishable from rocks or tree bark. Other animals which are poisonous or taste very bad warn potential predators with their bright coloring (red, blue, metallic green). Some animals hide their brightly colored parts and only display them if attacked. One butterfly's outer wings resemble a dry leaf, but its underwings flash two huge, glinting cat eyes. Several butterflies have a disagreeable taste to birds. Other butterflies which taste good imitate the coloring of the bad-tasting butterflies to gain protection.

Costa Rica abounds in cases of highly specialized inter-species relationships, due to her complex ecosystems. In many cases, both participating species co-evolve by modifying themselves to meet the needs of the other. Many flowers are designed to attract only certain animals which complete their pollination process. Bright colors attract a pollinizing agent with a strong sense of sight, like hummingbirds. If the pollinizing agent has a stronger sense of smell, like flies and some butterflies, the flower will be fragrant. Some of the most fragrant flowers emit their scent only at night. They attract animals with nocturnal habits, like bats. The flower will be shaped to accommodate the part of the body that its pollinizer uses to carry pollen away (beak, wings, feet, etc).

You can now see a walk-through diorama of a Costa Rican rainforest at the Milwaukee Public Museum. The twelve thousand-square-foot exhibit, opened in November 1988, was five years in the making. It is the largest museum exhibit portraying the complexities of tropical biology anywhere in the world. Its underlying theme is interdependency among living creatures and how that mutual dependence enables life to cope with an evolving environment. At the same time it shows how human activity, especially deforestation, ignores our relationship with the rest of nature and threatens our survival, as well as destroying biological diversity.

Deforestation

The ecological relationships that are so fascinating to observe in Costa Rica are a lesson for human beings in how to live cooperatively with nature, rather than exploiting, exterminating, and controlling, as we do now. Despite the richness of its forests, Costa Rica takes second place in Latin America for percentage of deforested land. In 1950, 72 percent of Costa Rica was covered in forest. In 1973, it was 49 percent, in 1978, 34 percent, and in 1985, 26 percent. At this rate, Costa Rica's unprotected forests will be destroyed by the year 2000.

One sees evidence of deforestation constantly. Huge trucks piled with massive tree trunks rumble along the highways from Talamanca, Osa, and Sarapiquí, all areas recently opened to roads. A flight to Tortuguero will show you the facts--a thin border of rich tropical forest lines the shore, and inland, where "nobody" sees, the land is naked. Only a few tall trees remain from the forest that is disappearing every day. Part of the Guanacaste region has become a desert due to four centuries of cattle raising and slash-and-burn agriculture.

According to a 1987 study, the reasons for this destruction are the following:

Spontaneous, unplanned expansion of agricultural frontiers, often in response to foreign credit possibilities (in the 1960's millions of dollars in loans were given to Costa Ricans by the US to stimulate beef production); lumbering activity, which often destroys large areas of forest to extract certain profitable (and often endangered) species of trees, leaving the rest to rot; a population that doubled between 1950 and 1970; the concentration of the best agricultural lands into large properties, forcing campesinos to clear and work land on hillsides for subsistence; laws which defined clearing of forest for agriculture as proof that the land was being "improved", a requisite for obtaining land titles; and lack of government ability to enforce deforestation laws.

The cattle raising encouraged by banks during the sixties and subsequent conversion of large tracts of forest to erosion-prone pasture have had particularly harmful ecological effects. Raising cattle requires less work and is less labor-intensive than agriculture, but a farmer can make 86 times as much money per acre with coffee, and 284 times as much with bananas. Yet, 23 times the amount of land used to grow coffee and bananas is devoted to cattle. It has been estimated that Costa Rica loses 2.5 tons of topsoil to erosion for every kilo of meat exported. Much of this meat ends up as hamburgers in North American fast-food restaurants.

As a consequence of this deforestation, Costa Rica faces not only erosion, but flooding, long-term hydroelectric shortages, sedimentation in canals and rivers, destruction of beautiful coral reefs from silt, climatic destabilization, loss of forest wildlife and valuable wood resources, loss of genetic reserves of incalculable value, scarcity of drinking water in some areas during the dry season and, of course, loss of natural beauty.

Tripled reforestation efforts, encouraged by government tax incentives, planted about 16,000 acres of trees in 1988. Most reforestation is directed toward planting fast-growing trees that can be sold in a few years for lumber or firewood. Although this form of reforestation is extremely valid and useful, it is important to understand that rain or cloud forest and the habitats they support cannot be reproduced by simple reforestation. Hundreds of years are needed to regenerate an ecologically viable rain forest. Very little effort is being made to replace the precious hardwoods found in natural rain forest, because investors would have to wait generations to reap the profits.

How to help

Despite this bleak picture, many people are working to reverse this situation, and visitors who admire Costa Rica's beauty are important collaborators in these efforts.

One of the most interesting groups is **Arbofilia**, a grass-roots organization in which Costa Rican tree-lovers are helping *campesinos* reforest one of the most environmentally degraded areas of the country. Biologists provide high quality seedlings and voluntary expertise in grafting, planting and greenhouse management. In return for the trees and the technical assistance, the *campesinos* provide voluntary work and make a *"compromiso con la naturaleza"* (commitment to nature), by vowing not to cut trees by water sources, not to burn fields (still a common practice in Costa Rica) and not to hunt endangered birds or animals. The group likes to use the term "ecological regeneration" rather than "reforestation" because they only plant native species and try to observe the patterns in which trees are found in nature. Jungle Trails (55-3486), a nature-tour company, takes visitors on a one-day trip to the Puriscal region, southwest of San Jose, to see Arbofilia in action. The tour fee includes the cost of a seedling which visitors can plant. You can contact Arbofilia at 36-7145, or make tax-deductible donations to them through:

The Audubon Society of Portland
5151 NW Cornell Rd.
Portland, OR 97210
(503) 29-6855

With the aid of international conservation groups like the Nature Conservancy and World Wildlife Fund, Costa Ricans have formed two sister foundations to address environmental issues. The **Fundación de Parques Nacionales** promotes management, protection and development of the national parks and reserves. **Fundación Neotrópica** promotes conservation and sustainable development of forests, wildlife, and soil and water resources in general. Both foundations are involved in environmental education and are developing programs in non-destructive land use, eco-tourism, coastal zone management, eco-agriculture and scientific research applied to conservation.

Their **Conservation Data Center** compiles and generates information on endangered species, providing scientific support for national planning and management. **Editorial Heliconia** publishes books, posters, postcards, slides, and T-shirts with ecological themes. British artist Deirdre Hyde's beautiful posters of the flora and fauna of the parks are published by Heliconia, and are favorite souvenirs ($7 each incl. postage). They also publish a bilingual photographic guide in paperback to the parks by Mario Boza, one of the founders of the park system ($12 incl. postage), a larger, beautifully done coffee-table version (Boza, *Costa Rica National Parks,* 1988, 271pp., hardback, $45 incl. postage) and a map showing park locations with photos ($8 incl. postage). All these books are much less expensive when purchased from Heliconia in San José (55-2984).

Their **Environmental Education Department** fosters national awareness of conservation and sustained development. Their publication *Socioeconomic Development and the Environment in Costa Rica* analyzes policy alternatives and defines national environmental issues. The **Lands Program** does the legal work involved in acquiring park lands. Much of the territory which has been designated as national parks and reserves is still unpaid for, and thus could revert back to private ownership. Donations are matched with endowment funds in Costa Rican government bonds through debt-for-nature swaps. The Foundations encourage international membership. Write or call:

Fundación de Parques Nacionales
Fundación Neotrópica
Apdo. 236
1002 San José, CR
(506)33-0003

The **Organization for Tropical Studies**, the **Tropical Science Center** and the **Monteverde Conservation League** are active in research, training, environmental education and stewardship of the forest and wildlife reserves they maintain in La Selva and Monteverde.

Tropical Science Center
Apdo. 8-3870
San José, CR
(506)22-6241

Orgaization for Tropical Studies
Apdo. 676, San Pedro
2050 San José CR
(506) 36-6696

Monteverde Conservation League
Apdo. 10165
1000 San José, CR
(506) 61-2953

US tax-deductible donations can be made to support the efforts of any of the above groups through the following organizations:

Costa Rica Program
World Wildlife Fund
1250 24th St NW
Washington, DC 20037, USA

Costa Rica Program
Conservation International
1015 18th St NW
Washington, DC 20036
USA

Costa Rica Program
The Nature Conservancy
International Program
1785 Massachusetts Ave NW
Washington, DC 20036, USA

Bibliography:

Bonilla, Alexander. *Costa Rica: La Típica Situación Ambiental de un País en Proceso de Desarrollo.* Bogotá, XV Congreso Interamericano de Planificación, 1985.

Ramírez, Alonso and Maldonado, Tirso. *Desarrollo Socioeconómico y el Ambiente Natural de Costa Rica: Situación Actual y Perspectivas.* San José, Fundación Neotrópica, 1988.

Valerio, Carlos E. *Anotaciones sobre la Historia Natural de Costa Rica.* San José, Editorial Universidad Estatal a Distancia, 1980.

hermit
hummingbird
and heliconia

PLANNING YOUR TRIP

NOTE: All information in this book is valid as of August 1989.

Weather and Clothing: One of the most surprising things for newcomers to San José is that it's not as warm as they thought it would be. The truly hot months are at the end of the dry season, March and April. December, January, and February are usually rain-free, but the weather can be downright chilly, especially at night or if a wind is blowing. During the rainy season, May to November, the days usually start out warm and sunny and cloud over by noon. The downpour usually starts around 2 or 3 pm and it can get pretty cold then, too. Usually a sweater and long pants are enough to keep you warm.

If you go down in altitude from San José's 3800 feet, you'll be able to wear the kind of clothes you hoped you could wear in the tropics. Just don't expect to be comfortable in shorts in San José. Culturally, too, shorts are not acceptable in the city, except for sports use. Costa Ricans are well-known for their appreciation of nice clothes and good grooming.

When it rains, it really *rains,* but afternoon downpours are usually short-lived. In San José during the rainy season, people usually carry umbrellas--brightly colored *sombrillas* for women and black *paraguas* for men. In the mountains, a lightweight rain poncho is usually more convenient. You'll be glad to have high rubber boots if you go hiking in the rain forest, especially in Corcovado or Sarapiquí. You can buy good ones here for under $7 at provincial supply stores. Bring boots with you from home only if you wear an especially large size.

Bring at least three changes of lightweight cotton or cotton-mix clothing when you go to the beach or rainforest, protected inside a plastic bag in case of sudden downpours. Even if you are going to the steamy lowlands, you often have to pass through high mountains to get there--Cerro de la Muerte on the way to the Osa, Braulio Carrillo or Vara Blanca on the way to Sarapiquí. You'll be happier if you have a zippered sweatshirt, long pants, and socks that can be peeled off as you get to lower altitudes. The sweatshirt also makes a good pillow for long bus trips.

Many hotels will let you store excess luggage while you adventure off. I can usually fit everything I need for a trip to the country in a day-pack. I start out in a bathing suit, jeans, a cotton overshirt, socks and running shoes. In addition, I bring 2 bathing suits or leotards, 2 pairs of lightweight pants, extra socks, 2 long T-shirts (one to sleep in), flip-flops, the zippered sweatshirt, and a scarf, as well as insect repellent, sulphur powder, a flashlight, a book, an umbrella or rain poncho, a towel and toilet paper. If you are going to Irazú, Poás, Chirripó or other high altitudes, you'll need a jacket on top of a thick sweater and warm socks.

When to come: Tourist season is Christmas through Easter, which corresponds to the dry season. You can almost depend on clear, sunny weather, but there are occasional unseasonal storms from the north, which can last for days. The rainy season usually takes awhile to get started in May, and often diminishes for a couple of weeks in July, a time called *el veranillo de San Juan,* "the little summer". The rains dwindle down in November.

There are certain advantages to coming during the off-season: The mornings are almost invariably clear and warm. The scenery is fresher and greener. The days are cooled by the rains, which for some people is a blessing, especially at the beach. The clouds usually clear in time for a magnificent sunset. Many hotels offer substantial discounts during the off-season, up to 50%. All places are less crowded, more peaceful. Less harm is done to the ecosystems in the parks when fewer people come trooping through at one time.

Since Costa Rica's tourist infrastructure is struggling to keep up with increased demand, many hotels are completely booked during the dry season, even small backpacker hotels and *pen-*

siones. This can add a bit of tension and disappointment to a "let's just explore and see what happens" kind of vacation. So be warned--during the dry season, plan way ahead.

What to bring: Things that are not made in Costa Rica are sold with a 100% import tax, and therefore are much more expensive here than elsewhere. Following is a list of items that are imported or impossible to find. Bring them with you. If you plan to stay in low-cost hotels, see also p. 110.

Film and camera equipment
Cassette tapes
Binoculars
Pocket alarm clock or watch
Pocket calculator
Swiss army knife
Good walking shoes
Insect repellent
Sulphur powder (sprinkle on socks to deter chiggers)
Sunscreen
Anti-itch ointment
Water purifying device
Small first aid kit
Contact lens solution
Diaphragms and diaphragm jelly
Vitamins

Customs: Tourists are permitted to bring two cameras, binoculars, and electrical items that are for personal use only, like a small radio, a hair dryer, etc. Personal computers, electric typewriters and other appliances are sometimes held in customs and taxed. To avoid that, you must prove that what you are bringing is for personal use. The items in question will be noted in your passport and you must have them in your possession when you leave the country. Check with the consulate nearest you for latest regulations.

Traveling expenses: Costa Rica is not as inexpensive for travelers as are México and other Central American countries. Although public transportation is cheap, restaurant and hotel prices are relatively high, but variable. If you are determined to spend as little money as possible, it is good to bring a tent and visit during the dry season, or visit during the rainy season and take advantage of the off-season rates. You can also find clean and decent rooms with shared baths for under $10 almost anywhere. Meals cost between $2 and $6 depending on the "atmosphere". Groceries cost about 2/3 as much as they do in the United States. Two people can travel for about $20/day each, including bus transport, comfortable lodging (double occupancy) and restaurant meals. If you go to the cheapest places, you can get by for $12-15 each. Camping out is cheaper still, except for the inconvenience of hauling around equipment and leaving your tent guarded at all times.

Airlines serving Costa Rica: Usually the cheapest and most direct flights to Costa Rica are through Miami. LACSA is Costa Rica's international airline. It is known for its almost accident-free record, and for jolly Costa Rica-bound flights where everyone gets tipsy on free wine or wired on Costa Rican coffee, and returning Ticos applaud as the plane touches down. LACSA's toll-free number in the US is 1-800-225-2272. In Canada it's 800-663-2344; England: 01499-6731; Japan: 445-48-74; Taiwan: 02-704-94-38.

Following are the airlines serving Costa Rica, their different ports of embarkation, and the stops they make on their way to San José:

Miami: Nonstop: LACSA, Eastern, PanAm.

With stops: SAHSA (via Belize, San Pedro Sula, Tegucigalpa), TACA (via Belize and San Salvador). PanAm and Eastern of course have connections to all the following cities, but their flights are always routed through Miami.

New Orleans: LACSA (via Cancún and San Pedro Sula), SAHSA (via Belize, San Pedro Sula, Tegucigalpa), TACA (via Belize and San Salvador).

New York: LACSA (via Guatemala and San Pedro Sula).

Houston: SAHSA (via Belize, San Pedro Sula, Tegucigalpa); TACA (via Belize and San Salvador).

Los Angeles: LACSA (via San Salvador and Mexico City); Mexicana (via Mexico City and Guatemala); TACA (via Guatemala and San Salvador).

San Francisco: TACA (via Guatemala and San Salvador).

Mexico City: Aeronica (via Guatemala and Managua), LACSA (via San Salvador or Guatemala), Mexicana (via Guatemala).

Europe: KLM (via Curacao and Aruba); Iberia (via Puerto Rico and Dominican Republic).

For information on **low-cost flights** to Costa Rica contact the above airlines, or:

González Travel	Americas Tours and Travel
4508 Academy Dr.	1218 Third Ave. Suite 2207
Metairie, LA 70003	Seattle, WA 98101-3058
(504) 885-4058	(206) 623-8850, Fx: 467-0454
Fx: (504) 443-4737	1-800-553-2513

Charter flights: Canadians have been flocking to Costa Rica because of the availability of charter flights. **Fiesta Wayfarer Holidays** in Toronto (416) 498-5566, and **Fiesta West** in Vancouver (604) 688-1102, charter planes from those cities year-round. The Montreal offices of **Go Travel** (514) 735-4526) charter planes to San José December through April. Tourists have the option of staying one, two, or three weeks.

Senior Citizens: Elderhostel, which sponsors cheap and interesting trips for people over 60 years of age, now includes Costa Rica in their itinerary. Find out more by writing them at 80 Boyleston St., Suite 400, Boston, MA 02116.

Cruises: Many cruise ships stop in Costa Rica. Ask your travel agent about them.

Entry requirements: Citizens of the United States and most Latin American countries can obtain a 30-day tourist card (US$2) from the airline issuing them a ticket. They must enter the country with at least $400 and a departure ticket. It is wise to have a passport. Citizens of Canada and almost all the European countries can stay for 90 days with a tourist card. Citizens of some Latin American, Asian, African and East European countries must obtain a visa from a Costa Rican consulate and pay a deposit upon entering the country, refundable when they leave. Check with the consulate nearest you for latest information.

Exit and extended visas: All tourists must pay an airport tax of $5 when they leave.

42

In addition to the airport tax, **if you overstay your 30 or 90-day visa, you will need an exit visa in order to leave the country**. An exit visa is good for 30 days from the date it is issued, so it is an automatic 30-day extension of your visa. If you do not use your exit visa within 30 days, you must buy a new one.

Get a Pensión Alimenticia stamp (\$.60) at the Tribunales de Justicia (c 17, a 6/8), which proves you are leaving no dependent children in the country. Take the stamp, your passport and your ticket out of the country to Migración on c 21, a 6/8 (open til 3:30pm). If you leave by air, an exit visa costs about \$12. If you leave by land, the exit visa costs about \$40. Allow at least 48 hours for processing of exit visas. They cannot be processed on weekends or holidays (see p. 55).

If you have stayed over 30 days when you apply for your exit visa, you will be charged \$4 for each month or part of a month that you were here without a valid tourist card.

If you wish to **extend your tourist visa**, you can request an extension of 30 to 60 days from the Departamento de Extranjeros at the Migración. At that time you must present three passport pictures, a ticket out of the country, and the results of a blood test that prove you do not have AIDS. The blood test is given at the Ministry of Health (c 16, a 6/8, open 7:30am-4pm) and takes 4 working days to process. You should also be prepared to show that you have at least US\$400 per month of extension (i.e., \$800 for 60 days). This money must be presented in the form of travelers checks or local bank statements in your name. Presenting the money in cash is not acceptable (you can have dollar accounts here). You can also present a notarized letter from a Costa Rican willing to guarantee your stay economically.

You will be required to leave your passport for a few days at Migración while your request is being processed. They will give you a receipt for it which is valid identification, but you should xerox the important pages of your passport (including date of entry) before you turn it in. A minimal fee is charged for each month of extension.

Children of any nationality who stay in Costa Rica for more than 30 days are automatically subject to Costa Rican laws which require that both parents request permission from the child welfare organization (Patronato Nacional de la Infancia) to take the child out of the country. Thus, if a child travels with a guardian or only one parent, written permission to travel from the other parent (notarized by a Costa Rican consul in the country of origin) must be presented to the Patronato in order for the child to leave Costa Rica. They are quite serious about this. Two passport photos of the child must accompany the Patronato exit request form, as well as the child's passport.

If you stay for more than 90 days, you must get a statement from the Ministerio de Hacienda, Departamento de Tributación Directa, proving that you do not owe taxes.

After you've gotten your exit visa and are ready to leave, be sure to **confirm your departure flight** 72 hours in advance.

You must get to the airport at least two hours ahead of flight time. Flights are often overbooked. The overflow from an 8am flight might be sent on a 10am flight, causing connection problems.

For further travel information, contact:

Costa Rican Tourist Board
1101 Brickell Ave.
B.I.V. Tower, Suite 801
Miami, FL 33131
Tel: 1-800-327-7033
(305) 358-2150 (within FL)
Fx: (305) 358-7951

Costa Rican Tourist Board
3540 Wilshire Blvd.
Los Angeles, CA 90010
Tel: 1-800-762-5909
1-800-762-5900 (within CA)
Fx: (213) 380-9326

Instituto Costarricense de Turismo
Apdo. 777
San José, CR
Tel: (506) 22-1090

SPECIAL WAYS
TO VISIT COSTA RICA

Nature Tours

The following agencies organize tours for nature lovers and birdwatchers. Bilingual naturalists accompany small groups into parks and reserves, and arrange for food, lodging and transportation, which are all included in the trip price. Costa Rica-based groups will arrange jaunts for groups of two to ten people, once you are here.

Costa Rica-based companies:

Horizontes
Apdo. 4025, a 1, c 1/3
San José, CR
(506) 22-2022
Nature tours to all locations as well as bicycle and hiking tours.

Geotur
Apdo. 469 Y Griega
1011 San José, CR
(506) 34-1867
Wildlife observation in Carara Biological Reserve, and Santa Rosa, Cahuita, and Braulio Carrillo National Parks

Interviajes
Apdo. 296
Heredia 3000, CR
(506) 38-1212
Low-cost tours to many locations

Tikal Tours
Apdo. 6398
1000 San José, CR
(506) 23-2811
Fx: (506) 23-1916
All locations

Costa Rica Expeditions
Apartado 6941
San José, CR
(506) 22-0333
All locations, specializes in white water rafting and Tortuguero.

Cosmos Tours
Apdo. 298, a 9, c 1/3
1000 San José, CR
(506) 33-3466

Jungle Trails
Apdo. 5941
1000 San José, CR
(506) 55-3486
Fx: (506) 55-2782
Camping, hiking, birdwatching
and tree-planting trips.

Finca Ob-La-Di, Ob-La-Da
Villa Colón, CR
(506) 49-1179
Horseback tours near
Villa Colón and Orotina

Costa Rica Sun Tours
Apdo. 1195
1250 Escazú, CR
(506) 55-3518, 55-3418
Fx: (506) 55-4410
To all locations, specializes
in Pavones and Arenal

US-based nature tour companies: (arranged by state):

Borderland Productions
922 E. 8th St.
Tucson, AZ 85710
(602) 882-7650,

Wings
PO Box 31930
Tucson, AZ 85751
(602) 749-1967
Fx: (602) 749-3175

Baja Expeditions
2625 Garnet
San Diego, CA 92109
(1-800) 843-6967
(619) 581-3311
Fx: (619) 581-6542

Betchart Expeditions
21601 Stevens Creek Blvd.
Cupertino, CA 95014
(408) 252-4910
(800) 252-4910
Fx: (408) 252-1444

Costa Rica Connection
958 Higuera St.
San Luis Obispo, CA 93401
(805) 543-8823
(800) 345-7422
Fx: (805) 543-3626

Extraordinary Expeditions
1793 Vía Rancho
San Lorenzo, CA 94580
(415) 276-1569

Forum Travel
91 Gregory Lane, Suite 21
Pleasant Hill, CA 94523
(415) 671- 2900, fx: 946-1500

Geo Expeditions
3237 Mono Way
Sonora, CA 95370
(209) 523-0152
(1-800) 351-5041

Natural History Tours
PO Box 1089
Lake Helen, FL 32744-1089
(904) 228-3356

Overseas Adventure Travel
349 Broadway
Cambridge, MA 02139
(617) 876-0533
(800) 221-0814
Fx: (617) 876-0455

Voyagers International
PO Box 915
Ithaca, NY 14851
(607) 257-3091
Fx: (607) 257-3699

Halintours
P.O Box 49705
Austin, TX 78765
(512) 499-0237

Americas Tour and Travel
1218 3rd Ave, Suite 2207
Seattle, WA 98101-3058
(206) 623-8850
(1-800) 553-2513
Fx: (206) 467-0454

Journeys, Inc.
904 W. Highland Dr.
Seattle, WA 98119
(206) 284-8890

Wildland Journeys
3516 NE 155th
Seattle, WA 98115
(1-800) 345-4453
(206) 365-0686

LANGUAGE LEARNING VACATIONS

Many people like the idea of learning Spanish on their Costa Rica vacation. There are many excellent language schools here, offering a variety of experiences. **Conversa** (see below) has a new lodge overlooking the beautiful Santa Ana valley with live-in instructors so that families and individuals can enjoy life in rural Costa Rica while studying. **Centro Lingüístico Latinoamericano** trains participants in international service programs as well as tourists. **Instituto de Lengua Española** is primarily for missionaries, but accepts other students when space is available. It is one of the most intensive and least expensive schools. The **Centro Cultural** sponsors many plays and concerts by Costa Rican and US performers. They also have a large, English-language library. Students must pass through security as they enter. **ILISA** offers courses incorporating specialized vocabulary in areas such as medicine, law, finance, tourism, agriculture, politics and culture, depending on students' needs (see p. 52 for info on their course in Central American History). Most schools arrange for students to live with Costa Rican families to immerse themselves in the language. They also set up weekend sightseeing trips for participants. Class size is 2 to 5 students. Intensive conversa-

47

tional methods are used for 4 to 6 hours a day in programs lasting one week to several months. Students are placed according to ability. All language schools assist their students in extending their tourist visas.

American Institute for
Language and Culture
Apdo. 200
1001 San José, CR
(506) 25-4313

Centro Cultural
Costarricense-Norteamericano
Apdo. 1489
San José, CR
(506) 25-9433

Centro Lingüístico Conversa
Apdo. 17 Centro Colón
San José, CR
(506) 21-7649, 33-2418

Centro Linguístico
Latinoamericano
Apdo. 151
Alajuela, CR
(506) 41-0261

Forester Instituto
Internacional
Apdo. 6945
1001 San José, CR
(506) 25-3155, fx: 25-9236

Instituto de Lengua
Española
Apdo. 100
2350 San José, CR
(506) 26-9222

Instituto Universal
Apdo. 219
2120 San José, CR
(506) 57-0441

Intensa
Apdo. 8110
San José, CR
(506) 25-6009

ILISA (Instituto Latinoamericano
de Idiomas)
Apdo. 1001
2050 San Pedro, CR
(506) 25-2495
Fx: (506) 25-9090
In US: (818) 843-1226

Central American Institute
for International Affairs
School of Languages
3540 Wilshire Blvd.
Los Angeles, CA 90010
(213) 383-1218
(506) 55-0859

STUDY PROGRAMS

Spanish, Latin American Culture, Politics, Economy, Literature, Tropical Biology, Ecology, International Relations, International Business--you can study nearly anything in Costa Rica.

There are several options for university-level students who want to spend a semester or a year here. All programs require advance planning, so start thinking about it early. Also, since there are two decidedly different seasons, choose your months according to your preferred weather.

Associated Colleges of the Midwest (ACM) is a competitive program run by and primarily for several private midwestern colleges. However, students at any accredited university or college can apply. The fall semester (September-December) offers an intensive course in Spanish and the social sciences (the topic of the course changes each year). Students can do research in an area of their particular interest. The spring semester (February-May) gives students an opportunity to do two months of field research in the social or physical sciences with some excellent professors. Students live with Costa Rican families. For information write:

> Associated Colleges of the Midwest
> 18 S. Michigan Ave, Suite 1010
> Chicago, IL 60603.

Friends World College maintains its Latin American Regional Center in San José. It focuses on understanding world problems through work and study in countries around the globe. Students in San José receive Spanish classes and design their own projects. They work in national ministries, with experimental agricultural projects, in rural communities, etc. Students receive credit based on a journal they maintain during their projects. For information write:

> Friends World College
> Plover Lane
> Huntington, NY 11743.

The **University of Kansas** runs a one, two, and three-semester study program that is open to students who are at least sophomores at any US college or university. Kansas students take full course loads at the University of Costa Rica (UCR) and live with Costa Rican families. The first semester group arrives for an orientation period in February, a month before UCR classes begin. The second semester group arrives in July and doesn't have an orientation. Kansas students like their program for the flexibility it offers them in choosing courses and for the contact they have with Costa Rican students. For more information, write:

> Office of Studies Abroad
> 204 Lippincott Hall
> University of Kansas
> Lawrence, KS 66045.

People who would like to enroll directly in the **University of Costa Rica** do so as "Special Students". All foreigners fall into this category for the first two years of their studies at the UCR. Admission fees are about double those for Costa Rican students, but the price is still quite low compared to US standards. There is also the option of being an *oyente* (auditing a class). The first semester runs March to June, the second July to December. The office is on the west side of campus, near the Oficina del Registro.

During the December-March break there is a series of *cursos libres* on many subjects. They are open to the public for a nominal registration fee. For more information contact:

> Oficina de Asuntos Internacionales
> Ciudad Universitaria Rodrigo Facio
> San José, Costa Rica
> 24-3660

The **University for Peace** is located on a beautiful tract of forested farmland in Villa Colón, southwest of San José. The goal of the University is to create pilot projects for peace studies programs in universities around the world. By exploring different aspects of peace education and the most effective methods of teaching them to cross-cultural groups, the University hopes to foment fundamental change in the orientation of university programs and to establish peace education in unions, churches and other community groups. Presently the University for Peace is offering two-year masters degree programs in Communications for Peace, Human Rights, and Ecology and Natural Resources. To request the University's bulletin write Apdo. 199, Escazú. To arrange a visit, call 49-1072.

The **Monteverde Institute** inaugurated its first courses in Tropical Biology and Ecology in March, 1987. Students do research at the cloud forest field station in the Monteverde Reserve. Spanish language study is included.

> Monteverde Institute
> Apdo. 10165
> San José, CR
> (506) 61-2550

The **Organization for Tropical Studies** is a consortium of universities and research institutions dedicated to education, investigation, and conservation in the tropics. They offer Tropical Biology: An Ecological Approach, a 2-month lecture/field experience course twice a year at their research stations in La Selva, Palo Verde, and Wilson Gardens, as well as several other courses. They also provide logistical support for dissertation research.

> OTS
> PO Box DM, Duke Station
> Durham, NC 27706
> (919) 684-5774
> In San José: 36-6696

The **Institute for Central American Development Studies** aims to stimulate critical evaluation of current development strategies, identifying and overcoming inherent "first-world" biases, and to search for alternative policies. They offer structured internships, in Costa Rica or Nicaragua, which help integrate theory with real-world experiences, and allow students to give something back to the host society through the projects on which they work. Courses include Spanish Grammar, Conversation and Culture, Women in Central America, Agriculture and Hunger in Central America, Ecological and Environmental Issues, and Multinationals and Foreign Investment.

> ICADS
> P. O. Box 145450
> Coral Gables, FL 33114
> In CR: (506) 25-0508

The **Central American Institute for International Affairs (ICAI)** gives students a chance to meet key decision makers and political thinkers in Central America from all sides of the spectrum in its course, Crisis in Central America--Issues and Perspectives on Peace. It also offers courses in Spanish (see p. 48), Central American Art (covering graphic arts, literature, music and folklore) and Education and Society in Costa Rica.

> ICAI
> Apdo. 3316
> San José, CR
> (506) 55-0859

ILISA offers an excellent course, in English, in Central American history, showing how the region's heritage exerts a decisive influence on today's crises. Besides seven fascinating lectures on the complex historical issues affecting the area, students have the opportunity to talk to Costa Rican, Nicaraguan and Salvadorean leaders.

> ILISA
> Apdo. 1001, San Pedro 2050
> San José, CR
> (506) 25-2495, fx: (506) 25-9090
> In US: (818) 843-1226

Mesoamerica (The Institute for Central American Studies) runs study tours to Nicaragua to promote a better understanding between U.S. citizens and the people of Central America. The tours help open eyes to the complexity of Central American issues. The 10-day tours include three days of orientation seminars in San José and six days in Nicaragua. Participants meet with high-level Sandinistas, opposition to the Sandinistas, journalists, Catholic Church hierarchy, academicians, etc. There are visits to an agricultural cooperative, historic sites, and local artisan markets.

For those interested in Central American politics, Mesoamerica is a great place to work as an intern. People who are willing to volunteer for at least 20 hours a week can read newspapers and journals, help maintain Mesoamerica's extensive clipping file, do research, and write articles for the monthly newsletter. College credit can be arranged. Write:

Mesoamerica
The Institute for Central American Studies
Apartado 300-1002
San José, Costa Rica.
(506) 27-9928

RETIREMENT SEMINARS

Jane Parker leads tours for those who want to investigate Costa Rica as a place to retire. Write:

Retirement Exploration Tours
P.O. Box 6487
Modesto, CA 95355
(209) 577-4081

GENERAL INFORMATION

Arrival and reservations: Costa Rica is becoming so popular that it is recommended that you call months ahead for reservations in the dry season. You can change money at the airport until 5 pm. Taxi service into San José is about $10 per taxi. A bus ($.20) goes into San José, but you can't take much baggage on it.

You might prefer to skip San José altogether and stay at the inexpensive **Hotel Alajuela** (41-1241), or the lovely mountain hotels, some of which offer airport pickup, like **Posada Pegasus** and **Pico Blanco** near Escazú (see p. 115), or **Chalet Tirol, El Pórtico, Cabañas Las Ardillas**, or **La Rosa Blanca** (see p. 128-9) above Heredia.

Currency: The currency unit is the *colón (¢)*. Bills come in denominations of ¢5 to ¢1000, and coins from 10 *céntimos* to ¢20. The current exchange rate is around ¢85 per US$1. After the *colón* was devaluated, the government also shrank the size of the coins, so you may be given change with both the older, larger and the newer, smaller coins.

It is illegal to exchange dollars for *colones* anywhere but in the national banks and in some hotels. If anyone offers to buy dollars from you on the street, be aware that you and he could be prosecuted for it. Costa Rica needs all the dollars it can get to pay off its external debt, so it is important for your dollars to go into national rather than private hands. Unless you are changing huge amounts of money, there is really very little economic advantage to exchanging on the black market. When you leave Costa Rica you will be able to change only a certain amount of *colones* back into dollars. Presently you can receive only up to $50 in cash. This amount may be subject to change.

Changing money: This is often a time-consuming process. Banks are open 9-3. There is always a special window for changing dollars. A branch of the Banco de Costa Rica (a 1, c 7) is open 8am to 6pm M-F. You can use a Visa or Mastercharge card to buy *colones* at the banks, otherwise travelers checks are acceptable. It is best to change money in San José before going to the provinces, and to carry small bills with you (not just 1000's) because everyone has a problem stocking enough change.

The larger hotels are authorized to change money and travelers checks for their guests. The Gran Hotel Costa Rica provides this service for non-customers too. This is much quicker than going to the bank but is subject to the fluctuations of their cash box. Ask the cashier at the reception desk.

Holidays: Costa Rica has 17 official holidays *(feriados)* per year, and they are taken quite seriously. Do not expect to find government offices, banks, professional offices and many stores open on *feriados*. Two times during the year, the whole country shuts down completely. These are Semana Santa (the week before Easter) and the week between Christmas and New Year's. Transportation stops totally Holy Thursday and Good Friday, making Wednesday's buses very crowded. Good Friday is the most important day of Holy Week in Costa Rica and is a day of mourning throughout the country.

Easter week is the time to see picturesque religious processions in the countryside. There are also large non-religious parades in San José on Labor Day, Independence Day and during Christmas week. The Tico Times will tell you where the most interesting events are. It's best to avoid visiting the beach during Easter week because it's the last holiday young *ticos* have before their school starts and they're all at the beach with their radios.

Following is a list of Costa Rica's *feriados:*

January 1: New Year's Day
March 19: Feast of Saint Joseph (San José's patron saint)
April 11: Anniversary of the Battle of Rivas
Holy Thursday through Easter Sunday
May 1: Labor Day
Corpus Christi
June 29: Saint Peter and Saint Paul

July 25:   Annexation of Guanacaste Province
August 2:   Our Lady of the Angels
August 15:   Assumption, Mother's Day
September 15:   Independence Day
October 12:   Día de la Raza (Columbus Day)
December 8:   Immaculate Conception
December 24, 25:   Christmas Eve and Christmas Day

Buses: Since most Costa Ricans don't have cars, buses go almost everywhere.   Most buses that travel between San José and the provinces are quite comfortable, and fares almost never run more than $2-4 to go anywhere in the country.   Some provincial buses are a bit rickety, but all buses are punctual. Buses from San José to the provinces are crowded on Fridays and Saturdays and the day preceding holidays or 3-day weekends.   Likewise it is difficult to get buses back to San José on Sundays, Mondays and the days following a holiday.   This is especially true of trying to make connections in Liberia, Puntarenas, Quepos and Limón.

Some buses don't have buzzers or bells to tell the driver when you want to get off.   When the bus gets close to your stop, shout *"La parada!"* or whistle loudly.   If you are traveling cheaply by bus, it is good to leave most of your luggage at a San José hotel and travel lightly.   Big suitcases are very inconvenient for bus travel.

The second half of this book gives detailed information on transportation including locations of bus stops and numbers to call to check schedules.   English is usually not spoken.

San José and suburban buses: The Sabana-Cementerio bus will take you through the area between downtown and the Sabana.   Downtown, it stops at Parque Central, at c 7, a ctl and at the Post Office.   The San Pedro buses (a 2, c 1/3) cover the eastern side of the city, through Los Yoses to San Pedro.   The northern and southern boundaries of downtown are only an 8-or 9-block walk from Avenida Central.   Most urban buses cost about $.05.   Suburban buses cost $.15-20 and run from 5 am to 10 or 11 at night.

If you are returning to San José by bus from the north or west, and want to get all the way downtown, get off early on Paseo Colón and hop on the Sabana-Cementerio.   That way you avoid going to the Coca Cola or some other bad neighborhood terminal. (The Coca Cola is a large bus terminal on c 16 between a 1/3. See map at back of book.)

Following is a list of *paradas* (bus stops) for buses to the suburbs:

Coronado: c 3, a 5
Escazú: a 6 c 12/14 (minibus), a 1, c 16/18 (big bus)
Guadalupe: a 3, c 1/3
La Uruca: c 6, a 3/5
Moravia: a 3, c 3/5
Pavas: a 1, c 16/18
Sabanilla: a 2, c 5/7
San Ramón de Tres Ríos: a 2, c 5/7
Santa Ana: Coca Cola
Villa Colón: Coca Cola

Buses to Panamá and Nicaragua: Since both Panamá and Nicaragua are in turmoil at this moment, it is essential to talk to people who have been there recently before going. Be sure to get an exit visa if you have been in Costa Rica over 30 days (see p. 43).

People who have only read about **Nicaragua** in the headlines are usually surprised by the friendliness of the Nicaraguan people, and their willingness to talk about their lives. Personal safety is usually assured in Nicaragua; however, you do have to watch out for contaminated water carrying amoebas or hepatitis. Because of the desperate economic situation there, it is good to bring simple things that people might need like toilet paper, pens, toothpaste, clothes, canned or dried food. Most nationalities don't need a visa, but must show that they have at least $200 in cash or travelers' checks, and change $60 into *córdobas* at the border. Check latest rules with the Nicaraguan consulate, 33-8747. Most car rental agencies will not allow you to rent a car to go to Nicaragua.

The SIRCA bus leaves San José for Managua at 5am Weds, Fri, Sun (c 11, a 2, 22-5541, $7, 12-hour trip). Tica Bus also goes to Managua Mon, Weds, Fri at 7 am, arriving around 5 pm (c 9, a 4, 21-9229, $8, better buses than SIRCA).

People used to go to **Panamá** to change dollars and buy film before continuing to South America, but the economic situation is very precarious there now. Between the police and the robbers, personal safety is not assured. You need a passport and visa to enter, and must present a return or ongoing ticket to get the visa. Check with the Panamanian consulate (25-3401, open 8am to 1 pm). Tica Bus leaves for Panamá on Mon, Weds, Fri, Sun at 11am, arriving at 5am (c 9, a 4, 21-9229, $18). Also, a TRACOPA bus leaves San José daily at 7:30am, and arrives in David, Panamá at 4:30pm (a 18, c 4, $7.50, 21-4214, 23-7685). Although we haven't been there, the Hotel Camino Real (D, a/c) and the Hotel Iris (B) have been recommended. Garlic chicken is supposed to be good in David, and seafood is recommended in its port, Pedregal, 8km away. From David you can get hourly buses to Panamá City (7 hours), or an express bus at noon and midnight (5.5 hrs).

You can also avoid at least 7 hours on the bus by flying with SANSA to Coto 47 on the Palmar route (Mon thru Sat, 10:40am, $11, see p. 59) and taking a taxi to Paso Canoas on the border, then catching a bus from there. The border closes for lunch from 12 to 2pm. It's very hot and muggy in Paso Canoas. International airfare from San José to Panamá is $108.

Trains are older, take longer and lurch from side to side more than buses, but they often go through wilder, less-inhabited country. Bathroom facilities are primitive to say the least. The **Puntarenas** train station is at c 2, a 20. Trains leave at 7am and 3pm return from Puntarenas at 6am and 3pm ($1, 26-0011). Trains leave for **Limón** at 10am daily from the Atlantic station on a 3, c 19/21. They return from Limón at 6am. Trip takes 7-8 hours as compared to 2.5 hours by bus. If you want to enjoy the most beautiful part of the ride, but don't intend to go to Limón, you can get off the train in Siquirres and take the 4pm or 6pm bus back. Siquirres is a hot, dilapidated town, but the **Centro Turístico Pacuare,** just south of town, is clean and has a good restaurant, pools and cabinas to make your wait more refreshing. You'll have to take a taxi to get there. Call 76-5196 to check Siquirres bus schedules, 23-3311 for train schedules. You can also take the Limón train to Cartago, Turrialba or Moín, but the best scenery is between Turrialba and Siquirres. Trip costs about $1.

The Tourism Institute (ICT) and the national train companies have collaborated on refurbishing vintage train cars, providing them with bar and restaurant service. These cars are much more elegant than the regular ones and so far are only available for tourists in organized tours. Of course, it's a much more expensive way to go but, depending on your tastes, might make the trip more enjoyable. Call the ICT (22-1090) or stop by their office under the Plaza de la Cultura for more information.

Planes: Because of Costa Rica's mountainous terrain, small aircraft transport is frequently used. A 20-minute flight can get you to Quepos and Manuel Antonio on the Pacific coast, instead of 4 hours by bus. SANSA, the local airline, flies to all corners of the country for $8 to $18 one-way. Here is their schedule:

Barra del Colorado (near Tortuguero N.P.): Tu, Th, Sat, 6am
Golfito (near Corcovado N.P.): Daily except Sun, 8:45am
Palmar and Coto 47: Mon, Wed, Sat, 10:40am
Coto 47: Tu, Th, Fri, 10:40am
Nosara: Mon, Fri, 6am
Quepos (Manuel Antonio National Park) : Daily except Sun at 9:30 am
Tamarindo: Mon, Wed, Fr, 1:10pm with connection to Sámara

Extra flights are added during the dry season, so check current timetables before making plans. Flights can be crowded, so make reservations at least 2 weeks in advance during the dry season (33-0397, 33-3258, fx: (506) 55-2176). You must pay for your ticket the day before you leave. A microbus will take you to the Juan Santamaría Airport from the SANSA office on calle 24, north of Paseo Colón. SANSA planes leave from the smaller terminal west of the main air terminal. In some places, like Quepos, SANSA buses will pick you up at your hotel for the return trip. SANSA also offers some of the cheapest tour packages around to the areas they serve (23-4179, 33-2714, fx: 55-2176).

Small 5-passenger planes can be rented for about $120 an hour from VEASA (32-1010) or Trans Costa Rica (32-0808), at the Tobías Bolaños smallcraft airport near Pavas ($2.50 by taxi from San José). They go places inaccessible by larger aircraft. The price can be divided by the number of passengers.

The only drawback to air travel is that sometimes flights are delayed by climatic conditions, and passengers must wait at either end. With luck this won't happen to you, and you'll have the thrill of seeing Costa Rica's symphony of mountains, sea and sky as you fly next to the clouds.

Taxis are relatively inexpensive by northern standards. Drivers have just begun to use computerized meters, called *marías*. If your taxi does not have one, or if you are going more than 12 kilometers, agree on a rate with the driver before you get into a taxi. Official rates are $.50 for the first kilometer and $.15 for each additional km in San José, $.20/additional km in the provinces. Each hour that a *taxista* waits for you costs $4.

Taxis can come in handy if you want to visit hard-to-get-to places but do not want the expense of renting a car. You can take an inexpensive bus trip to the town nearest your destination and hire a jeep-taxi to take you the rest of the way. Usually taxis hang out around the main square of any small town. It's best to ask several drivers how much they charge in order to make sure you are getting the going rate.

Hitching: Since there is bus service almost everywhere, most people prefer to take buses. Hitch-hiking is rare but possible on the major highways. In the country, where bus service is infrequent or nonexistent, cars often stop to pick up pedestrians.

Car rental for 3 days costs $50/day including insurance and mileage (4-wheel drives cost $70/day). You can usually get a 10% discount during the dry season. Valid foreign drivers licenses are good in Costa Rica for 3 months. If you don't have an Amex, Visa or Masterchage card, you must leave a US$700 deposit. All repairs must be okayed first with the main office, or you will not be reimbursed. Some agencies will rent tents, coolers, portable tables, trailers and even surfboards by the day. It is best to reserve a car a few days in advance, or even to telex before your arrival. All major rent-a-car agencies have branches in Costa Rica.

Renting a car, of course, makes exploring easier and is less time-consuming than taking the bus. However, renting a car just to get around San José is more hassle than it's worth. Cars are very vulnerable to theft. They must be left in parking lots at all times. Traffic is crazy. Left turns from right lanes are not uncommon. Taxis or buses are much cheaper and easier for city travel. If you do rent a car for trips, do not leave anything in it unless it is in a well-guarded place.

Gas: The best place to fill up before leaving San José going west is at the gas station on the right at the end of Paseo Colón. There are no other gas stations on the highway between San José and the airport. There are several gas stations on Avenida Central going east from downtown. Gas costs about $1.50/gallon. There are no self-service stations in Costa Rica.

Accidents: 27-7150 and 27-8030 are the numbers to call for a traffic official if one doesn't appear. Do not move vehicles until you are authorized to do so by an official. Offer paper and pencils to witnesses to write their names and *cédula* numbers (legal identification).

Do not remove badly injured people from the scene. Wait for the Red Cross ambulance (21-5818). Make no statements on the cause of the accident except to the official or a representative of the National Insurance Institute (INS).

Make a sketch of the area and the positions of the vehicles before and after the accident. Make note of the principal characteristics of the other vehicles involved, as well as the damage to your car and others. Avoid further damage by staying with your car. You must report the accident to the local municipality or Tribunal de Tránsito within 8 days. A copy of this report must be presented to the INS, along with your drivers' license, insurance policy, police report and information about injuries and witnesses (23-5800, 23-3446, a 7, c 9/11).

Foreign **insurance** policies are not effective in court and only the INS can provide local service for defense or adjustment of claims. Insurance is included in car rental fees.

Road trouble: By law you should have fluorescent triangles to place on the road in front and in back of your car in case of road trouble. Probably the best service to call in case of road trouble is Coopetaxi Garage (35-9966). Some operators understand English. Do not abandon your car, if you can possibly avoid it. If you don't speak Spanish well, have someone explain your location in Spanish when you make the telephone call. If a wrecker is needed, it can be called by Coopetaxi radios.

Telephones: Pay telephones are frustrating to use. Most of them only take small ¢2 coins, so bring a stack of them. Put a coin in the groove at the top of the box. Pick up the receiver and dial. The phone starts to beep. When the person answers, the call is sometimes cut off. Go to another phone. This one probably has a long line of people waiting in front of it. They already know that the phone you tried to use is *malo*. When you finally get through to the person you're calling, be prepared for a second series of beeps after a few minutes. These beeps mean that you are about to be cut off. Drop in another ¢2 piece if you want to talk for awhile. It's wise to tell the person you're calling the number of your pay phone so they can call you back and you can talk uninterruptedly. The number is often above the phone on a yellow sign. Good luck.

In rural areas, like Puerto Viejo or Monteverde, hotels and *pulperías* have phones to call out on. They do the dialing and charge you for the length of time you speak.

International calls: There are three public phones on which you can make collect or credit card calls directly to the United States: at Juan Santamaría Airport, in the Hotel Aurola lobby (c 5, a 5), and at Radiográfica (c 1, a 5). No coins are required. Just pick up the phone and give the operator the number desired.

If you have access to a private phone, direct dialing is easy from Costa Rica. The telephone directory has a list of codes for various countries. To dial the US or Canada directly, for example, dial 001 first, then the area code and number. Dial 116 for an English-speaking operator. For international information, dial 124. If you don't have access to a phone, go to Radiográfica, c 1, a 5, open 7 am to 10 pm.

Radiográfica also offers telex and fax services. You can send or have faxes sent to you at their number: (506) 23-1609. Call them at 87-0513 or 87-0511 to check if you have received a fax, or have your correspondent include the number of your hotel, and Radiográfica will notify you.

Mail: The main Post Office (Correo Central) is located on c 2, a 1/3. Mail letters from a post office. There are hardly any mailboxes on the streets, and they are seldom used.

Beware of having anything other than letters and magazines sent to you in Costa Rica. A high duty is charged on all items arriving by mail, in an attempt to keep foreign merchandise from entering illegally. Receiving packages can mean two trips to the Aduana in Zapote, a suburb of San José. The first trip is to unwrap and declare what you have received. The second one, 3 to 5 days later, is to pay a customs charge on every item in the package before you can take it home. Personal photographs can be received duty-free if just a few are sent at a time. Individually-sent cassette tapes can also make it through. Usually anything that fits in a regular-sized envelope will arrive duty-free. But you will have to pay outrageous fees for Hershey bars, several blank checkbooks sent together, the sweet little cap your Aunt Hilda knitted for you to remind you she still thinks of you--in short, beg your loved ones not to send you anything. Of course if you don't pay for it, the package will be sent back within a few months, but you wouldn't want to hurt Aunt Hilda's feelings, would you?

You can send most things from Costa Rica to North America or Europe with no problem, although postal rates for packages are pretty expensive. Mail packages from the entrance to the far left of the main entrance as you face the Post Office. Surface mail *(marítimo)* is somewhat cheaper than *correo aéreo* (airmail), and takes 4 to 6 weeks to arrive.

There is a General Delivery service *(Lista de Correos)*. If you are planning to stay in Costa Rica for awhile, rent a post office box *(apartado)* or have your mail sent to a friend's box. It is much more common for people to have post office boxes here than elsewhere, because delivery to an *apartado* is quicker and more secure than home delivery.

Carry your passport: Never, never go anywhere (not even to the post office) without your passport or tourist card. The huge influx of foreigners makes it necessary for immigration officials to perform routine identification checks. They can walk up to you anywhere (they might even knock on your hotel room door) or at anytime (they might greet you walking down the street at 11pm). They will courteously ask you to present your identification, including tourist card or visa. Not having it with you could mean a trip to the police station.

Bombetas: If you hear two very loud explosions in rapid succession, don't run for cover--that's just the Tico way of celebrating momentous occasions. Usually the fireworks are from the neighborhood church which is celebrating a Saint's Day, or are to announce events at a town fiesta *(turno)*. Sounding all the sirens in town is another way of expressing joy, as when the Pope or Tico astronaut Franklin Chang Diaz arrived in San José.

Avoid theft: So far, San José is much safer than most other cities, except for theft. The zippered compartments of backpacks are excellent targets in the area around the Coca Cola. It's best not to wear them on your back downtown. Don't carry a lot of packages at once. Purses should be zippered and have short shoulder straps so that you can protect them with your upper arm. Wallets and passports should not be carried in your back pocket, and expensive watches, chains and jewelry should not be worn. If on a bus or in a crowd you feel yourself being jostled or pinched between several people at once, don't just be polite. Protect your purse or wallet and elbow your way out of the situation immediately. Don't leave tents or cars unguarded anywhere. Don't leave cameras or binoculars in sight of an open window, even a louvered one. A pole can be stuck in and they can be fished out. If you follow these precautions, you probably won't have any trouble.

Notes for women: Even if you consider yourself a little on the chunky side in other cultures, you'll have plenty of admirers here. Ticos like to *piropear* (make flirtatious compliments to) women, especially unaccompanied ones. As you walk down the street, they will direct little comments at you, like *guapa* (pretty), *machita* (if you are blond), *mi amor* (my love) or will just lean toward you with a meaningful *adiós*. If they are farther away from you, they hiss as you pass. This can be quite tiresome, but they mean no harm and there's not much you can do about it. Complete obliviousness is the best policy.

Ticos can be very compelling in their professions of eternal devotion. Whether they're married or not doesn't seem to have much to do with it. Real romantic relationships and friendships usually take a long time to develop in Costa Rica, so take anything that is too rash with a large grain of salt. Foreign women are regarded as loose and easy game *(conquistas)* by Latin men, but their hearts belong to *la Virgen Purísima*. Don't become another notch on another *gringa*-chaser's gun. If you act like a lady, most Tico men will respect you.

Notes for men: Costa Rican women are sought out by foreign men because of their loveliness and their reputation for being *chineadoras,* i.e., able and willing to take care of men as if they were babies. Many men, frustrated from trying to "deal with" more assertive women back home, dream of a pretty Tica wife who won't give them any problems. These dreams may come true for awhile, until deeply ingrained cultural differences arise, causing major communication problems which can lead to *gringos* being taken to the cleaners in divorce courts. Of course there are many successful inter-cultural marriages as well. This is just a warning that, as in any aspect of life, you cannot leave an unresolved problem behind and expect it not to resurface in another form elsewhere.

Prostitution is legal in Costa Rica, and the women are given medical tests on a regular basis. Some prostitutes however have been found to be carrying AIDS. Others have been known to gang up on men in the street and rob them. Recently, there have been various cases of men being drugged and robbed after having invited women to their apartment or room. Be careful, guys.

Student Travel: OTEC is Costa Rica's student travel agency, affiliated with the International Youth Hostel Federation. If you are under 26 years old or have a student or teacher ID card, you can become a member for ¢600 and a photo. Affiliated youth hostels exist in San José, Lake Arenal, Rincón de la Vieja National Park and Guayabo National Monument. An OTEC membership can get you discounts on international flights, and at stores, restaurants and hotels in Costa Rica. OTEC is on the third floor of the Victoria Building, a 3, c 3/5, 22-0866. The Toruma youth hostel coordinates low-cost trips to other hostels in the country (a ctl, c 29-31, 24-4085).

You can get up to a 40% discount on PanAm flights to Costa Rica with an IYHF card. Also the Council on International Educational Exchange (CIEE), of which OTEC is an affiliate, sponsors a Work-Travel program in which *gringos* can work in CR and *ticos* can work in the US. Find out more from

CIEE
205 E. 42nd St.
New York, NY 10017
(212) 661-1414

Water: Water is safe to drink in San José. Bottled water is recommended in the suburbs of Escazú and Santa Ana, and in Puntarenas and Limón. *Soda blanca* is the term to use when asking for soda water, the closest thing to mineral water here.

Laundry: Laundromats are scarce in Costa Rica because most people have maids or relatives who do their laundry for them. Mid- and upper-range hotels have laundry services. Most cheaper hotels have large sinks *(pilas)* where you can wash your own clothes, or they can connect you with a lady who will wash for you for about $.80 an hour--less in the countryside. There are many *lavanderías* in San José, but they are quite expensive. The only self-service laundromat we know of is **Lava Más** in Los Yoses, next to Spoon (25-1645), where it costs about $3.25 to wash and dry one load of clothes.

Health Care: The following hospitals have emergency X-ray, laboratory and pharmacy services available to foreigners: Clínica Bíblica (a 14, c ctl/1, tel: 23-6422), Clínica Católica (Guadalupe, tel: 25-9095), Clínica Santa Rita (specializes in maternity care, a 8, c 15/17, tel: 21-6433).

According to a United Nations study, Costa Rica holds first place in Latin America for development of preventive and curative medicine. It is ranked near the United States and Canada among the 20 best health systems in the world. Many Costa Rican doctors have been trained in Europe and the United States, and the University of Costa Rica Medical School is considered one of the best in Latin America.

The Social Security system makes low-cost medical care available to those who need it, but doctors also have their private practices in the afternoons. A gynecological exam including papsmear costs around $15; a sonogram costs about $25; a complete cardiac stress exam runs about $45. Dental care is also considerably less expensive here than elsewhere. All the above services are available to foreigners.

Facelifts and other plastic surgery cost a fraction of what they do elsewhere, and post-operative care is also a lot cheaper.

The low cost of health care and labor make full-service custodial care of the elderly less expensive. **Golden Valley Hacienda** offers specialized care for Alzheimer's patients, and **Villa Confort Geriatric Hotel** provides a comfortable atmosphere for the elderly who just need help in everyday living.

Both are in converted homes near Alajuela, about 20 minutes from San José. Monthly cost includes round-the-clock care, meals, two visits a week from a geriatrician, laundry and basic medicines (Apdo. 2627, 1000 San José, (506) 21-6381, 43-8191, 43-8575).

The **Centro Victoria** offers innovative holistic treatment for addictions. One month of personal psychiatric care in a clinic is $5000 (33-8374, 23-6422 ext. 415, Apdo. 1307, 1000 San José).

Amoebas, etc.: Even though Costa Rica's water is as well-purified as possible, visitors sometimes get intestinal problems. If they are persistent, they might be due to *amibas* or *giardia*. If you get a strong attack of diarrhea, it's wise to take a stool sample to a local lab to have it analyzed. Put it in a clean glass jar, and deliver it immediately. Amoebas can't be found in samples that have been left overnight. Hospital labs are open on weekends and holidays (Clínica Bíblica, 23-6422; Clínica Americana, 22-1010. Dr. Gil Grunhaus, across from Hospital San Juan de Dios, 22-9516, gives the most complete reports). Your results will be ready the same day, especially if you bring your sample before noon ($3.25 in advance). If results are negative, take up to three samples--sometimes the offending organisms are not found the first time. The most dangerous one is *entamoeba histolytica*. This can migrate through your system and cause eventual liver damage.

It is not necessary to go to a doctor unless you want to. A pharmacist can give you the needed drug based on your lab results. We have not found that natural methods cure amoebas. It's best to take the chemicals and be done with the bugs. Be sure and ask for the literature that goes with the medicine. Even if you get over your diarrhea, the organisms can still be doing damage to your system unless you've taken medicine. This often shows up in a tendency towards constipation and a feeling of depression and low energy.

To avoid amoebas and giardia when traveling outside San Jose, avoid drinks made with local water or ice, and avoid lettuce, tomatoes and other fruits and vegetables which cannot be peeled.

Insects: Mosquitos can be a problem even in breezy San José at night during the dry season. Anti-mosquito spirals can be bought at supermarkets and *pulperías* for about $.40 a box.

Smaller stores will often sell you just a pair for about $.12. Be sure to ask for the little metal stand *(soporte)* that goes with them. Light up the spiral and circle it several times over your bed, then put it as far away from your bed as possible, or even outside the window or door. They usually work pretty well.

If you have been on the Atlantic coast, beware of sandfly bites that seem to become infected and grow instead of disappearing. This could be a sign of *papalomoyo,* (Leishmaniasis) a disease that can be life-threatening if untreated. See a tropical disease specialist immediately.

Bring sulphur powder from home to sprinkle on your socks to discourage chiggers, or buy *azufre sublimado* here and let it dissolve under your tongue. It gives your sweat a smell that chiggers can't stand.

Africanized **bees** have been working their way north from Brazil, and can attack humans with fatal results if their nests are disturbed. It is wise to be aware of this when exploring hot, dry areas, where bee colonies are ten times denser than in rainforests. If attacked, run as fast as you can in a zigzag direction, or jump into water. Bees don't see well over distances. Never try to take cover; don't crawl or climb into a precarious position from which you cannot make a quick exit. Throw something light-colored over your head to protect your eyes and nose; keep your mouth closed. If you know you are allergic to bee stings, talk with your doctor before you come and carry the proper medication with you. For more detailed information, contact the OTS, 36-6696.

Snakes: If you want to be able to recognize a poisonous snake if you run across it in the wilds, visit the **Serpentorium** on a 1, c 9/11 (2nd floor, open 10am-7pm daily, $1 entrance fee). Live native poisonous and non-poisonous frogs, snakes and reptiles are on exhibit there, as well as foreign snakes, such as the black cobra and a 19-foot python. At first we thought that the reptiles were very realistic plastic replicas, because they move so little, but after awhile we'd see that their positions had changed slightly. Some of the snakes and frogs are difficult to spot in the camouflaged environment, but you get better at picking them out as you go along.

BEACH SAFETY--HOW TO HANDLE RIP CURRENTS

Each year, hundreds of ocean bathers suffer serious near-drownings or death due to their ignorance about rip currents, a phenomenon found on wave-swept beaches all over the world--including Costa Rica.

Ironically, they can be fun if properly understood--yet they are responsible for 80 percent of ocean drownings, or four out of five.

Water safety expert Don Melton defines rip currents as "a surplus of water put ashore by waves, that finds a channel to drain and reach equilibrium".

All rip currents have three parts: the feeder current, the neck, and the head.

The feeder current is water moving parallel to the beach. You know you're in one when you notice, after a few minutes, that your friends on the beach have moved down 30 to 50 yards, yet you thought you were standing still.

At a depression in the ocean floor, the water turns out to sea. This can occur in knee- to waist-deep water, where the "neck" begins. The neck, which is very swift, can carry a swimmer out to sea at three to six miles per hour, faster than a strong swimmer's rate of two to four miles per hour.

"It's like being in a river, and can move a person 100 yards in just a moment," says Melton, a coastal archaeologist who has

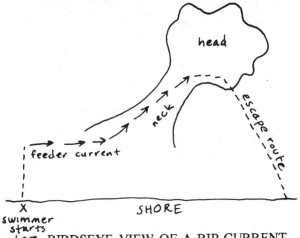

BIRDSEYE VIEW OF A RIP CURRENT

studied the ocean's currents for years. "It is typical to experience panic when caught in the neck, and it is here that most drownings occur."

The rip current loses its strength just beyond the breakers, dissipating its energy and eventually delivering the swimmer to relatively calm waters. This area, known as the "head", may appear to have a mushroom shape from the air, as debris picked up by the current is dissipated.

Here, the water is deep, but calm. The swimmer can get back to shore by moving parallel to the beach in the direction of the bend of the current, and then back to shore at a 45-degree angle rather than straight in, to avoid getting caught in the feeder current again. (See diagram).

As a safety precaution, Melton recommends that before you even go into the water, you should throw a buoyant object like a coconut or a stick into the water and watch where the current carries it, for this is the direction you will have to go to get back to shore.

"There is definitely one direction that is better than the other," he says.

The weak swimmer should call for help as soon as he notices that a current is moving him and making it difficult for him to walk in towards land.

"Most drowning victims are caught in water just above waist level," Melton explains. "When a person realizes he can't walk directly in, he should turn and walk sideways, leaping towards the beach with every wave, to let the water 'push' him towards shore."

Once a person is no longer touching bottom and in a rip, he should not fight against the current in a vain effort to get back to shore, for this is like "swimming up a river" and will sap his strength.

Floating conserves energy. Everyone should learn to float, Melton says, because "every minute that you can salvage gives someone the opportunity to make a rescue."

"There's a crashing surf than can throw you off balance," he adds. "One of the signals of someone who's in danger is one who turns his back to the crashing surf."

"Once off balance, a swimmer is unable to get traction on the ocean floor and can be dragged out four or five feet into deeper water with each swell," he says. After a few swells he may be in over his head, and it becomes even more important to float--arching his back, head back, nose pointing in the air. "The human body is buoyant," Melton notes. "Even more so in salt water."

If water gets into the lungs of the person in trouble, he sinks out of sight, feeding the myth of a fearsome "whirlpool" that pulls one down. This myth is "responsible for hundreds and hundreds of deaths", according to Melton. He estimates there have been "over 300 rescues by persons who recognize the difference between rip currents and *remolinos*".

There are four different types of rip currents: permanent, fixed, flash, and traveling.

Permanent rips occur at river mouths, estuaries, or by small streams, and can be quite wide. They also occur at finger jetties designed to prevent beach erosion, where the water's lateral drift is forced to turn seaward. Fixed, flash, and traveling rips are caused by "wind-generated waves," according to Melton.

Fixed currents, which appear only on long, sandy, surf-swept beaches, can move up or down the beach depending on shifts in the ocean floor, "but they are generally stable in one spot, staying there for hours to a day," according to Melton.

Flash or temporary rips are created when "an increased volume of water is brought to shore from sudden wave build-ups" according to *Lifesaving and Marine Safety,* a publication of the United States Lifesaving Association. Melton explains that these currents can occur on a warm, sunny day, generated by storms whose waves do not lose their energy until they crash on a distant shore. The excess water build-up has no opportunity to drain and reach equilibrium while the unusually large and fast waves are coming in; a flash rip current therefore forms during a lull in wave action.

A traveling rip current is just what the name implies. According to Melton, "You'll see it in front of you, and in five minutes it may move 15 yards up or down the beach. They can move 30 yards in a minute." They occur on long, sandy beaches where there are no fixed depressions on the ocean floor.

Some beaches, such as Espadilla at Manuel Antonio, are known to have rip currents and must be approached with caution at all times. The currents can be spotted by the trained eye as a brownish discoloration on the surface, caused by sand and debris carried by the current, or there can be a flattening effect as the water rushes out to sea, making it appear deceptively smooth.

Melton insists that rip currents are not dangerous to people who understand them.

"The more you know about the ocean, the more fun they can be," he asserts. Surfers use the rip currents as an energy saver since they provide "a free ride out" to sea just beyond the breakers.

In his studies of rip currents, Melton has many times sought them out, and encouraged others to do so under controlled conditions with experienced trainers.

"As long as you swim in the ocean, you're going to be caught in one sooner or later, and it's critical that you know what to do when you run into one," he says.

° Weak swimmers should avoid surf-swept beaches and swim instead at safer beaches like the 3rd beach at Manuel Antonio.
° Inexperienced swimmers should not swim alone.
° Always be prepared to signal for help at the earliest sign of trouble.

For more information, contact Don Melton or Anita Myketuk at 77-0345 in Quepos.

The above article was reprinted with permission from The Tico Times.

FISHING
By Jerry Ruhlow

With two oceans, beautiful freshwater lakes and endless miles of magnificent rivers--all only a few hours' drive or minutes by air from the capital city of San José--Costa Rica offers anglers some of the most fantastic and diverse sportfishing in the world.

For the freshwater angler, Lake Arenal and many of the rivers provide outstanding action on rainbow bass *(guapote)*, beautiful, fine-eating fish that may run eight pounds or more and are fished just as you would largemouth bass. **Posada Arenal**, a comfortable new fishing lodge, has just opened at the lake--for information, write or call: Posada Arenal, Apdo. 1139, Escazú 1250, San José, CR, 28-2588, 46-1881, fx: (506) 28-2798.

There are rainbow trout in the mountain rivers, and a range of such exotic species as the *machaca, bobo, mojarra* and *vieja* to be found in lower elevation waters.

But Costa Rica's greatest claim to fame is the incredible deepsea fishing for billfish and other gamesters on the Pacific Coast, and what is without doubt the world's finest tarpon and snook angling on the Caribbean.

Interest in Costa Rica sportfishing has increased dramatically in recent years, resulting in a tremendous expansion of the sportfishing industry, with new areas opening, improved and expanded facilities, and the introduction of world-class boats and equipment.

The Quepos area, for example, has long been a commercial fishing center, but it wasn't until 1988 that **Sportfishing Costa Rica** put in three new boats for sportsmen, offering packages for fishing local waters and the virgin grounds around Caño Island. The local boats raised 20 to 30 sails a day during the first three months' operation beginning in March, most of the action in only 30 minutes running time.

Further north, **Bahía Pez Vela, Flamingo Bay Pacific Charters, Ocotal** and **Papagayo Excursions** all added new, modern boats to their fleets, while on the Caribbean, Costa Rica Expeditions added eight new rooms to **Tortuga Lodge,** a popular tarpon and snook area that recently iced the cake with two new IGFA records for cubera snapper taken on the reef just outside the Tortuguero River mouth.

CARIBBEAN COAST

If you have never battled a tarpon, you have a surprise and perhaps a shock in store. When those silver rockets, weighing an average of 80 pounds each, take to the air, jumping and twisting and turning and tumbling, and then running halfway to hell and back, only to start jumping again... well, all I can say is, "try it."

You fish the tarpon from 16-foot outboards, and much of the action is in quiet jungle rivers and lagoons where you're likely to see bands of monkeys in the trees overhead, alligators basking along the shoreline and a host of brilliantly-plumed birds flitting through orchid-draped tropical growth.

Traditional season for tarpon is March through mid-May, but they're around all year and for the past several seasons we have had the best action in July and August.

Like tarpon, snook can be taken year around, with 17 to 25 pounders common and a generous share of big fish (including the IGFA all-tackle world record) coming from the area. Peak season for big fish is usually late August into November. From late November through January, the area enjoys a run of smaller snook (known locally as *calba),* that average about five pounds and pour into the river in huge numbers. Catches of 30 or 40 a day are not unusual.

In addition to the tarpon and snook, Caribbean coastal waters abound in mackerel, jack crevalle, saltwater catfish, sharks, grouper, snapper and more, while exotic freshwater species provide great light tackle action up river and in the lagoons.

Five lodges provide accommodations, boats and guides for visiting anglers. For information and free brochures, contact:

Casamar: Apdo. 825 Centro Colón 1007, San José, CR, (506) 41-2820.

Río Colorado: Apdo. 5094, 1000 San José, CR, (506) 32-8610, fx: 31-5987. In USA call 1-800-243-9777, fx: (813) 933-3280.

Parismina Tarpon Rancho: Apdo. 149 Moravia, CR, (506) 35-7766.

Tortuga Lodge: Apdo. 6941, San José, 1000, CR, (506) 22-0333.

Isla de Pesca: Apdo. 8-4390, San José, 1000, CR, (506) 21-5396 or 23-1973.

PACIFIC COAST

Sailfish are found along the Pacific Coast all year, with the heaviest action centering off Quepos in the early Spring. Action peaks further north, from Cabo Blanco through the offshore waters off the Gulf of Papagayo, from July through September.

Such dates are very general, however. In 1988, for example, the fishing was not to be believed in May, when 63 anglers in the International Sailfish Tournament caught and released 455 sails in four days. The previous year's tournament, in July, posted a score of 417 sails for 66 fishermen.

Marlin season (mostly blacks and blues, with some striped) are also caught year-round, but the peak months are January, February, May, July, August and September. Three charter boats out of Guanacaste took "Super Grand Slams" in 1988, catching all three varieties of marlin and a sailfish on the same day.

Dorado (dolphin fish) season traditionally corresponds to that of the sailfish, and wahoo usually peak from June through September. Roosterfish peak in May and June; rainbow runners from late Spring through the Summer.

Best action for small yellowfin tuna is normally late Summer, but they are sometimes abundant through most of the year, and a few big tuna in the 100-pound-plus bracket are caught every season by anglers trolling for billfish. There are always other tuna-like fish around, including bonito and skipjack.

Other popular game fish include jack crevalle, mackerel, *corvina,* big Pacific dogtooth snapper and several varieties of smaller snapper.

For information, reservation or free brochures, contact the following operators on the Pacific Coast:

Sportfishing Costa Rica: At Quepos. Apdo. 115-1150 La Uruca, CR, (506) 38-2729, 38-2726, fx: (506) 38-4434.

Costa Rican Dreams: Apdo. 79, San Antonio de Belén, 4005 Heredia, CR, 39-3387, 77-0593, fx: (506) 39-3383. Out of Quepos.

Oasis del Pacífico: Across the Gulf of Nicoya via ferry from Puntarenas, Apdo. 200, Puntarenas, CR, (506) 61-1555.

Hotel Flor de Itabo: Apdo. 32, Playas del Coco, Guanacaste, CR. (506) 67-0111, 67-0292, fx: (506) 67-0003.

Hotel Ocotal: Apdo. 1013, San José 1002, CR, (506) 22-4259, 67-0230. Near Playas del Coco.

Flamingo Bay Pacific Charters: 121 Nurmi Dr., Fort Lauderdale, FL 33301, (305) 987-5860 or 467-0532. In Costa Rica, (506) 31-4055, 32-6519, 68-0906. At Flamingo Beach.

Hotel Hacienda Las Palmas: Apdo. 136, San José 1007, CR, (506) 31-4343. Near Playa Brasilito.

Flamingo Beach Resort: (506) 68-0976.

Tom Bradwell: Apdo. 109, Santa Cruz, Guanacaste, CR, (506) 68-0942. Based at Flamingo Beach.

Papagayo Excursions: Apdo. 35, Santa Cruz 5150, Guanacaste, CR, (506) 68-0859, 68-0652, 32-6854. At Tamarindo Beach.

Hotel Villaggio La Guaria Morada: At Punta Guiones de Garza, near Nosara, 68-0784.

Diving Safaris: c/o Hotel Ocotal, Apdo. 1013 San José 1002, (506) 67-0230. Offers dive trips, rentals and instruction at Hotel Ocotal.

Fresh water **fishing permits** can be obtained from the Dirección de Vida Silvestre, c 19, a ctl/2, 55-0192, 33-8112, open 8 am-4 pm. They cost $10 and are valid for 60 days. Sportfishing permits for salt water fish are obtained from the Dirección de Pesca, Dept. de Protección y Registro, c 24, a 2, 21-7135. They cost $2 and are valid for one year.

Fishing equipment and tide tables are sold at La Casa del Pescador (c 2, a 18/20) and Deportes Keko (c 20, a 4/6). They can also give you good advice on which lures to use.

SPORTS

Soccer: Costa Ricans are very sports-minded. There isn't a district, town or city where *fútbol* (soccer) isn't played. It's said that Costa Ricans learn to kick a ball before they learn to walk! There are teams all over the country in every imaginable category including all ages and both sexes, although only men play on the major teams. *La Selección Costarricense de Fútbol* competes in international tournaments in many countries. Nationally, there is a major league made up of first-class teams backed up by second and third divisions. Each town has a team and each province competes for national championship. Play-offs begin in April and end in December every year. Various teams have their own stadiums, but the largest is the National Stadium in La Sabana.

Tennis: Among the most important international tennis matches here is the World Friendship Tournament at the Cariari Country Club in March and April. The Costa Rica Country Club hosts the Coffee Cup Tournament. Los Reyes Country Club (La Guácima), the Costa Rica Tennis Club (Sabana Sur), Cariari and La Sabana courts offer programs for learning and practicing tennis. Most beach and mountain hotels have tennis courts.

Golf: The Costa Rica Country Club in Escazú and the Los Reyes Country Club in La Guácima, Alajuela each have nine holes and professionals to teach the game. The only 18-hole golf course in the country is at the Cariari Country Club. Cariari hosts the Friendship Golf Tourney and the American Professional Golf Tourney which attract PGA professionals. Cariari rents equipment and provides pros for golf lessons. Tango Mar

Surf and Saddle Club, a private resort on the Gulf of Nicoya near Tambor, also offers a golf course.

Gyms: There are plenty of gymnasiums in the San Jose area, which you can use for $12 to $25 per month. Look for them in the telephone directory under "Gimnasios".

Running: There are many marathons throughout the year, including the one sponsored by the University for Peace each April. The Hash House Harriers, a world-wide organization devoted to running and beer-drinking, also meets here once a week. Call Bill Barbee at 28-0769 for info.

Horses: Finca Ob-la-di, Ob-la-da (49-1179) combines horseback riding with visits to beautiful waterfalls in the Villa Colón and Orotina areas. They will pick you up in San José.
  The **Portón del Tajo** at Hotel Cariari offers riding and jumping lessons, dressage and trail riding (39-2248). International horse riding competitions are held each year at **Club Hípico La Caraña** in Río Oro de Santa Ana, west of San José (28-6106, 28-6754). **Club Paso Fino** in Santa Ana specializes in purebred Paso Fino horses and gives instruction in the techniques needed to ride this special breed. Horse lovers can also stay at the Club, which is decorated with riding memorabilia and offers creative gourmet meals (49-1466).
  Most beach and mountain resorts rent horses.

Whitewater sports: Rafters, canoers and kayakers are beginning to flock to Costa Rica because of its exciting rivers. The Río Pacuare, considered world-class by sportspeople, is threatened with being dammed for a huge hydroelectric project. **Ríos Tropicales** (33-6455), **Costa Rica Expeditions** (22-0333), and **Aventuras Naturales** (25-3939) will take you on one- to three-day rafting trips, with challenges graded to your level of skill and experience. The one-day trip is $65 including transportation, lunch and expert guides. Ríos Tropicales also offers sea-kayaking trips, and is starting an "Adventure School" with classes in skin-diving, kayaking and jungle survival (55-0194, fx: (506) 55-4354). **Rancho Leona** takes beginners on river kayaking trips down the Río Puerto Viejo in Sarapiquí (71-6312).

Surfing: Recently Costa Rica has become famous for its great waves, which have been described by surfers as "tubular Hawaiian", "epic", and "totally king". The Pacific coast waves are mostly beach breaks, and surfing season is July through December. The Atlantic coast waves are formed by coral reefs, and the season is November through March and again in June and July. Serious surfers usually bring big boards for the Atlantic and small ones for the Pacific. The nearest surfing beach is **Boca Barranca**, between Puntarenas and Puerto Caldera, known for long waves. About a half hour to the south are **Playa Jacó** (good for beginners) and **Playa Hermosa** (not to be confused with Playa Hermosa in Guanacaste), where an international surfing contest is held each year. The whole area between Jacó and **Playa Dominical** to the south has many excellent surfing spots. **Playa Pavones,** south of Golfito on the Golfo Dulce is said to have a left wave "so long you can take a nap on it". **Playas Nosara, Junquillal** and **Tamarindo** in Guanacaste have areas for surfing as well as swimming and snorkeling spots. SANSA has inexpensive, half-hour flights to Tamarindo and Nosara. **Playa Naranjo,** in Santa Rosa National Park, is known for **Witch Rock**, an island which causes tubular waves. If you don't have 4-wheel-drive you have to hike 13km with your surfboard on your back, and camp out. On the Atlantic coast, **Playa Bonita,** just north of Limón, offers waves which are very thick, powerful and dangerous. There is an international competition there each year. **Puerto Viejo**, south of Limon, is famous for "La Salsa", a challenging ride responsible for many a broken surfboard. See the Index for more information about the above beaches. Most surfers say they can't decide which coast they like best. The **Mango Surf Shop,** 25 mts. west of the Banco Popular in San Pedro, buys and sells surfboards and accessories, as does **Tsunami** in Los Yoses. There are surfboard rental shops in Puntarenas, Jacó, Manuel Antonio, Limón and Cahuita. Many car rental agencies and hotels give discounts to surfers, especially in the off-season.

For more information, get **Surf Guide Magazine** at the above stores, or by writing Apdo. 694, 1100 Tibás, San José, CR.

Hunting: This is definitely not encouraged in Costa Rica. However, hunters do play an important ecological role in Guanacaste, where they are welcomed by farmers to shoot white wing doves which flock to the rice and grain fields between November and March. Without the hunters, farmers would use poison against the birds, which also kills other birds and wildlife. Trek International Safaris, Box 19065, Jacksonville, FLA 32245-9065, (904) 733-3236, can arrange flights, permits, lodging, etc.

NATIONAL PARKS, RESERVES
AND WILDLIFE REFUGES

Costa Rica's 46 national parks, reserves and wildlife refuges protect jewels of the country's rich but diminishing wilderness. They occupy approximately 27% of national territory, when added to Indian reserves and forest buffer zones. Most national parks have camping facilities. Most reserves and wildlife refuges do not.

It is wise to call the departments in charge of each area before going there. Parks and reserves are run by Parques Nacionales. Wildlife refuges are run by Vida Silvestre. Radio operators at 33-5473 maintain 24-hour contact with the national parks and can give you current information on weather and facilities (Spanish only). There is a National Park Information Center in the zoo, Parque Bolívar, that sells books and maps (c 9, a 11, 33-8841, 33-5284). If you need specialized information on scientific aspects of the parks, contact Editorial Heliconia at the Fundación de Parques Nacionales, c 20, a ctl/1, 55-2984. You need a permit to go to some reserves, like Cabo Blanco. Nominal fees are charged for entering the parks, as well as for camping and anchorage.

If you call ahead, park and refuge personnel can sometimes take time to show you around. If you speak Spanish, you can call them by radio at 33-5473 for the National Parks, or 55-0192, 33-8112 for the refuges. Emil Montero, a guard at Tapantí, loves to take people exploring in the parks and refuges on his days off (45-0187, Spanish only).

All national parks, reserves and refuges are indicated on the map of Costa Rica in the back of this book, and are described in the sections on the various regions.

The Association of Volunteers for Service to Protected Areas helps visitors donate support services to the severely understaffed parks and reserves. Volunteers receive free transportation and lodging, but sometimes have to chip in on food. They should understand basic Spanish, and provide two letters of reference from organizations abroad or individuals in Costa Rica. Contact Stanley Arguedas, 33-5055.

Warning: Although Costa Rica has been described as a "Disneyland" of ecological wonders, you must be aware that here you are dealing with Mother Nature in all her harsh reality. Five foreigners were reported missing in 1989, and only three were found.

Three German hikers were lost in unseasonal fog and rain for 11 days on Barva Volcano on the west side of Braulio Carrillo National Park. Their goal was a simple day-hike around the crater lake, but landslides blocking the trails threw them off course. Costa Rica's famous parks are victims of the country's budget deficit, and trails are not maintained with the same rigor foreigners are used to. Tropical weather itself makes trail maintenance a full-time job. The three hikers could keep each other warm and encouraged, and survived their ordeal well, but two older tourists disappeared without a trace, one on Coco Island National Park, the other in Cahuita National Park. Both were hiking or swimming alone when they disappeared. See beach safety information, pp. 69-72.

Maps: The ICT has put out a new road map which is one of the most accurate available. It shows principal highways in green, secondary paved roads in red and dirt roads in white. It includes the locations of most national parks, reserves and wildlife refuges. The only problem is that so many roads are in the process of being paved that the map is already out of date. Meanwhile, other paved roads are in a state of deterioration. The best policy is to call a hotel at or near your destination and ask about current road conditions and travel times. They will also have current bus schedules. Ask for the road map ($.50) through the ICT offices listed on page 44.

Topographical maps can be purchased at Librería Lehmann (c 3, a ctl/1), Librería Universal (a ctl, c ctl/1), or the Instituto Geográfico Nacional (a 20, c 5/7). Ask for *mapas cartográficos.* You'll be shown a little map of Costa Rica divided up into 20 x 30 km. sections. Indicate which one you want. Maps show roads, trails, water sources including rapids, and contours at every 20 meters. They cost ¢90 a section.

Small yellow posts mark the distance in kilometers from San José on Costa Rica's highways.

You can buy **camping and snorkeling equipment** at several stores: Aro (c 9, a ctl/3), Carlos Luis (a ctl, c 2/4), El Palacio del Deporte (c 2, a 2/4). Ferretería El Clavo (c 6, a 8) sells *gasolina blanca* (kerosene) for camping stoves. Many places sell sealed canisters for alcohol stoves.

FRUITS AND VEGETABLES

The abundance of fresh, delicious fruits and vegetables in Costa Rica is amazing. You can get an idea of it by elbowing your way through the **Mercado Borbón** (c 8, a 3/5), a two-level circus of fruit and vegetable vendors in a rough-and-tumble part of town. Or you can go to any of the Saturday morning *ferias del agricultor,* where streets are shut off and truck farmers bring their fresh produce to the neighborhoods. In San José the Saturday morning market is west of Plaza Víquez (c 7/9, a 16/20). There you will find fresh homemade wholewheat bread and pastries, eggs, chickens, fish, cheese, and honey, as well as every imaginable fruit and vegetable. Bring your own shopping bags.

Unfortunately, pesticide use is still unregulated in Costa Rica, and most farmers are not aware of organic gardening. However, a small group of farmers from the Cartago area is experimenting with organic methods. You can buy their beautiful, fresh organic produce at **Club Vida Natural**, 100 m south of Restaurant La Nueva China in San Pedro. Call 24-8713 or 73-6079 for more info.

Here are some tips on how to identify and choose the best produce:

A ripe **papaya** will always be slightly soft, but a too-soft papaya is to be avoided. It is customary for papaya vendors to cut a triangular piece out of the papaya to show you its color. Some people are fans of the rounder *amarilla* or yellow-orange papaya. Others will swear that only the more elongated and red-orange *cacho* papaya is worthy of the name. You do not have to buy a papaya just because the vendor cut a piece out of it for you to taste. At least, Ticos don't. Just make sure you feel it first.

Ticos judge the ripeness of a pineapple by giving it a slap. A good **piña** should sound firm and compact. The yellow pineapple is best for eating. The white pineapple is more acid and is used in cooking and to tenderize meats. It produces a hollow sound. A green color on the outside does not necessarily reflect unripeness. You should be able to easily pluck a leaf from the top of a ripe piña.

Watermelons are also considered sweeter if they produce a firm rather than a hollow sound. The best watermelons come from the hot coastal zones. One of the nicest parts of driving to Puntarenas is stopping at the fruit stands in Esparza for a delicious **sandía**.

Don't make the mistake of a friend of ours who, on a hot San José afternoon, came home with what he thought was a delicious, red, juicy watermelon. "And what a bargain!" he said as he thirstily cut into the **chiverre**, only to find a mass of whitish spaghetti-like pulp. Chiverre looks just like a watermelon from the outside. You'll see them sold on the roadsides during Semana Santa. Their pulp is candied with *tapa dulce* to make special Easter treats.

Cantaloupe, **melón** in Costa Rica, is also judged for sweetness by its firm sound, but a fragrant smell is the best indication of a fully ripe melón.

Mangos should be slightly soft and red and yellow in color, without any brown or mushy spots. By far the most delicious are the large *mangas,* given feminine gender because of their voluptuous size. The neatest way to eat mangas is to slice them close around the flat oval seed to get two meaty halves. With the skin-side down, score each piece into one inch divisions without cutting through the skin. Now gently turn each half inside out, and you will have a bunch of delicious bite-sized pieces offering themselves to you (see diagram).

Ticos love to eat green mangoes sliced and sprinkled with lemon and salt. Some people get a rash or irritation around their lips from eating mangos. This can be avoided by cutting off the part of the fruit nearest the stem, as the irritation is caused by the sap.

Four types of **limones** (lemons) grow here. The seedless *verdelio* is rare. The *criollo* is small, juicy and greener. The *Bencino* is more the size of a North American lemon but is green and has much less juice than the criollo. The *limón mandarina* looks like a bumpy tangerine, and is very sour and juicy. It's good for making lemonade.

Blackberries are called **mora** and are used mainly in *refrescos* and ice cream. You have to liquefy moras in a blender and then strain and add sugar and water to the sour juice.

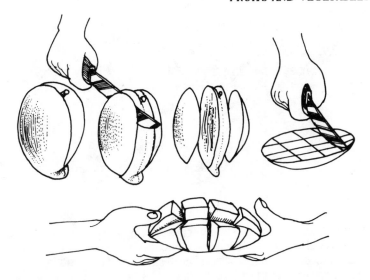

Guayabas (guavas) are plentiful in Costa Rica from September through November. Their pink fruit is used for jam or guava paste.

Cas is a little round fruit similar to the guayaba whose tart tropical flavor is popular in *refrescos* and sherbets. Try the *nieve de cas* at Pop's.

Tamarindo is a tart and sweet *refresco* made from the seed pod of the tamarind tree. You will see the orange-sized balls of brown tamarindo seeds and pulp at the markets. The seeds are put in hot water so the sticky tamarindo washes off. Then sugar and cold water are added. The resulting light brown *refresco* is somewhat similar in flavor to apple juice.

Granadillas (passion fruit) are yellowish-red and slightly larger than an egg. They have a crisp but easily-broken shell. Inside are little edible seeds surrounded by a delicious, delicately-flavored fruit which is first slurped and then chewed.

Mamones are little green spheres which you can break open with your fingers or teeth, to expose a large seed covered with a layer of fruit which tastes like a peeled grape.

Mamón chino is the mamon's exotic cousin, sporting a red shell with soft spines growing all over it. It resembles a fat, round, red caterpillar and has an even larger delicious grapelike fruit inside its outrageous shell.

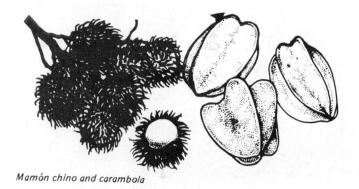

Mamón chino and carambola

When you slice a yellow **carambola**, the pieces look like five-pointed stars. It makes a delicious *refresco* and has been made into a substitute for cranberry sauce at Thanksgiving.

Marañón is an unusual fruit. Its seed, the cashew nut, grows on top of it in a thick, rubbery shell. Don't try to bite open the shell; it's very bitter. Cashews must be roasted before they can be eaten; they are poisonous when raw. If you take the train to Puntarenas, people will try to sell you home-roasted cashews. The ripe fruit can be eaten or made into a *refresco* or fermented into wine. The dried fruit is like a cross between a prune and a fig and is sold in supermarkets. You can make a quick and elegant dessert with half a dried marañón topped with a dollop of cream cheese and a cashew.

Avocados are called **aguacates.** They are usually a little less buttery and flavorful than their North American counterparts. They are soft when ripe, but if bought green can be left inside a paper bag to ripen.

Zapotes look like big brown avocadoes, and their texture is avocado-like, but their pulp is bright red-orange and sweet. Some places make zapote ice cream.

Nísperos have brown-paper-bag skin like zapotes, but they are smaller than an orange and have a delicate, honey-colored fig-like fruit.

Fresh coconut meat (**coco**) can be found at fruit stands downtown. *Pipas* or green coconuts are popular with Ticos on hot days at the beach. They are sold whole, with a straw stuck through a hole in the outer shell so that the coconut water can be drunk.

The best way to get coconut meat out of its shell is to hack it open with a machete or a hammer and then heat the shells on top of the stove in a pan. This makes the meat shrink a little bit so that it is easier to remove.

Pejibaye, a relative of the coconut, is one of Costa Rica's most unusual treats. Pejibayes grow in clusters on palm trees, like miniature coconuts. The part that you eat would correspond to the fibrous husk, while the hard pejibaye seed, when cracked open, reveals a thin layer of bitter white meat around a hollow core. The bright orange or red pejibayes are delicious boiled in salted water, then peeled, halved and pitted and eaten alone or with mayonnaise. You'll see them sold on San José streets year-round. Their flavor is difficult to describe. They are not sweet, but more a combination of chestnut and pumpkin with a thick, fibrous texture. You can buy a *racimo* (bunch) of raw pejibayes at the Mercado Borbón and boil them up for parties, or you can buy them in the supermarkets peeled and canned to take home as souvenirs.

Pejibaye

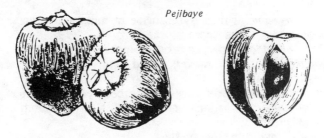

Palmito (palm heart) is another delicacy worth trying. It is sold raw in the supermarkets or tenderly pickled in jars or bags. It is the succulent inner core of small palm trees. Even though whole trees must be cut so that you can savor palmito, the trees are cultivated as a crop, so are replaced.

As human nature would have it, the most highly prized fruits in Costa Rica are imported apples, grapes, and pears. They signify the advent of the Christmas season, and Ticos pay big prices for them.

COMIDA TIPICA (NATIVE FOOD)

Sodas are small restaurants where you can get inexpensive snacks and light meals. They line the streets of San José and fill the Mercado Central. These are some of the foods you'll run across at sodas or at the Fiesta de Maíz in La Garita (see p. 124).

arreglados: sandwiches, usually made of meat, on a tasty but greasy bun.

arroz con pollo: rice with chicken and vegetables.

cajeta de coco: delicious fudge made of coconut, *tapa dulce* and orange peel.

casado: a plate of rice, black beans, cabbage and tomato salad, meat or egg, *picadillo,* and sometimes fried plantains.

ceviche: raw seabass cured in lemon juice with *culantro* (chinese parsley) and onions. Delicious.

chorreados: corn pancakes, sometimes served with *natilla.*

cono capuchino: an ice cream cone dipped in chocolate. A Pop's delicacy.

dulce de leche: a thick syrup made of milk and sugar.

elote asado: roasted corn on the cob.

elote cocinado: boiled corn on the cob.

empanadas: corn turnovers filled with beans, cheese, or potatoes and meat.

gallos: meat, beans or cheese stuck between two tortillas.

gallo pinto: the national breakfast dish of rice and beans fried together.

guiso de maíz: fresh corn stew.

horchata: a sweet drink made of corn and cinnamon.

masamorra: corn pudding.

melcochas: candies made from raw sugar.

milanes and *tapitas:* small, foil-wrapped, pure chocolate candies, available in corner stores and restaurants all over the country. Beware: these delicious little things are addictive.

natilla: sour cream, often more liquid than northern sour cream.

olla de carne: literally "pot of meat", but actually a meat soup featuring large pieces of *chayote* (a green, pear-shaped vegetable that grows on vines), *ayote* (a pumpkin-like squash), *yuca, plátano,* etc.

palomitas de maíz: "little doves". Popcorn.

pan de maíz: a thick, sweet bread made with fresh corn.

pan bon: a dark, sweet bread with batter designs on top. A Limón specialty.

patacones: fried, mashed green plantains, served like french fries with meals on the Atlantic coast.

patí: flour-based *empanadas* filled with fruit or spicy meat, sold on the Atlantic coast.

picadillo: a side dish of fried vegetables, which often contains meat.

plátanos: plantains. They look like large bananas, but cannot be eaten raw. Sweet and delicious when fried or baked. Also sold like potato chips. A Central American staple.

queque seco: pound cake.

refrescos: cold fruit drinks. Most refrescos are made with a lot of sugar. If you order a refresco that is not made in advance, like *papaya en agua, papaya en leche,* or *jugo de zanahoria* (carrot juice), you can ask for it *sin azúcar* (without sugar) and add your own to taste. Similarly an *ensalada de frutas* (fruit salad) might come smothered in jello and ice cream. You can ask for it *sin gelatina, sin helados.*

sopa de mondongo: tripe soup.

sopa negra: soup made from bean gravy, with hard-boiled egg and vegetables added.

tacos: a bit of meat topped with cabbage and tomato salad.

tamales: cornmeal usually stuffed with pork or chicken, wrapped in banana leaves and boiled. A Christmas tradition.

tamal asado: a sweet cornmeal cake.

tamal de elote: sweet corn tamales, wrapped in corn-husks.

tapa dulce: native brown sugar, sold in a solid form that looks like an inverted flower pot. It's grated with a knife or boiled to make syrup from which is made *agua dulce,* a popular campesino drink.

torta chilena: a many-layered cake filled with *dulce de leche.*

tortas: sandwiches on a bread roll.

tortilla de queso: a large, thick tortilla with cheese mixed into the dough.

tortilla: may mean the Costa Rican thin, small, corn tortilla, but also another name for an omelette.

yuca: manioc, a thick tuber, another staple of the Central American diet. *Enyucados* are *empanadas* made from a yuca-based dough.

People who don't eat meat should be aware that the word *carne* generally refers to beef. Some restaurants will say a dish *"no tiene carne"* when it does contain pork, chicken, or fish.

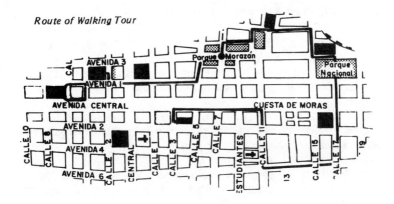

Route of Walking Tour

GETTING TO KNOW SAN JOSE

As you can see from the map, San José's streets are laid out in a very logical system: odd-numbered streets *(calles)* are east of Calle Central, even-numbered streets are west. Odd-numbered *avenidas* are north of Avenida Central and even-numbered avenues are south. So if an address is on c 17, a 5/7, it is in the northeastern part of the city.

Perhaps because Costa Rica is a small country in transition from rural to urban, most Ticos completely ignore the street numbering system. *Calles* and *avenidas* appear in the phone book, and that's about it. The accepted way to give directions is from *puntos cardinales* or landmarks. If you call for a taxi you have to give the name of a church or a *pulpería* (corner store) or a well-known business (like Pollos Kentucky). Then you state how many *metros* you are from there and in what direction. *Cien (100) metros* roughly corresponds to one city block. These are some examples of typical ways of giving directions: *"De la pulpería La Luz, cien metros al norte y cincuenta al oeste."* (From the La Luz grocery store one block north and half a block west.) *"De la Iglesia La Soledad, doscientos al sur y trescientos al este."* (From the Soledad Church, two blocks south and three blocks east).

The area bordered by *Calle 4* on the west, *Avenida 9* on the north, *Calle 23* on the east and *Avenida 2* on the south is the heart of downtown culture and nightlife, and is usually quite safe (always follow precautions on p. 64, however).

RULES OF THUMB FOR PEDESTRIANS

1. When crossing streets in downtown San José, always look over your shoulder at the cars coming from behind you. In practice, the pedestrian does not have the right of way. Drivers love to whip around corners whether or not people are trying to cross.

2. When a traffic light for oncoming cars changes from green to yellow or red, do not take it to mean that the cars will stop. Look at the cars, not the light. When you see that the cars have stopped, run across real quick. This habit is easily developed because another loveable characteristic of San José is that traffic lights are hung so that pedestrians cannot see them. *Buena suerte.*

3. Street numbers are attached to the sides of buildings near intersections. Not all corners have them, but keep looking and you're bound to find one.

4. To orient yourself in cities and villages, remember that most Catholic churches have their entrances on the west so that the altar faces east.

WALKING TOUR

The following tour can take several hours to one day, depending on how involved you get.

We will start out at the **Central Post Office** *(Correo Central)* on calle 2 between avenidas 1 and 3. The entrance is in the middle of the block. The stamp windows are directly in front of you as you enter. Slots for mailing letters abroad are directly to your left. Philatelists will be interested in visiting the commemorative stamp department on the second floor. The Correo is open from 8 am-midnight M-F and 8 am-12 noon Saturdays.

Walk two blocks west on avenida 1 and you're at the **Mercado Central**, entering through the flower section. The market is a crowded, bustling maze of shops, restaurants, and produce stands covering the whole block between avenida central and 1 and calle 6 and 8. Although there are quite a few more sedate places to buy souvenirs, at the Central Market you can get a glimpse of the lives of everyday Costa Ricans. Everything from leather goods to hammocks and fresh fish to mangoes is sold there. Of special interest are the stands where herbs are labeled with their medicinal uses. It's easy to get quite disoriented in the market, but try to come out at the southeast entrance on avenida central and start walking east again. If you don't like crowds, skip the market.

Between calles 6 and 4, you'll pass **La Gloria,** Costa Rica's largest department store. Across from that is the huge black marble **Banco de Costa Rica.** You can take an elevator there to the eighth floor to get a bird's eye view of the city. Turn left at calle 4 and you'll pass a branch of **Pop's,** Costa Rica's excellent chain of ice cream stores. At calle 4, avenida 1, turn right, heading for the Post Office again. You'll pass the **Banco Nacional** on your left. It often has interesting art exhibits. Continuing on avenida 1, a block and a half past the Post Office, you'll pass the **Librería Universal** where you can buy almost anything. They sell large-scale maps which are helpful for hiking.

Look to your left at the intersection of calle 1 and avenida 1. Two blocks north is **Radiográfica,** where you can make long-distance phone calls, send telegrams, or send and receive faxes. **LACSA** airline ticket offices are across from Radiográfica.

But you are still on avenida 1. In the next block after calle 1 is The **Bookshop,** which sells newspapers, cards and books in English. Continue east to calle 5. Turn left. You'll pass two excellent crafts stores: **Magia,** on your right in the middle of the block, and **Suraja** on your left at the corner of avenida 3. Both merit a browse.

Now **Parque Morazán** is on your right, with its music temple patterned after Le Trianon in Paris. On the northwest corner of the park is the **Hotel Aurola Holiday Inn,** with its mirrored panels that reflect San José's changing skies. The third floor features a swimming pool and gym. One block south of the **Music Temple** is the popular **Hotel Amstel,** with its quiet bar and excellent, reasonably-priced restaurant. Across from the Amstel (a 1, c 7) is a smaller branch of the **Banco de Costa Rica** where you can cash traveler's checks. It's open until 6 pm weekdays. Three blocks north of the Music Temple is the entrance to **Parque Bolívar, San José's zoo,** which also houses the **Information Center of the National Park Service.** There you can buy maps and posters and consult about your special areas of interest. To enter the zoo, go to the right at the intersection of calle 7 and avenida 11 and follow the avenida as it curves to the left (adm. $.25, open 8am-4pm Tues-Fri, 9am-5pm Sat and Sun).

Go back to the Music Temple. Pass the green **Escuela Metálica** on your left, which was bolted together from parts shipped from France. Enter **Parque España** with its venerable and beautiful trees. Continue to avenida 7 and the tall **National Insurance Institute** (INS) which houses a fine exhibit of jade, ceramics and art in the **Jade Museum** on the 11th floor (open 9am-3pm, Mon-Fri).

Continuing east on avenida 7, you will pass the **Casa Amarilla** with its wide stairways. It houses the country's Department of Foreign Relations. This building and the park in front of it were donated by Andrew Carnegie. Local artists display their works in the park on Sunday mornings.

On the east side of the park is the **National Liquor Factory**, founded by President Juan Rafael Mora in 1856. Guided tours of the building, including generous samplings of their products, are available after 4pm during the week. Call 23-6244.

Now we're going east again on avenida 7, up a gentle hill, passing the Mexican Embassy on the north and arriving at the intersection of avenida 7 and calle 15. Turn right towards the **National Library** (Biblioteca Nacional). On its western side is the **Galería Nacional de Arte Contemporáneo**, which often has good exhibits (open 10am-1pm, 2pm-5pm, Mon-Sat). Entrance to the library is on avenida 3.

The library faces **Parque Nacional**. To the east of the Park are the railroad and bus stations for the scenic trip to Limón. In the center of the Park is the massive **Monumento Nacional**, depicting the spirits of the Central American nations driving out the despicable William Walker. The statue was made in the Rodin studios in France and shipped to Costa Rica. Across the street from the park you will see a statue of **Juan Santamaría**, holding aloft his torch in front of the **Legislative Assembly** building, the Costa Rican Congress. Inside is a small library and an exhibit recounting the momentous decisions in Costa Rica's legal history.

Two blocks south of the Parque Nacional, on calle 17, is the **Museo Nacional,** housed in the former Buenavista Fortress. There are bullet holes in the turrets from the 1948 civil war. A giftshop is to the left of the entrance. Inside are exhibits of indigenous gold and ceramics, colonial religious objects and furniture, political history and art. Open Tues-Sun, 8:30am-5pm, admission $.25).

One block south of the Museum are the **Tribunals,** the **Police Department,** (O.I.J., pronounced o-ee-hota) and the **Supreme Court Building.** When you reach them, turn right, on avenida 6. Three blocks west, at calle 11, turn right again, and you'll see the **Mercado Nacional de Artesanía,** a good and inexpensive place to shop for souvenirs. Continue north on calle 11 until you reach avenida central. You might be ready for a bite to eat at the **Balcon de Europa** or **Finisterre** (a ctl, c 7), or coffee and cake at **Spoon** (a ctl, c 5/7). **ANDA** (a ctl, c 5/7) features crafts made by Costa Rican Indians.

Now you're coming to the **Plaza de la Cultura** on avenida ctl, calle 5/3. Down the grassy steps on calle 5 is the **Tourism Institute's Information Center** to the left. There too is the entrance to the excellent exhibition rooms and **Gold Museum** below the Plaza (open Tues-Sun).

Cross the Plaza to the famous **National Theatre.** In 1890 the world renowned prima donna, Adelina Patti, appeared with a traveling opera company in Guatemala. She could not perform in Costa Rica because there was no appropriate theater. Newly-rich coffee merchants offered to finance the construction of a theater with a tax on every bag of coffee exported from the country. Belgian architects were called in to design and supervise the building, and metal structure was ordered from Belgian mills. Painters and decorators were brought from Italy, along with that country's famous marble. The Teatro Nacional was inaugurated in 1894 with Gounod's *Faust.* The opening night cast included singers from the Paris Opera. A source of cultural pride for many years, the Theater was made into a national monument in 1965. Extensive restoration work has recently renewed its beautiful ceiling paintings and sumptuous decor. Current plays, dance and music concerts are announced at the entrance. Tickets are sold at a booth on the northeast side of the building. Guided tours are available. The **Café del Teatro Nacional,** to the left as you enter the building, has changing art exhibits. They specialize in exotic coffee combinations and desserts. Sit down there, you deserve a rest.

CREATIVE ARTS

Costa Ricans are well known for their interest in culture and the arts. The Ministry of Culture stimulates activity by sponsoring theater, choral music, opera, dance, literature, poetry, art, sculpture and film.

Music: Since 1972, Costa Rica has had the only National Youth Symphony in Latin America. It was inaugurated by ex-President Figueres' famous quote: "We need to concern ourselves not only with the standard of living but the quality of life as well. Why have tractors without violins?" Many of the young musicians trained in the Youth Symphony have graduated to participate in the **National Symphony,** which performs Thursday and Friday nights at 8 and Sundays at 10:30am in the National Theater. Call 21-5341 to check showtimes. Internationally famed guest directors and soloists are often featured in their programs. Entrance fees are kept low so that people of all economic levels may enjoy the concerts. The least expensive seats are in the *galería* section which is up three flights of stairs through an entrance on the left side of the Teatro Nacional. The *butacas* are in the first tier of boxes above the *luneta* (orchestra) section. The *palcos* are on the second tier at the same level as the President's box. The symphony season starts in April and ends in December.

Retired musicians, amateurs and some symphony members play together for fun on Monday nights in Heredia. Foreigners are welcome to join. Call German Alvarado at 21-1185 for information.

Since economic difficulties have limited the Ministry of Culture in recent years, the **Ars Musica Foundation** has been formed to generate international and local funding for valuable projects like the Youth Symphony. (Ars Musica, Apdo. 1035, San José, 33-9890).

Radio Universidad at 870 AM and 96.7 and 101.9 FM plays classical music all day, interspersed with educational programs. **Radio Azul**, 99 FM, plays a lot of new age music and jazz.

Peñas and **La Nueva Canción:** The *peña*, literally "circle or group of friends", is a tradition brought to Costa Rica by Chilean and Argentinean exiles. People of all nationalities come together at a favorite cafe and sing the moving and inspiring songs that have become the themes of today's Latin America: *La Nueva Canción*. **Luis Angel Castro, Rubén Pagura** and **Juan Carlos Ureña** are some of the favorite leaders of *peñas* these days. The **Toruma Youth Hostel** (a ctl, c 29, 24-4085), **La Rayuela** (100 m north and 100 m east of the San Pedro Church) and **Baleares** (25 m east of La Nueva China in San Pedro) often have *peñas*. Also keep your ears open for concerts by **Adrián Goizueta** and his Grupo Experimental, **Cantares** and **Canto America.**

Theater: Ticos are great actors. It is said that Costa Rica has more theatre companies per capita than any other country in the world. Even if you don't understand Spanish, it might be worth it to go, just to see the energy and creativity that these people bring to the stage. Proof of Costa Rica's democracy is the excellent **National Theater Company,** whose plays sometimes poke fun at the same government that pays their salaries. The *Tico Times* and the *Viva* section of *La Nación* will tell you what is playing. Admission is about $1.50. Theater addresses are listed below:

Teatro de la Aduana, c 25, a 3/5
Teatro del Angel, a ctl, c 13/15, 22-8258
Teatro Bellas Artes, east side of University of Costa Rica campus.
Teatro Carpa, a ctl, c 29, 34-2866
Sala de la Calle 15, a 2, c 15
Teatro Chaplin, a 9, c 1/3
Teatro Laurence Olivier, a 2, c 28, 23-1960, 22-1034
Teatro La Mascara, c 13, a 2/4
Teatro Melico Salazar, a 2, c ctl/2, 21-4952
Teatro Tiempo, c 13, a ctl/2, 22-0792
Teatro Vargas Calvo, c 3/5, a 2, 22-1875

The English-speaking community also puts a lot of energy into their **Little Theatre Group,** which presents musicals and comedies several times a year. See the *Tico Times* for schedules. Plays benefit the Youth Symphony.

Films: North American movies dominate the film scene here, and are usually shown 3-6 months after they appear in the States, with Spanish subtitles. The **Sala Garbo** (a 2, c 28) features excellent international films with Spanish subtitles. Next door, the **Teatro Laurence Olivier** offers films, plays and concerts as well as a gallery and coffee house. Recently local jazz groups have been playing in their Shakespeare Gallery. Take the Sabana-Cementerio bus (c 7, a ctl/2) and get off at the Pizza Hut on Paseo Colón. The two theaters are one block to the left (south). You can walk there in 25 minutes from downtown. All movie theaters charge about $1.50. Check schedules in the *Tico Times* or *La Nación*.

Art: True to form, the Ticos converted their former air terminal into the **Museum of Costa Rican Art.** Located in the Sabana at the end of Paseo Colón, this tastefully done museum displays the works of the country's finest painters and sculptors as well as international exhibits. Open 10am-5:45pm. Admission $.30. Free Sundays, closed Mondays.

Check *La Nación* and the *Tico Times* for exhibits at the many galleries downtown. The Centro Cultural has monthly art exhibits. Their openings are a good place to meet people.

MISCELLANEOUS INFORMATION

Newspapers and magazines: English-language newspapers and magazines are sold at the Candy Shop of the Gran Hotel Costa Rica (c 3, a ctl/2), The Bookshop (a 1, c 1/3), the Automercado (c 3, a 3/5), the Hotel Aurola (c 5, a 5), Yaohan's (across from the Hotel Corobicí), the Hotel Amstel Shop (c 7, a 1), the Hotel Bougainvillea, and Librería Lehmann (a ctl, c 1/3). Most of them carry the *New York Times*, the *Wall St. Journal* and the *Miami Herald,* as well as *Time* and *Newsweek.* You can also have the above periodicals delivered to your home by calling Publiserisa, 55-3883, 55-3996.

The best source of local news in English is the *Tico Times,* available for $.25 at the above places and at many hotels. Winner of the 1981 Interamerican Press Association award for distinguished service to the community, the *Tico Times* offers a well-researched synthesis of weekly events in Costa Rica and Central America as a whole. They are without comparison in their coverage of local environmental and political issues, and also give an excellent rundown of cultural activities. Published Fridays. Apdo. 4632, San José. Tel: 22-8952 or 22-0040. **Casey's** (c ctl, a 7/9) sells and trades used books in English.

Meeting places: The **Friends' Peace Center** in San José is a network for the various groups working for peace in Central America. It provides meeting space, coordination of activities, a library and educational programs as well as a weekly meditation time in which peace workers can renew their spirits. The staff of the center is made up of both Central and North Americans, most of them volunteers. They welcome donations of time or funding from interested people. The Peace Center is located on c 15, a 6 bis. Tel: 33-6168.

The Women's Club, Bridge Club, Newcomer's Club, Republicans Abroad, Democrats Abroad, American Legion, Disabled American Veterans, Retired Officers Association, Masonic Lodge, Amnesty International, Lions, Rotary, Women's Aglow Fellowship, Christian Women's Club, Amateur Fishing Club, Canada Club, Cricket Club, Coffee Pickin' Square Dancers, the Canoeing/Kayaking Club and the US Citizens Concerned for Peace all meet regularly in San José. Current hours and numbers are listed in the *Tico Times*.

Supermarkets: Name-brand products from the U.S. are flooding Costa Rican supermarkets. Because they are imported, they are extremely expensive. Right next to them on the shelf will be a comparable locally-made product for a quarter of the price.

Stores are often closed between 12 and 2 during the week. They usually open only half day on Saturday. The **Mas x Menos** supermarkets are exceptions: most are open 8 am to 8 pm and do not close for lunch or on Sundays. Ask at your hotel for the nearest one. The **Automercado**, less crowded, cleaner and more expensive than the Mas x Menos, is open 8:15am to 7:30pm and closed Sundays.

Yaohan's, a large Japanese-owned supermarket across from the Hotel Corobicí, Sabana East, is also open on Sundays. It has one of the best produce sections in San José. Most *pulperías* (corner stores) stay open during lunch and on Sundays. Often they also have excellent produce if you get there early in the day (see p. 81).

Orchids and butterflies: Orchid lovers should plan to visit during March or September when the annual **National Orchid Show** is held. Write the *Tico Times* for exact dates. Butterfly enthusiasts will enjoy the **Museum of Entomology** at the University's *Facultad de Agronomía,* UCR campus, San Pedro. Open Weds and Thurs, 1-6 pm, admission free.

PLACES TO JOG OR WALK IN SAN JOSE

La Sabana: We know of no other city which has converted its outgrown international airport into a metropolitan park with sports facilities. The National Gymnasium was built on the southeast corner of the former airfield; the National Stadium on the northwest corner. A small lake, which had been filled in, has been restored and residential districts have been built on three sides of La Sabana (the flatland). The Air Terminal Building is now the National Art Museum.

With an Olympic swimming pool, jogging and walking paths, tennis, volleyball, basketball courts, soccer and baseball fields, La Sabana has become a favorite recreation area on weekends and a training ground for joggers during lunch hours (showers provided). In an effort to build good driving habits, a miniature town has been built to teach traffic laws to little kids in battery-driven cars with brakes. There's a hill for kiteflying. People fly-cast in the lake. There are lots of trees for relaxing in the shade. Take the Sabana-Cementerio bus (c 7, a ctl; or c 2, a 3).

Behind the Zoo: Walk through Parque Morazán and Parque de España to the Casa Amarilla. Go north on calle 11, which becomes a winding, quiet, tree-lined street along the upper border of Parque Bolívar. Keep winding around until you come to the railroad tracks and a rural guard station. Climb the steps and you're in Barrio Aranjuez, a nice, older neighborhood. You'll be walking east on avenida 11. Go to your left two blocks after the tracks and soon you'll be at the edge of a cliff with cement stairs going down it. You'll see basketball courts and a soccer field with a track around it, free from San José's diesel fumes.

The back way to San Pedro: Walk through Parque Nacional to the Limón train station. Follow the tracks going east, across calle 23 and on past some graceful old houses with lovely flower gardens. Follow the tracks one block past the *pulpería* Ambos Mares till you see a sign that says *"Final del Patio"*. After this point there is no sidewalk, so keep jogging to your left and head east at the next block. You'll only have to zigzag once; then, after the Colegium Fidelitas (notice the Centro Cultural Costarricense-Norteamericano to your right), it's a short zigzag and you're heading east again. This street ends across from one entrance to the University of Costa Rica campus. A circular drive one mile long goes around the campus and is pleasantly shaded by beautiful trees. If you go early in the morning you'll see joggers, walkers, and a lot of birds.

Parque del Este: This park above San Pedro in San Rafael de Montes de Oca is a great place to escape from pollution and crowds for a few hours. It's an expansive green area cleared out of a lush canyon. There's a Vita Course jogging and exercise trail with little signs that tell you to do all sorts of strenuous things along the way. There's also a pool, basketball courts, a soccer field, picnic tables, playgrounds, a lookout point with a sign that identifies the mountains on the horizon, and a zigzagging nature trail. Get there on the San Ramón de Tres Rios bus that leaves from a 2, c 5/7 and passes through San Pedro. The park is open until 4 pm, closed Mondays, and pretty crowded on weekends and holidays.

RESTAURANTS

Coffee Shops

Below are some of the best places we've found to eat a quick meal or have a cup of coffee. The traditional Tico way to serve coffee is in two separate pitchers, one filled with strong black coffee and the other with steaming hot milk. You can mix them to suit your taste. Many establishments have stopped this practice for economic reasons, but Las Cuartetas, Manolo's, Spoon, and Giacomín have retained the tradition.

Abacus: Crepes, salads, yummy desserts. Moderate. Next to Tega on the road to Escazú; 28-5350.

Azafrán: Interesting and delicious sandwiches and desserts, often made to go. Los Yoses, 25m east of Panadería Pancel. Open Mon-Sat 11am-7pm.

Café del Teatro Nacional: Quiet and elegant. Walls display changing exhibits of Costa Rican art. To the left as you enter the Theatre. Open weekdays 10:30-6.

Las Cuartetas: Their little pastries are exquisite and cheap, c 2, a 3/5. Open every day 8am-8pm.

Giacomín: Their upstairs tea room is the most charming and peaceful place to enjoy coffee and delicious pastries or homemade candy. Next to Los Yoses Auto Mercado, a 20-minute walk from downtown towards San Pedro. Open 8am-12, 2pm-7pm, Mon-Sat.

Café Ruisenor: Quiet, informal atmosphere, delicious pastries and quiches made with pure, healthful ingredients. Los Yoses, 150m before the three fountains. Open 11am to 7pm, Mon-Sat. A 25-minute walk from downtown towards San Pedro.

Spoon: Outrageous desserts. Three locations: Downtown, a ctl, c 5/7; Los Yoses, one block south of Cancún, before the three fountains; Pavas across from the US Embassy.

La Casa del Angel: Delicious pizza and incredible cinnamon-flavored coffee. Inexpensive. San Pedro, 100 m. north, 150 m. east of the San Pedro Church.

El Escorial: Lunch for $1, good buffet for $3. Open Mon-Sat 11 am-2pm, 5 pm-11 pm; a 1, c 5/7.

Finisterre-Food World: A good place to go for breakfast or a quick sandwich at lunch. Next door to the Balcón de Europa, a central, c 7, 21-4841.

Manolo's: Clean, quick service. Two locations: a ctl, c ctl/1 and a ctl, c9/11. Open 7 am-10:15 pm Mon-Sat.

Soda La Casita: Small, clean, homey. Good for a quick breakfast or lunch; a 1, c ctl/1. Open weekdays.

Soda Central: Specializes in thick chicken empanadas; a 1, c 3/5.

VEGETARIAN RESTAURANTS

Don Sol: Pleasant vegetarian restaurant. Try their *energético,* a delicious natural fruit salad; a 7B, c 15, northeast of the Casa Amarilla.

Gopal: Run by the local Hare Krishna community, c 1, a 6.

Restaurant la Macrobiótica: Healthful meals in a pleasant older building, a 1, c 11-15. Open Mon-Sat 8am-3 pm, 5-10 pm. Health food store around the corner on c 11, a ctl/2.

La Mazorca: Macrobiotic fare. An extensive array of delicious wholewheat pastries and natural food products. A good place to spend an afternoon writing letters. 100 m. north, 200 m. east of the San Pedro Church. Open 9am-8pm Mon-Fri, 9am-2pm Sat, 24-8069.

Shakti: Vegetarian goodies, open 7am-4pm M-F, c 13, a 8.

Vishnu: Centrally located, inexpensive, generous servings; c 3, a ctl/1.

La Nutrisoda: Pure vegetarian food; homemade natural ice cream. Open 11-6; 55-3959; Edificio Las Arcadas, next to Gran Hotel Costa Rica.

DINING OUT

All restaurant bills include a 10 percent tip and a 10 percent tax. Therefore, tipping is not customary, but is certainly appreciated, especially when service is good.

Ambrosia: A quiet cozy place for lunch, tea or dinner. Vegetarian and non-vegetarian fare, all specialties named after Greek deities. Open Tues-Sat 11:30am to 10:30pm, Sun and Mon 11:30am to 4:30pm, 53-8012, Centro Comercial de la Calle Real, San Pedro.

Hotel Amstel: Well known for its reasonably-priced, excellent meals and service. On c 7, a 1/3, 22-4622.

Arirang: Korean specialties, Edificio Colón, 23-2838.

Ave Fénix: Authentic Chinese cuisine, Szechuan specials. Moderate. 200 m. west of the San Pedro church, 25-3362.

Balcón de Europa: Homemade fettucine, delicious cheeses. Chef Franco Piatti does his best to make you feel at home; a ctl, c 7/9, 21-4841.

Beirut: Middle Eastern specialties. Open Tues-Sat 11:30 am-11 pm, Sun 11:30-6; a 1, c 32, 1 block north of Pollos Kentucky on Paseo Colón. Moderate prices. 57-1808.

Le Bistrot: One of our favorite places, very small, with a relaxed French *savoir faire*. 100 m. east, 20 m. north from San Pedro Church, 53-8062.

Hotel Bougainvillea: The Barrio Tournón and new Santo Domingo Bougainvilleas, well-known as fine hotels, have excellent restaurants as well. Tournón: 33-6622, Santo Domingo: 36-5310.

Chalet Suizo: A San José landmark with a traditional European menu. Crowded at lunch; c 5/7, a 1, 22-3118.

Chalet Tirol: Near the cloud forest above Heredia, a truly elegant restaurant with two French chefs specializing in *nouvelle cuisine*. Open 8am to 11pm every day, closes around 8pm on Sunday. Call for reservations, 39-7070, 39-7050.

Le Chandelier: Fancy French cuisine. Paseo Colón west of Banco Anglo, 21-7947.

Flor del Loto: Delicious Hunan and Szechuan Chinese specialties. Open every day for lunch and dinner. East side of ICE building, Sabana Norte, 32-4652. Moderate.

Restaurant La Galería: Excellent European cuisine. One of the best. Call ahead for reservations. Los Yoses, 34-0850.

Greta's: Creative, excellent, expensive. San Pedro, 53-3107.

L'Ile de France: Excellent French cuisine, superb service. Expensive, but you don't have to order a whole meal there; c 7, a ctl/2, 22-4241.

Kudamm: One of the only places in San José open Sundays besides the hotel restaurants. Their generous Sunday buffet is served from 11am to 6pm, but getting there earlier is better. $8 for all you can eat. German specialties. Open the rest of the week 11:30-2:30 and 6-11. Curridabat, 53-7601.

Lai Yuin: Specializes in Chinese seafoods. Curridabat, across from Indoor Club. Moderate, 53-5055.

La Mallorquina: Spanish and French cuisine; Paseo Colon, 23-7634.

La Masía de Triquell: Spanish cuisine in a lovely colonial atmosphere. Expensive, elegant; c 40, a 2, 21-5073.

Mirador Ram Luna: This large, family-style restaurant in the mountains 15km S of San José is famous for tender steaks and fantastic views of the central valley. Jukebox, dancefloor, playground equipment for kids. Go through Desamparados to Aserrí and follow a lovely winding road 5 km up from there, or take an Acosta (c 8, a 12/14) or San Gabriel (c 10, a 12/14) bus to the Mirador. Tel: 30-3060 (see map, p 122).

La Nueva China: One of San José's best Chinese restaurants. Try their fish soup. San Pedro, across from the Banco Popular, 24-4478.

Paprika: Delicious soups, salads, omelettes, main dishes and desserts. Very rich. Quiet, comfortable atmosphere. Open for lunch and dinner; a ctl, c 29/33, 25-8971.

La Petite Provence: French cuisine accompanied by Nicole's *ballades*. Open 12-2:30, 6:30-10:30, closed Sun. On the road to San Pedro next to Pizza Hut (a ctl, c 27), 55-1559.

Sakura: Costa Rica's only authentic Japanese restaurant. Expensive. At the Sheraton Herradura Hotel near the airport, 39-0033, ext.258. Open 11:30am-3pm, 6-10pm, closed Mon.

Valerio's: Delicious pizza and lasagne, great desserts, reasonable prices. Los Yoses, in the shopping center next to Cancún, 25-0838.

Vía Veneto: Excellent Italian food, elegant atmosphere, delicious pastries. Curridabat, across from Indoor Club, tel: 34-2898.

Villa Franken: Homemade sauerkraut, paté, apple strudel and other German specialties. Open 12-2:30pm, 6:30-10:30pm, Sun 12-3:30pm, closed Weds. 100m E, 75 S of Banco Popular, San Pedro, 24-1850.

Zermatt: Swiss specialties, including fondue. 100 m. north, 25 e. Santa Teresita Church, 22-0604.

NIGHTLIFE

These are some of our favorite nightspots. Most of them serve the traditional *bocas,* little plates of food that accompany each drink. *Ceviche* (raw fish "cooked" in lemon juice), fried fish, pork and beans and *mondongo* (tripe) are common bocas. Usually they are free. As for national beers, we recommend Bavaria, Imperial, or the more expensive Heineken.

Amstel Hotel Bar: Simple, elegant, *quiet,* c 7, a 1/3.

Antojitos: Good Mexican food, great mariachis. Paseo Colón near Pizza Hut, and in Los Yoses.

Bar México: One of San José's most revered traditional nightspots where *boca*-making has been elevated to an art. Here you pay for the *bocas.* Live mariachi bands. To get there from downtown you have to walk through a bad neighborhood, so it's better to take the Barrio México bus at c 7, a ctl. A cab will take you there for about $1. It's kitty-corner from the Barrio México church.

Chelles: As far as atmosphere goes, there's not much, but if you're a people-watcher, you'll enjoy hanging out at Chelles. Probably because it remains open 24 hours a day, seven days a week, Chelles has become a landmark. You'll see actors, musicians and dancers from the National Theater there having a midnight snack. You'll see middle-aged Costa Rican men amusing each other with toothpick tricks. You'll be asked to buy wilted roses from intriguing old ladies and persistent young boys. There are free *bocas* with every drink. For those who tire of the glare of Chelles' bare lightbulbs, there is **Chelles Taberna** around the corner, where you can hide in booths. The Taberna has better *bocas* too. Chelles Lite, a ctl, c 9, Chelles Dark, c 9 a ctl/2. Overpriced.

Charleston: Nice 1920's decor, often have good vintage jazz tapes, c 9, a 2/4.

Crocodile Club: Friendly bar featuring gringo-style hamburgers. Huge video screen, dance floor; San Pedro, across from Banco Anglo.

El Cuartel de la Boca del Monte: By day a quiet, artistically-decorated restaurant featuring Costa Rican dishes. By night, the bar in the back becomes one of the most popular in San José. The *bocas* aren't free, but they're good. Most fun are their fantastic cocktails, extravagantly decorated with tropical fruit and sometimes even sparklers. Reasonably priced; a 1, c 21/23.

Dennie's: Quiet bar and restaurant, featuring live music and Caribbean food. Excellent curry, generous *bocas*; a ctl, c 19/21.

La Esmeralda is lots of fun. It's the new home of the Mariachi Union. Groups of musicians stroll between the tables while their vans wait outside to transport them to emergency serenade sites. I'll never forget the best party I ever went to in Costa Rica--my landlady's 80th birthday. After eating, drinking and dancing till 1:00, I was ready to retire, but that's not the way Ticos celebrate birthdays. At 2 am the mariachis arrived to serenade her with guitars, harps, trumpets and violins. But I digress. La Esmeralda offers good, reasonably-priced food as well as fun; a 2, c 5/7. Open round the clock every day but Sunday.

El Pueblo is a huge maze of Spanish colonial style alleyways and tiled roofs. You can spend hours wandering around there, getting lost and spending money. **Montego Bay** and the **Kacatúa** feature live calypso, reggae, and jazz. There is a small bar where you can hear authentic Argentinean tango. **Lety's** has a variety show with Costa Rican native dancers, comics and singers.

A skating rink and three discotheques also await you at El Pueblo. **Lukas** is a popular place to go for a late dinner or snack; **Rias Bajas,** one of San José's most elegant seafood restaurants, is also there. At the **Cocina de Leña** you can eat Costa Rican native dishes in authentic *campesino* atmosphere. The rest of El Pueblo is full of more restaurants, nightclubs, boutiques, galleries and offices. Most nightspots have a cover charge, especially on weekends or holidays, but it's fun to go and wander there anyway. It's across the river north of downtown, next to the Hotel Bougainvillea. Walk, or take a Calle Blancos bus from c 1, a 5.

Los Lechones: You have to buy the bocas here, but the atmosphere is great when a calypso band plays weekends; a 6, c 11/13.

Soda La Perla, Soda Palace: Like Chelles, these two restaurants are not special in themselves. They are mentioned as places where budding novelists can go to polish their powers of character description. Apparently the 1948 insurrection was planned over fried fish bocas and beer at the Soda Palace. It's open all night. Roving calypso bands come in, take a table, and play for everyone just for the joy of it. The restaurants are on either side of the Teatro Melico Salazar, a huge auditorium run by the Ministry of Culture as a forum for local artists. Be careful in the Soda Palace neighborhood. Parque Central can be dangerous at night (a 2, c ctl/2).

SOUVENIRS

Moderately priced souvenirs can be found at the government crafts cooperatives: **CANAPI** (c 11, a 1) and the **Mercado Nacional de Artesanía** (c 11, a 2b, behind the Soledad Church), as well as in the **Mercado Central** (a ctl/1, c 6/8), and **La Casona** (c ctl, a ctl/1). One of the most charming, complete, and inexpensive souvenir shops is in the converted home of one of Costa Rica's ex-presidents, now the **Hotel Don Carlos** (c 9, a 9). **Arterica**, a small shop next to the entrance of the Teatro Melico Salazar (a 2, c ctl/2) is a showcase for crafts-people who are revitalizing Costa Rican native artisanry, such as weaving, basketmaking, ceramics and woodcarving. They also offer free courses in native crafts through the University of Costa Rica, and give workshops in the countryside to people wishing to develop their skills. You can also see indigenous crafts at **ANDA** (a ctl, c 5/7).

If you have a little more money to spend, visit **Magia** (c 5, a 1/3), **Suraska** (c 5, a 3), or **La Galería** (c 1, a ctl/1) where more artistic items are sold, including the innovative woodwork of two North Americans, Barry Biesanz and Jay Morrison. Biesanz specializes in exquisitely-crafted bowls and boxes, as well as furniture, which can be seen at his workshop in Bello Horizonte, above Escazú (28-1811). Morrison's creative hardwood furniture is also displayed at his showroom, Tierra Extraña, in Santa Ana (28-6697).

Another extraordinary woodworker is Paul Smith, one of the early settlers in Monteverde. His lovingly-crafted stringed instruments are made of European wood aged for ten years. You can find Paul at his Monteverde workshop (61-2551, 44-6990).

The capital of Costa Rican woodcraft is **Sarchí**, about an hour northwest of San José (see p. 126). Everything from salad bowls to rocking chairs to miniature oxcarts can be purchased there. The capital of Costa Rican leathercraft is Moravia, a suburb of San José, where you'll see shops like **El Caballo Blanco, La Rueda** and **El Potro** around the main square. Moravia buses leave frequently from a 3, c 3/5.

Tiny *huacas*, copies of precolumbian jewelry representing frogs, lizards, turtles and humanesque deities, are relatively inexpensive and make lovely necklaces, earrings and tiepins. Some nice copies of precolumbian jadework and ocarinas are sold around the National Theater. Authentic precolumbian artefacts are not allowed to be taken out of the country, so don't believe anyone who tells you something is original. If it is original, the item has been stolen from an archaeological site.

If you need lightweight souvenirs, there are plenty of T-shirts, woven hemp shoulder bags, and jewelry made of wood and metal. Colorful scarves, hats, blouses, bags and sun visors made by Go Bandannas are unusual souvenirs, with motifs of

107

native flora and fauna. Their creative coloring and activity book, *Let's Discover Costa Rica*, is the answer for the kids on your souvenir list. They are sold almost everywhere, but if you go to the **Bandanna Republic Jungle Shop** in Villa Colón between December 1 and April 1, you can enjoy a free swim at Finca Ob-La-Di, Ob-La-Da's spectacular 75-foot waterfall. Call for arrangements and directions, 49-1179.

If you're staying for awhile, take advantage of the low prices and excellent work of local tailors and seamstresses. They make fine formal clothes, or can copy your favorite designs. Ask a well-dressed Tico whom he or she would recommend.

You can buy freshly ground coffee or coffee beans at the Central Market. It is usually ground finer than percolator coffee, for use in the *chorreador,* a filter bag that hangs from a wooden stand. There are percolator grinds available in supermarkets, where you'll also find **Caferica**, a delicious coffee liqueur, as well as dried bananas, coconut twirls, macadamia nuts, cashews, and yummy El Angel jams, fruit leathers and pastes. A *tapa dulce,* the native hard brown sugar, can be grated to add a rich flavor to baked goods or used in cereals or coffee. We've heard of tourists who take home cases of **Salsa Lizano**, a tasty bottled sauce that Ticos love to sprinkle on their *gallo pinto.*

If you are going to Monteverde, save some of your souvenir budget for **CASEM**, the women's craft cooperative there, which specializes in embroidered and hand-painted clothing depicting cloud forest wildlife. You'll see it on the right as you enter Monteverde. There is also a new crafts cooperative on the main square in Ciudad Quesada.

The beautiful handicrafts of Guatemala and El Salvador can be found at **Sol Maya** on Paseo Colon across from Hospital San Juan de Dios. Guatemalan textiles are also sold on Calle 3, a 3/5, next to the Automercado (closed weekends).

Wicker, raffia and woven palm leaf items should be spray varnished when you get home. Don't be tempted to buy tortoise shell or alligator skin goods--they are made from endangered animals which are internationally protected. Customs officials will confiscate these items at your home country airport.

HOTELS

Our hotel rate categories, based on *double* occupancy, and including the 13% tax, are as follows:

XL $80-125	A $40-50	D $12-20
LL $60-80	B $30-40	E $7-12
L $50-60	C $20-30	F under $7

Most hotels that are trying to cater to tourists are listed with the Tourism Institute. If there is any doubt about what you are being charged, the ICT-approved rates (without 13% tax) should be posted at the main desk and on the back of the door in each room, including info on where to complain in case of an overcharge or bad service.

The following codes are used to describe hotel facilities in the rest of the book, especially when referring to low cost places. You can assume that any room in the D category or above will have a private bath, but only the most expensive places at the beach have hot water.

pb: private bath
cb: communal bath
hw: hot water, either referring to an electric device which warms the shower water, or hot water from regular water tanks.
cw: cold water
a/c: air conditioning
tf: table fans
cf: ceiling fans
nf: no fans

We should clarify the meaning of various terms which you'll see throughout the book referring to lodging. *Hotels* usually have more than one story, but not always. *Cabinas* are the most common form of lodging at the beach or in the mountains. They can be either separated, or connected in rows or duplexes. They roughly correspond to what a North American would call a "motel". However, here, *motel* refers to a small number of establishments, mostly on the southeastern side of San José, which couples use for clandestine romantic trysts. The couples are often married, but not to each other. The motels rent by the hour. *Villas* and *chalets* are fancy cabinas, usually separated. *Pensiones* and *hospedajes* are usually converted houses which often serve family-style meals. A *posada* is an inn.

You can find clean, fairly comfortable rooms almost anywhere for under $10 for two. Atmosphere costs more. If you can afford it, there are plenty of places with great atmosphere, equipment and service. If you are traveling cheaply, you will find the following items handy:

Your own cup
A universal plug for the sink
A cotton sheet or two (some hotels have nylon or polyester covers which are uncomfortable in the humid heat at the beach)
String and clothespins for hanging up wash
Toilet paper
Towel, washcloth and soap
Flashlight
Earplugs

Of course, most places, even cheap ones, supply towels and soap, but there is an occasional one that doesn't. Our main complaint about many hotels, even some expensive ones, is that you're often subject to noise pollution from somebody's high-powered sound system, usually a nearby dance hall, or neighbors with a loud radio. A place can seem perfectly *tranquilo* when you arrive during the day; the thumping disco across the river only comes on at night. The best solution is to get up and dance. Places that are owned by foreigners are generally quieter than places owned by Ticos, who regard loud music as *alegre*.

We cannot emphasize enough that you should make reservations a month in advance during the dry season, and 3 months in advance for Christmas or Easter. Then be sure to confirm the reservations 3 days before you need them. Beach and mountain hotels often give substantial discounts in the rainy season. Discounts are often given for stays of more than a week as well. If you are staying in one place for longer than a week, consider renting a house. See the Tico Times for current listings, or ask at a local *pulperia*.

In the great tradition of Bambi ("If you can't say something nice, don't say nothing at all") we mention only places that we consider basically decent and worthwhile.

DELUXE HOTELS: All except L'Ambiance are large convention centers and are in category XL ($80-125 double occupancy).

L'Ambiance: Small, exclusive hotel in an old Spanish style home with courtyard and fountain, very quiet, filled with antiques, gourmet restaurant, continental breakfast incl., cable TV, complete *concierge* service for travel arrangements, symphony and theater tickets, emphasis on service, 22-6702, c 13, a 9/11, SJ, CR.

Aurola Holiday Inn: Downtown, indoor pool, sauna, gym, cable TV, gourmet restaurant on top floor, non-smoking floor, firesafe, earthquake-proof, 33-7233, 33-7036, fx: (506) 55-1036, Apdo. 7802, 1000 SJ, CR.

Cariari: Resort hotel (golf, tennis, pools, exercise classes, horses, cable TV, bus service to downtown).   Located on airport highway 20 min. from San José; 39-0022, fx: (506) 39-2803, Apdo. 737, 1007 CC, CR; telex: 7509 Cariari.

Corobicí: Tennis, sauna, pool, cable TV.   Northeast corner of La Sabana; 32-8122, fx: (506) 31-5834, Apdo. 2443, 1000 SJ, CR.

Sheraton Herradura: Cable TV, health spa, golf, tennis. Airport highway 20 min. from San José. 39-0033, fx: (506) 39-2292.   Apdo. 7-1880, 1000 SJ, CR; telex: 7512 Herratel.

FIRST CLASS HOTELS.   Most are downtown, so look for the quieter rooms off the street.

L RANGE: $50-60 double occupancy

Balmoral: Convention center patronized mostly by businesspeople. Central, cable TV, sauna; 21-1919, 21-5022, fx: (506) 21-7826, a ctl, c 7/9, Apdo. 3344, 1000 SJ, CR; telex: 2254 Balmor.

Bougainvillea: Quiet, well-appointed rooms, excellent restaurant and service. Recommended.   Two locations: Barrio

Tournon, north of downtown (33-6622, fx: 22-5211) and Santo Domingo de Heredia, 9km from San Jose (36-8822, fx: 36-8484), Apdo. 69, 2120 Guadalupe, SJ, CR.

Europa: Distinctive traditional European style, light and airy, indoor pool, cable TV, central, streetside rooms discounted, 22-1222, fx: (506) 21-3976; c ctl, a 3/5; Apdo. 72, 1000 SJ.

Gran Hotel Costa Rica: Across from National Theater, 24-hr restaurant, salad bar, being remodeled to preserve its 1930's flavor, cable TV; 21-9706, fx: (506) 21-3501 a ctl/2, c 3; Apdo. 527, 1000 SJ, CR; telex: 2131 Hotel Costa Rica.

Irazú: Attractive rooms, casino, pool, cable TV, tennis, sauna, bus service; 15 min from downtown on airport highway, 32-4811, fx: (506) 32-3159; Apdo. 962, 1000 SJ, CR; telex 2307 Irazú.

President: Casino, discotheque, glitzy decor, good service, cable TV, central, 22-3022, fx: (506) 21-1205, Apdo. 2922, 1000 SJ, CR.

Tennis Club: Pool, tennis, gym, sauna, skating rink, parking, southwest side of La Sabana Park, 32-1266, Apdo. 4964, 1000 SJ, CR; telex: 3206 Tennisur.

Torremolinos: Quiet, pool, sauna, cable TV, near Sabana, shuttle bus to downtown, 22-5266, 22-9129, fx: (506) 55-3167; c 40, a 5 bis, Apdo. 2029, 1000 SJ, CR; telex: 2343 Hotomol.

A ($40-50) AND **B** ($30-40) **RANGE** (double occupancy)

Ambassador: Staying here gets you a discount at discotheques, restaurants and jewelry stores. A 20-minute walk from downtown. No extra charge for kids under 12. Paseo Colón, c 26/28; Apdo. 10186, 1000 SJ, CR; 21-8155, fx: (506) 55-3396, telex: 2315 Ambassador; A.

Amstel: Best known for its excellent restaurant, central, quieter rooms on east side of building. 22-4622, fx: (506) 33-3329, c 7, a 1/3; Apdo. 4192, 1000 SJ, CR; telex: 2820 Amstel; B.

Casa María: Pool, cable TV, breakfast incl., kitchen privileges, some shared baths. One km east of Escazú church, in residential neighborhood, 28-2270, fx: 28-0015, B-LL.

Don Carlos: European-style bed and breakfast. Charming decor, pleasant historical neighborhood. Cable TV, gym, tour videos, great souvenir shop, 21-6707, fx: (506) 55-0828, c 9, a 9 No. 779; Apdo 1593, SJ, CR; B.

Gran Vía: Streetside rooms with balconies, back rooms quieter. Very central, clean and light; 22-7737, a ctl, c 1/3; Apdo. 1433, 1000 SJ, CR; B.

Plaza: Small rooms, clean, restaurant open 6 am-10 pm, 22-5533, fx: (506) 22-2641, a ctl, c 2/4, B.

Royal Gardens: Casino, authentic Chinese food, central, 57-0022, 57-0023, telex: ROAGA, Apdo. 3493, 1000 SJ; B.

APARTHOTELS: As the word implies, these are a cross between an apartment and a hotel. All have kitchens, telephones and TV. Discounts for weekly or monthly rental. They tend to lack atmosphere, although the Lamm, D'Galah, Don Carlos, and Maria Alexandra are exceptions.

Castilla: c 24, a 2/4, 22-2113, near Paseo Colon, 21-2080, Apdo. 4699, SJ, CR; B.

D'Galah: Across from the Facultad de Farmacia of the University of Costa Rica campus in San Pedro. Quiet, friendly, music room, sauna, cheaper rooms w/o kitchens, 34-1743, 53-7539, Apdo. 208, 2350 San José, CR; C.

Don Carlos: Cable color TV, views, c 29, a ctl/8, 21-6707, fax: (506) 55-0828, Apdo. 1593, SJ, CR, B.

El Conquistador: Los Yoses, near shopping, quiet, 25-3022, Apdo. 303, 2050 San Pedro, CR; B.

Lamm: c 15, a 1, 21-4920, near parks and museums, large, clean, attractive older apartments, traffic noise, Apdo. 2729, 1000 SJ, CR; B.

La Perla: La Uruca, color TV, 32-6153, C.

Los Yoses: Very clean, pool, parking, breakfast incl, 25-0033, Apdo. 1597, 1000 SJ, CR; B.

María Alexandra: Escazu, west of San Jose. Cable TV, washing machine, a/c, pool, sauna, excellent restaurant, quiet, very clean, 28-1507, fx: 28-5192, Apdo. 3756, 1000 SJ, CR; B.

Napoleón: c 40, a 5, near shopping and Sabana Park, pool, kind of stuffy, 23-3252, Apdo. 86340, SJ, CR; B.

Ramgo: Near Sabana, 200m W, 100m S of Tennis Club, 32-3823, Apdo. 1441, SJ, CR; B.

San José: a 2, c 17/19, 21-6684, fx: (506) 33-3329; B.

MID-RANGE HOTELS, $17-30 double occupancy

Alameda: Near Coca Cola and other bus stops, simple, friendly; a ctl, c 12/14, 21-3045, 21-6333, C.

Cacts: In a neighborhood west of the Coca Cola, quiet, very friendly, helpful with travel arrangements, breakfast incl., airport pickup, 50% deposit requested when making reservations, 21-2928, fx: (506) 21-8616; a 3 bis #2845, c 28-30, Apdo. 379, 1005 SJ, CR; D.

Costa Rica Inn: Central, small rooms, some with windows that open onto a corridor. Discounts for weekly and monthly stays, 22-5203, c 9, a 1/3, D.

Diplomat: Clean, well-run, central, a favorite with foreigners, 21-8133, c 6, a ctl/2, D.

Fortuna: Clean, borderline neighborhood, 23-5344, a 6 c 2/4, D.

Galilea: Light, airy rooms, especially on 3rd floor, clean; English-speaking staff, near Plaza de la Democracia and Museum; 33-6925, a ctl, c 11/13, C.

Musoc: Peace Corps hangout, next to Coca Cola bus station, bad neighborhood, clean, well-run, noisy; c 16, a 1/3, 22-9437, D, cheaper with shared bath, hw.

Pico Blanco: Very lovely small mountain hotel with a great view. Clean, charming rooms, restaurant, friendly atmosphere, recommended. San Antonio de Escazú, 8 km west of San José, 28-3197 (Spanish), 28-1908 (English), Apdo. 900, Escazu, CR; C and B.

Posada Pegasus: "Dedicated to serenity, individuality, natural beauty." Light meals served. Jacuzzi. San Antonio de Escazú, next to Pico Blanco, 28-4196, C, lower weekly rates. Apdo 370, Escazú, CR.

Ritz: Small hotel, English library, hw, not the best neighborhood; 22-4103, c ctl, a 8-10, D.

Talamanca: Adequate 52-rooms, restaurant, parking, casino, 33-5033, a 2, c 8/10, D.

INEXPENSIVE, SIMPLE HOTELS ($3-12, double)

Astoria: Quiet, funky religious decor, small dark rooms, a 7, c 7/9, 21-2174, E with shared baths, D private bath, lower weekly rates.

Bellavista: Has a lot of chintzy charm for a cheap hotel, but not a lot of fresh air. Most windows open onto a corridor. Friendly owners run Dennie's restaurant next door, famous for Caribbean cooking; 23-0095, a ctl, c 19/21, near Limón bus stop and Museum, E.

Boruca: Clean, quiet, family-run, secure though neighborhood not good, near buses, very cheap, shared baths, recommended; c 14, a 1/3, 23-0016, F.

Capital: Clean, private baths, phones, hw, central; c 4, a 3/5, 21-8497, E.

Central: Clean, pb, central; a 3, c 4/6, 21-2767, F.

Cocorí: Private baths, hw, close to Guanacaste bus stops, noisy; c 16, a 3, 33-0081, E.

Gran Hotel Centroamericano: Good for wheelchairs, inexpensive cafeteria, private baths, a 2, c 6/8, 21-3362, E.

Marlyn: Borderline neighborhood near old penitentiary but central and fairly clean--an old house with beautiful tiled floors chopped up into rooms. Private baths, most with hot water, c 4, a 7/9, 33-3212, F.

Morazán: Older building, big bare rooms; near Parque Morazán, Parque Nacional; a 3, c 11/15, 21-9083, F.

Otoya: Dark and dingy, but cheap and friendly. Central location, c ctl, a 5/7, 21-3925, E, pb; F, cb, hw.

Petit: 9 blocks from Sabana Park, good neighborhood yet close to buses, light kitchen privileges; c 24, a ctl/2, 33-0766, D, pb; E, cb, hw.

Príncipe: Rooms have big windows, private baths, telephones, secure but borderline neighborhood, 1 block south of Parque Central, a 6, c ctl/2, 22-7983, E.

Roma: Near buses, noisy, cheap; c 14, a 1, 23-2179, F, cw.

HOSTELS

Toruma: Headquarters of the Costa Rica Youth Hostel Network.   Dormitory-style rooms, washing machine, kitchen, inexpensive soda open 7:15 am-9 pm. Sometimes Toruma holds Friday night *peñas* with local bands. $2.50 with an OTEC or International Student Card, $3 without; a ctl, c 31/33, tel: 24-4085.

The **Friends Peace Center** is opening a small *pensión* next to the Center on a 6 bis, c 15, with some individual rooms, one bunkbed room, shared baths with hot water and kitchen privileges (D, 33-6168).

Renting a room with a Tico family is a good way to get to know the people and practice your Spanish. The going rate for a room, two or three meals a day and laundry service is around $150 per month. Call the language schools, look for signs at the University or contact Sra. Soledad Zamora (24-7937) who specializes in connecting renters with rooms. Be prepared for a lot of hospitality. If noise bothers you, check first to see if your family leaves the TV or radio on all the time.

View with sombrilla del pobre.

DO-IT-YOURSELF TOUR PLANNING

The following chart will help you plan your own tour based on your interests and the time you have available. If you have only a short time, we have starred six places that will give you a great variety of beautiful landscapes, a chance to see birds and wildlife, and are easily accessible with reasonable accommodations. Travel time to and from San José plus time to relax and explore are calculated into the "Days Required for Trip" column, but should be regarded as the *minimum* relaxed travel time possible. Tours, when available as marked, can be arranged through the travel agencies listed on p. 45-6, or with agencies recommended by the ICT in their information office on Calle 5, under the Plaza de la Cultura. Places and transportation are described on the pages indicated. "Good for Children" means either that there are activities designed for children, or that, in the case of beaches, there are gentle waves.

Have a great time exploring Costa Rica!

THE CENTRAL VALLEY	Birdwatching	Botany	Crafts	Fishing	Hiking	Churches	Volcanoes	Water sports	Wildlife	Good for children	Camping	Days required for trip	Tours available	Page number
Ojo de Agua								x		x		1/2	x	123
La Garita	x											1/2		124
*Poás National Park	x				x		x			x		1	x	124
Sarchí			x									1	x	126
Zarcero					x	x						1		127
Heredia, Barva						x	x					1/2	x	127
Braulio Carrillo N.P.					x				x		x	1/2	x	. 131
San Jerónimo					x							1/2		131
Irazú National Park					x		x					1/2	x	132
Prusia					x						x	1/2		133

	Birdwatching	Botany	Crafts	Fishing	Hiking	Churches and archaeology	Volcanoes	Water sports	Wildlife	Good for children	Camping	Days required for trip	Tours available	Page number
Orosi Valley	x			x	x	x		x				1/2	x	133
Lankester Gardens		x										1/2	x	133
Turrialba		x										1	x	134
Guayabo	x					x				x		1, car 2, bus	x	136

THE ATLANTIC COAST

	Birdwatching	Botany	Crafts	Fishing	Hiking	Churches and archaeology	Volcanoes	Water sports	Wildlife	Good for children	Camping	Days required for trip	Tours available	Page number
*Cahuita N.P. and Puerto Viejo	x		x	x	x			x	x		x	3	x	142
*Tortuguero N.P.	x			x					x			3	x	150

THE NORTHERN ZONE

	Birdwatching	Botany	Crafts	Fishing	Hiking	Churches and archaeology	Volcanoes	Water sports	Wildlife	Good for children	Camping	Days required for trip	Tours available	Page number
La Selva	x	x			x				x			2	x	154
Rara Avis	x	x			x				x			3	x	157
*Arenal Volcano and Lake Arenal				x	x		x	x			x	2	x	159

GUANACASTE

	Birdwatching	Botany	Crafts	Fishing	Hiking	Churches and archaeology	Volcanoes	Water sports	Wildlife	Good for children	Camping	Days required for trip	Tours available	Page number
Lomas Barbudal	x	x			x			x	x	x	x	2		164
Palo Verde N.P.	x				x						x	2	x	164
Rincón de la Vieja N.P.	x				x		x		x		x	3	x	166
Santa Rosa N.P.	x	x			x			x	x		x	3	x	169
Guanacaste N.P.	x	x			x	x	x		x			3		171
Beaches near Liberia				x				x		x	x	3	x	173
Beaches near Santa Cruz				x				x		x	x	3	x	177
Nicoya, Guaitil			x			x						2		179
Nosara	x			x	x			x	x			3	x	180
Ostional	x								x					181
Sámara, Carrillo				x				x		x	x	3	x	182
Barra Honda N.P.	x				x			x			x	2	x	183

THE CENTRAL PACIFIC	Birdwatching	Botany	Crafts	Fishing	Hiking	History, archaeology	Volcanoes	Water sports	Wildlife	Good for children	Camping	Days required for trip	Tours available	Page number
Gulf of Nicoya				x				x				1	x	187
San Lucas Island			x									1		187
Bahía Ballena				x				x		x	x	2		188
Montezuma	x				x			x	x		x	3	x	189
Cabo Blanco Reserve	x				x				x			3		191
*Monteverde	x	x			x				x		x	3	x	191
Carara Reserve	x				x				x			1	x	196
Jacó, Herradura								x			x	1		197
*Manuel Antonio N.P.	x				x			x	x		x	3	x	199

THE SOUTHERN ZONE

	Birdwatching	Botany	Crafts	Fishing	Hiking	History, archaeology	Volcanoes	Water sports	Wildlife	Good for children	Camping	Days required for trip	Tours available	Page number
Copey de Dota	x				x							1		206
San Gerardo				x	x							2	x	207
Chirripó N.P.	x				x						x	4		208
Dominical				x				x			x	3		211
Boruca			x		x							3		212
Corcovado N.P.	x				x				x		x	4	x	213
Marenco	x	x			x			x	x			3	x	217
Golfito	x			x				x				3		218
Wilson Gardens	x	x			x							3		220
La Amistad N:P:	x			x	x				x		x	3	x	221
Isla del Coco Reserve	x							x				4	x	222

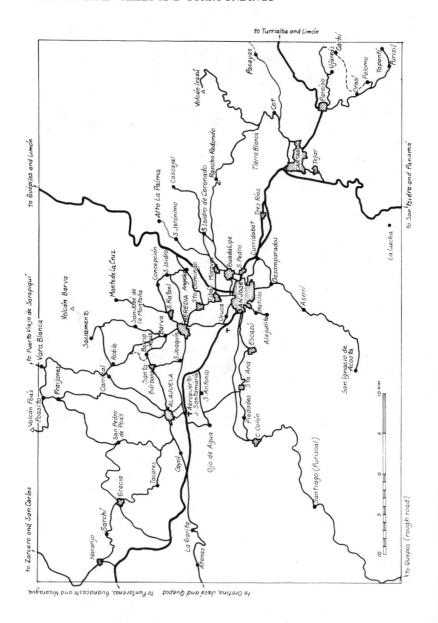

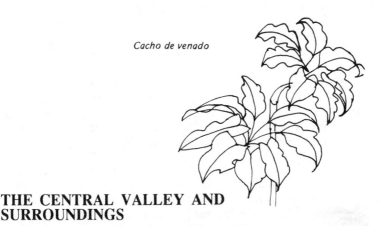

Cacho de venado

THE CENTRAL VALLEY AND SURROUNDINGS

Although only 20 km from San José, **Alajuela** is 200 meters lower, and so considerably warmer. It is full of shady parks. On Sundays, oldtimers sit in the Parque Central and entertain each other by thinking up nicknames for passersby. The **Juan Santamaría Museum,** housed in the former jail one block north of Parque Central, features relics of the 1856 rout of William Walker, including his incursion order and defense plea in English. It is open Tuesday through Sunday from 2 pm to 9 pm. Admission is free. In San José, buses leave continuously for Alajuela from a 2, c 12/14.

Hotels: The Juan Santamaría International Airport is about 5 minutes from Alajuela, and the elegant resort hotels, **Cariari** and **Sheraton Herradura** are just before the airport (see p. 111). **Hotel Alajuela,** 25 meters south from the SW corner of Alajuela's Parque Central, is an alternative for folks who want to avoid San José's bustle and pollution and still be close to the airport and buses. It's a friendly hotel with clean, pleasant rooms (C) and some very reasonable apartments in the older part of the building (D, hw, pb, 41-1241).

Ojo de Agua is a recreational complex about half an hour outside of San José. Cold, clear water gushes up from an *ojo de agua* (spring) and is pumped down an artificial waterfall into large swimming pools. There's a man-made lake where you can rent rowboats, grassy fields for soccer, volleyball, sunbathing and picnics, and a big *soda*. It is very crowded on weekends, but not so bad during the week. The lowering of the water table due to deforestation is starting to affect Ojo de Agua at the end of the dry season.

Buses leave at least once an hour for Ojo de Agua from c 18/20, a 1, a half block west of Coca Cola.

La Garita is the home of **La Fiesta del Maíz,** a restaurant where you can sample the wide variety of foods that Costa Ricans make from corn. Everything is delicious and homemade. The waitress will offer you little samples of the dishes if you ask (open Thurs-Sun). To make a day of it, visit the zoo of exotic birds in La Garita **(Zoo-Ave)**. There you'll see giant scarlet macaws, parrots, rosy-cheeked cockatoos, peacocks, pheasants, toucans, tanagers, orioles, swans, ostriches, falcons, owls, a tiger heron, and African crested cranes--all for $.50. If you have kids, they'll love the **Bosque Encantado,** an amusement park also in La Garita (tel: 48-7050). It's a lake surrounded by a medieval castle, fairytale figures, playhouses and horseback riding trails.

To get to La Garita, take the Atenas bus from the Coca Cola (it leaves once an hour), or go to Alajuela first and take the La Garita bus from there. La Fiesta del Maíz is about 2.5 km on the left after you make the Atenas turnoff from the main highway. The Bosque Encantado is 1.5 km to the left at the Fiesta del Maíz. There's a sign. The Zoo-Ave is about 3.5 km to the *right* after the Atenas turnoff. You might be interested in stopping at some of the *viveros* (greenhouses) along the way.

Poás is one of the few active volcanoes on the continent that is accessible by a good road. The 37 km trip from San José is full of beautiful scenery, with lookouts over the Central Valley. It is the most developed of the national parks, with a visitors' center and auditorium featuring slideshows about the park, and well-maintained nature trails.

The main crater of Poas is 1.5km wide and 300 meters deep, one of the largest in the world. There was a hot, sulphurous lake at the bottom, but it recently evaporated due to increased volcanic activity. Geysers and active fumaroles are visible from the lookout point above the crater. A 20-minute uphill hike takes you to another lookout over jewel-like Botos Lake, which fills an extinct crater. Unfortunately, that trail is currently closed.

Volcan Poás is entering an active phase, apparently part of a 40-45 year cycle. The volcano spewed a 4000-meter column of water and mud in 1910, sending ash as far as Puntarenas.

Lava flow increased also in 1953. In May 1989 Poas shot ash a mile into the air, but still it is quiet compared to Arenal and former explosions of Irazú.

Scientists believe that Poas has a relatively open passage from its magma chamber to its huge crater, so it can let off steam more easily than other volcanos and doesn't build up the pressure that causes large eruptions. Nevertheless, the volcano is under close observation these days, and the park is sometimes closed to visitors because of sulfur gas emissions from the crater which combine with steam to make sulfuric acid. Local residents have experienced breathing problems and irritation to their eyes, skin and stomachs due to the sulfur gas, and the local coffee crop has suffered.

Check with Parques Nacionales to see if the Park is open (33-8841, 33-5284). They recommend that visitors not stay more than 20 minutes at the crater. You should take glasses to protect your eyes, and a handkerchief soaked in a vinegar and water solution to neutralize the effect of the sulfuric acid if it becomes difficult to breathe. While the volcano is under observation, the park is open Tues through Sun, 9am to 2:30pm.

Poás National Park protects the headwaters of several rivers which feed the Río Tárcoles to the southwest and the Río Sarapiquí to the north. While the active crater is full of subtle, moonscape colors, the rest of Poás is intensely green, with a great variety of wildflowers, bromeliads, ferns, mosses and lichen. One of the most interesting plants there is the *sombrilla del pobre* (poor man's umbrella) which has thick fuzzy leaves up to two meters in width. Hummingbirds are among the 26 species of birds most easily seen along the highway or on the trails.

The average temperature on misty Poás is 50°, dropping as low as 22° and climbing as high as 70°, so it is important to dress in layers. Bring raingear. If you get there too late in the day clouds will have covered the crater, so the earlier the better. When it's clear you can see Poás on the horizon to the northwest of San José. If you can't see it, it's probably too late to go. There are no restaurants at the park, but local ladies sell homemade food there on Sundays.

If you do go to Poás, be sure to stop at **Chubascos,** one of the nicest places we know for native Costa Rican food. Set in a hillside garden with covered outdoor tables, their large $3 *casado* can't be beat, especially accompanied by *refrescos* made

125

from local strawberries and blackberries, and topped off with homemade cheesecake. It's about 16 km above Alajuela. **El Recreo** and **Restaurant Volcán Poás**, farther up toward the volcano, are also nice places to stop for a snack.

About 14km east of the Park, near Vara Blanca, is **Albergue Volcán Poás** (C, 55-3486, hw), a bed-and-breakfast especially for hikers and birders who like to get out and roam around the countryside.

Getting there: Take the Alajuela turnoff about 15 minutes from San Jose. It leads you past Alajuela's Central Park and the Juan Santamaría Museum. Stay on the same road till you get to Fraijanes Lake and Chubascos. About 1.5 km beyond the restaurant you connect with the road from San Pedro de Poás, which leads you to the volcano.

A bus leaves *Sundays only* from Parque de la Merced in San José (a 2, c 12) at 8:30 am. Buses leave from Alajuela's Parque Central continuously between 8 and 9am Sundays (41-0631, $3.30 roundtrip). Get there early to assure yourself a seat. The bus arrives at the volcano around 11 am. Check with the driver for departure time. Many tour companies offer day trips to Poás for $15-25.

You can also catch a bus any day from Alajuela to San Pedro de Poás. It leaves from the Parque del Cementerio every hour on the hour. From there you can take a taxi (about $10 one way) or hitchhike the remaining distance. **Restaurant La Cabaña**, 50 m uphill from the Central Park in San Pedro is a good place to eat.

Sarchí is a pretty little town, painted everywhere with the bright mandala-like designs that adorn the famous oxcarts. On the way in, you'll pass a shop on the left with a big red oxcart sign and ARTESANIA written large in front. Here you can watch workmen turning out Sarchí's beautiful wooden crafts. The most inexpensive place to buy is at the cooperative a few minutes by bus on the other side of town, on the right. It has a big wooden wheel out front.

To get to Sarchí, take the hourly Grecia bus from the Coca Cola. In Grecia, connect with the Alajuela-Sarchí bus. You can catch the latter bus in Alajuela, but it takes a long, roundabout route to Grecia. By car, take the Grecia exit on the Puntarenas highway, 30 min. west of San José.

Zarcero is one of the most charming Costa Rican towns. Perched on the hills that divide the Central Valley from the San Carlos plain, Zarcero's climate is fresh and invigorating. Its ruddy-cheeked inhabitants are famous for their peach preserves and homemade white cheese, but Zarcero's real claim to fame are the fancifully sculpted bushes in front of its picturesque little church. Gardeners shape them into gigantic green rabbits, horses, oxcarts and elephants. When we were there, a huge rainbow guided us down the country roads above Zarcero to the town plaza, then remained in a perfect arc directly over the church. Zarcero is a good place for a Sunday walk in the hills. There are no real hotels in Zarcero, but if you ask around, you'll probably find a family who will put you up for a modest fee.

The Zarcero bus leaves from the corner of c 16 and a 3 near Coca Cola at 9:15 every morning, or you can take any of the hourly San Carlos buses in the Coca Cola. The trip lasts two hours. It's easy to catch a bus back to San José, or on to Volcán Arenal and the hot springs at Tabacón. Soda Los Amigos to the south of the park has the local bus schedules. Just before you reach Zarcero, there is a group of stands selling cheese, candied fruit and flowers. **Restaurant La Montaña** on the right specializes in hearty Italian dishes. By car, Zarcero is 1.5 hours from San José. Take the Naranjo-Ciudad Quesada exit on the highway to Puntarenas.

Founded in 1706, **Heredia** has retained a friendly, small town atmosphere. Its colonial church built in 1796 has a pretty facade and a peaceful garden. There are concerts Thursday nights in the music temple in the Parque Central. In the **Mercado Florense** (300 m. south and 50 m. west of the Church) there's an inexpensive place to have a good seafood lunch. Near the National University are some popular student bars, especially **La Choza** and **El Bulevar**. **Hotel Verano** (F, 37-1616, cb, cw, c 4, a 6) on the west side of the market in Heredia is clean, friendly and very inexpensive.

Buses to Heredia leave every 5-10 minutes from c 1, a 7/9 in San José from 5:20 am to 10:30 pm (through Tibás) and from a 2, c 12 every 20 minutes (through La Uruca).

The mountains above Heredia are full of evergreen forests and pastureland. It's exhilaratingly chilly there all year round, and a bright, sunny day can turn into a rainy one in minutes,

127

especially after noon. From these mountains you can see the sun glinting off the Gulf of Nicoya in the west. A hike to **Monte de la Cruz** gives you an incredible panorama of the entire Central Valley and beyond. Take a picnic lunch, an umbrella and a sweater. There is a restaurant there, open 10am to 11pm every day, but the menu is not too interesting. If you wish to enjoy the view in a more formal setting, visit **El Castillo,** a posh country club with an ice-skating rink, pool, gym, barbecue pits, go-carts, and a miniature train. The $5/person entrance fee lets you use all facilities and entitles you to a free lunch in the dining room, which overlooks the skating rink as well as the Central Valley. The small, wrought-iron sign at the entrance to El Castillo is hard to spot, but you'll see its well-manicured lawns on the right a few hundred meters after a large sign for Residencial El Castillo.

Before you get to El Castillo, there is a sign for **Bosque de la Hoja.** Go left, down a beautiful wooded road 2 km. The entrance says "Bar las Chorreras". Bosque de la Hoja protects the water supply for Heredia. It is not developed for tourism, apart from some rusting playground equipment, a gloomy bar and some makeshift latrines. The roads are terrible, so leave your car where a guard requests a minimal admission fee. There are trails through cool, fresh forests of *ciprés,* and lovely meadows for picnics. Camping is allowed.

The turnoff to Bosque de la Hoja is 5 km north of **San Rafael de Heredia.** El Castillo is 1 km farther, and Monte de la Cruz is 2 km beyond that. An hourly bus leaves from behind the Mercado Florense in Heredia from 8am to 8pm. The 9am, 12 and 4pm buses go to a fork in the road 1 km from the entrance to Monte de la Cruz.

Going *left* at that fork takes you in about 1km to **Hotel Chalet Tirol,** charming 2-story vine-covered cabins with hand-painted Tyrolean designs and an elegant French restaurant (B, bathtubs, hw, electric heating, room service, airport pickup, 39-7070, 39-7050). The hotel, at 1800m (5900 ft) is surrounded by a cloud forest reserve that borders Braulio Carrillo National Park. Two hiking trails are accessible from the reserve, one of which leads to a moss-covered cliff where a dozen small waterfalls cascade into as many small pools before joining the river below. It's a beautiful place to be, and amazing for being so close to San José. Another trail follows the Río Segundo into Braulio Carrillo amidst a carpet of ferns and ancient trees covered with orchids and bromeliads. A great place for a day hike or for a weekend, and you can warm up with a hot chocolate and *quiche lorraine* or pastry on the second floor of the Chalet's restaurant, or stay for their excellent *nouvelle cuisine* specialties.

All the above-mentioned places are about 35 minutes from San José by car. Take the San Isidro exit to the left about 14 km down the Guápiles highway. When you reach San Isidro, turn right in front of its pretty, white church and go 2 km to Concepción (ignore any previous Concepción signs). This area has a real flavor of *campesino* life, since these towns were pretty much off the beaten track until the highway opened in 1987. San Isidro and San Joaquín de las Flores, to the west of Heredia, are known for their colorful Easterweek processions. Continue a few minutes more to San Rafael, where again you turn right at the church to reach Bosque de la Hoja, El Castillo, Chalet Tirol, and Monte de la Cruz.

Barva de Heredia, 2 km north of Heredia, was recently declared Costa Rica's first historic town. Architects, historians, and construction workers are combining efforts to restore Barva's colonial atmosphere.

You can see how coffee was and is produced at the **Coffee Museum,** 400 m north of the church in San Pedro. Take a Santa Bárbara por Barrio Jesús bus from Heredia (San Pedro is 6 km NW).

Just before you get to Santa Barbara is the entrance to **La Rosa Blanca,** certainly the most comfortable and beautiful bed-and-breakfast in Costa Rica. Each room has a theme, and the architecture and hand-crafted furnishings are full of fantasy and delightful, creative touches. The honeymoon suite (XL) features a tower room with a 360 degree view and a bathroom painted like a rainforest, with the water for the bathtub bubbling out of a rocky waterfall (LL, pb, hw, breakfast and transportation incl, 39-9392).

One of the most pleasant hotels in Costa Rica is **El Pórtico.** Graciously designed, it offers quiet rooms with large windows, a lovely lounge, a pool, sauna, jacuzzi and restaurant (B, 37-6022). Down the road are **Cabañas Las Ardillas,** cozy, ivy-covered cabins with kitchens, fireplaces and views of hilly pastureland. A round restaurant serves Costa Rican specialties (B, hw, lower weekly and monthly rates, 22-8134). Across the road is **Hotel Cypresal,** with cabins, pool, and restaurant (C, 37-4466). There are two ways to reach these hotels. North of Barva, there's a fork in the road. Take the left fork 4 km to Birrí, turn right at the Pulpería El Buen Precio, and continue 5 Km, all on good road. Or, take the right fork above Barva to lovely **San José de la Montaña,** and continue 5 km beyond it. You'll see signs for Braulio Carrillo National Park on the right. Continue past the signs about 1 km to the hotels. The road has quite a few potholes, but goes through less developed country than the road from Birrí. The Barva-Birrí road continues north 1/2 hour to Vara Blanca, where you can turn left to go to Volcán Poás.

Hourly buses leave for San José de la Montaña from behind the Mercado Central in Heredia. At 6 am, 12 and 4 pm, they continue up to Paso Llano, the start-off point for hikes to Volcán Barva.

Quetzal

Volcán Barva is on the western edge of Braulio Carrillo National Park. Follow the road above Barva through San José de la Montaña to Paso Llano and on to Sacramento. The country people who live in those foggy mountains sell fresh eggs, sour cream and baked goods along the way. There are now camping facilities at the entrance to the park, about a half hour hike from Barva's scenic crater lake.

Quetzales are sometimes visible there. They migrate to forests over 3600 feet above sea level, where they nest in the hollows of the tallest and oldest trees. Males and females share the incubation of eggs and feeding of their hatchlings. The females sit on the eggs at night and at mid-day, and the male sits with his beautiful green tail hanging out of the nest during the rest of the day. They cannot live in captivity. Also heard on Volcán Barva is the black-faced solitaire, which has been compared to the nightingale for the sweetness and delicacy of its song.

To climb Volcán Barva you should catch the 6 am San José de la Montaña-Paso Llano bus from behind the Mercado

Central in Heredia. At Paso Llano (Porrosatí), you'll see signs for the park entrance 6.4 km to the left. Bring raingear, a compass, and waterproof shoes or boots even in the dry season. (see p. 80). Be sure to make it back for the 5 pm Paso Llano bus to Heredia.

By car, go to San José de la Montaña (see above) and continue beyond it until you see signs to Sacramento and Braulio Carrillo.

The founding of **Braulio Carrillo National Park** in 1978 represents a compromise between ecology and development. Environmentalists were concerned that the opening of a highway between San José and Guápiles would result in the ecological disasters that have followed the opening of other roads: indiscriminate colonization and deforestation. The government agreed to make 80,000 acres of virgin forest surrounding the highway into a national park.

The Guápiles highway, opened in May 1987, makes Braulio Carrillo the national park most accessible by car. The scenery is inspiring. Hopefully it is an education in itself for all the motorists who pass through it on their way to the Atlantic coast--mountains of untouched rainforest as far as the eye can see. And just 30 years ago, most of Costa Rica looked like that!

In order to hike the trails accessible from the highway, you must stop and pay a minimal entrance fee, either at the administration buildings before the Zurquí tunnel, or at the station on the right as you leave the park (coming from San José). The trail before the tunnel is steep and strenuous; the La Botella trail 17 km beyond the tunnel is easier. Parts of the trail are muddy, and snakes are a danger, so wear boots. Porcupines, margays, tapirs, monkeys, coatis, kinkajous, peccaries, pacas, ocelots, sloths and raccoons live in Braulio Carrillo though chances are you won't see them. More visible are the 500 species of birds there.

Take the hourly Guápiles bus (c 12, a 7/9, Coopetragua, $1). The La Botella trail is 2.5 km before the Quebrada Gonzales station at the far end of the park.

Minor Keith built a highway in 1881 to connect the central valley with the Atlantic railway, which in those days went only as far as Carrillo, 41 km. from San José. With the completion of the railway, this road fell into disuse. Today it provides a beautiful day hike through the Paso de la Palma. Take a bus marked **San Jerónimo de Moravia** from a 3, c 3/5 in San José (45 min, $.20). Take the small road going north from San Jerónimo. After walking about 45 minutes, you'll notice the old stone pavement of the *Carretera Carrillo,* built to withstand the constant traffic of coffee-laden oxcarts. You can follow the road for about 9 km before reaching one of the boundaries of Braulio Carrillo. Access to the park is not permitted from the Carretera Carrillo at this time because of efforts being made to preserve the old road. But the hike through rolling dairylands to the park boundary is very pleasant, especially if you go early in the day.

Though **Cartago** was the birthplace of Costa Rican culture and the capital for 300 years, many of its historical buildings were destroyed in the earthquakes of 1823 and 1910. The 1910 quake prevented the completion of a cathedral in the center of town. The ruins of that church have been made into a pleasant garden. On August 2, every year, thousands of Costa Ricans walk from San José to Cartago in honor of *La Negrita,* the Virgin of Los Angeles, who appeared to a peasant girl in 1635. She has become Costa Rica's patron saint, and her shrine is surrounded by offerings from grateful pilgrims she has miraculously cured. Tiny metal arms, legs, hearts, etc., decorate the walls near her statue inside the **Basílica,** an imposing structure on the east side of town.

Volcán Irazú is 32 km north of Cartago. On a clear morning, the trip up its slope is full of breathtaking views of farmland, native oak forests and the valley below. The craters are bleak and majestic. On March 19, 1963, the day John F. Kennedy arrived in Costa Rica on a presidential visit, Irazú erupted, showering black ash over the central valley for the next two years. People carried umbrellas to keep the ash out of their hair, roofs caved in from the weight of piled-up ash, everything was black. Since then, the volcano has been dormant. Some gases and steam are emitted from fumaroles on the northwestern slope, not visible from the crater lookouts. It is said that you can see both the Atlantic and the Pacific from Irazú's chilly 3800 m (11,000-foot) summit. This is true on occasion, but often the Atlantic side is obscured by clouds.

A good place to go for a day hike is **Area Recreativa Jiménez Oreamuno,** a reforestation project started after the 1963 eruption. It's located about halfway up the west side of the volcano, near **Prusia.** The hike to the forest is very beautiful, through uninhabited, steep hills covered with oak and pine. Once there, you'll find trails and picnic tables.

Getting there: Bus service to Irazú has been discontinued, so you have to drive or take a tour. If you want to try to catch the view of both oceans, it's a must to go early. Bring warm clothes, raingear, food and something to drink. There are no restaurants at the park, but there is a good place to stop for breakfast on your way down--the first place on your right. **Hotel Gestoria Irazú** (D, 53-0827, cw, cb) is a large, charmingly gloomy building that has seen better days, located about 2/3 of the way up the mountain. Call for reservations. Their restaurant is not recommended.

Developed by English botanist Charles Lankester, **Lankester Gardens** display the hundreds of varieties of orchids and bromeliads for which Costa Rica is famous. The gardens are run by the biology department of the University of Costa Rica.

Take the Paraíso bus from Cartago. Ask the bus driver to let you off near the gardens. There is a cube-shaped sign on the highway. The entrance is about 100 meters down a road to your right, then right again. The gardens are open every day from 9:30 to 3:30.

Orosi Valley, south of Cartago, is one of Costa Rica's jewels. You can visit the peaceful ruins of Costa Rica's oldest church at **Ujarrás,** then walk about 1/2 hour to **Charrarra,** ICT's tourism complex on the banks of Cachí Dam. Charrarra offers lakeside trails, a swimming pool, basketball courts, picnic facilities, a pleasant restaurant, and access to boating on the lake. Take the Cachí bus from Cartago and ask to be let off at Ujarrás. On Sundays, the buses go all the way to Charrarra at 8 am, 11 am, 2 pm.

South of Cachí Dam is the town of **Orosi,** with its colonial church, whose beautiful wooden altar and shrines were carved with a special grace. It is one of the few places in Costa Rica that has survived enough earthquakes to preserve its original atmosphere. A small museum of colonial religious history next door is open Tues-Sun 9-12, 1-5.

From Orosi, nature lovers can hire a jeep-taxi ($3.25 one way), hike, or drive the 10 km full of potholes to **Tapantí Wildlife Refuge**. Tapantí protects the rivers which supply San José with water and electricity. There's great birdwatching, trout fishing (see p. 76 re permits), and river swimming. It's open every day except Thurs and Fri. If you call ahead, one of the guards might be able to accompany you on the nature trails. Ask for Don Emil Montero, an excellent guide (Dirección de Vida Silvestre has radio contact with Tapantí, 55-0192). There are some nice cabins near the entrance to Tapantí--ask guards about them.

Motel Río (E, cw; D, hw, kitchens, pools, 73-3128, 73-3057), about 3km beyond Orosi on the Río Palomo is the famous, traditional place to go for a fresh fish lunch. It's open 8:30-5 every day. Signs indicate the turnoff to the left. The Orosi minibus goes all the way to the motel about once an hour on weekends, and at noon weekdays.

Getting there: All Orosi buses are 100 meters east of the church ruins in Cartago, and 300 m south. Cachí buses are on the same street.

If you rent a car for one day and start off early, you can easily visit Irazú, Lankester Gardens, Ujarrás, Charrarra and Orosi, stop for lunch at Río Palomo and continue on to Tapantí. Lankester is SE of Cartago on the road to Paraíso. Ujarrás and Charrarra are 6 km east of Paraíso; Orosi, Motel Río and Tapantí are south. A gravel road between Palomo and Cachí circles the dam and connects Orosi with Ujarrás, but it's not worth the wear and tear on your kidneys. There is a *mirador* on the way to Orosi with picnic and barbecue spots and a beautiful view.

Turrialba is becoming known worldwide as the perfect winter training ground for kayakers. The town, which used to be the main stopping place on the old San José-Limón road, suffered an economic depression with the opening of the Guápiles highway, which bypassed the zone completely. Now, however, it is a haven for international whitewater fans who rent houses there or stay with local families. Young Turrialbans are becoming interested in kayaking but most of them do not have the means to outfit themselves for the sport.

Turrialba is definitely "off the beaten track", and offers many possibilities for an interesting day or weekend trip, especially now that the road to Guayabo National Monument is paved. You can get there on the Limón train (3 hrs from San José) or by bus (2 hours). If you have a car, you can take a delightful, newly-paved back road which starts slightly south of the town of Cot on the slopes of Volcán Irazú, and skirts Volcán Turrialba, passing through the towns of Pacayas and Santa Cruz before arriving in Turrialba itself. The trip takes less than 2 hours from San José. Once in Turrialba, there are several restaurants worth visiting:

The charming and folkloric **Turrialtico** is high on a hill about 8km east of town. As you drive up, you'll see wonderful gargoyles popping out of carved branches of coffee wood bordering the spacious open-air diningroom with its magnificent view of the valley. Native food is their specialty. Above the restaurant are comfortable rooms with the same view (C, 56-1111, hw, pb, playground equip., brkfst incl.)

Two km farther down the road is **Pochotel**, on an even higher hill with an almost 360 degree view of the entire area, including Cerro de la Muerte and Chirripó to the south, and volcanoes Irazú and Turrialba to the north. You can climb up their observation tower and see even more. They'll send your refreshments up to the tower on a mini-ski-lift contraption they've invented. They also rent cabinas (C, 56-0111, pb, hw, playground equip., camping allowed) and specialize in native food.

Just outside Turrialba is **Restaurant Kingston,** whose Limonese owner and chef has made it famous. We didn't have a chance to eat there, but were told it's the best in town.

If it's hot, you might just want to take a dip at **Balneario Las Américas,** two large pools for kids and adults (adm. $.75) with a bar-restaurant. You'll see signs for it on the main road, a few blocks toward town from Kingston. To the west of town, 600m from the church, is **Parque La Dominica**, a pleasant place to stop for a picnic. There are swings, basketball courts and a swimmable river.

Turrialba is the home of the Centro Agronómico Tropical de Investigación y Enseñanza (**CATIE**). Established in the 1930's, it is one of the five major tropical research centers in the world. Its extensive library houses Latin America's largest collection of agricultural literature in English.

CATIE's 27,500-acre facilities include greenhouses, orchards, forest plantings, experimental agricultural projects, a dairy, an herbarium, seed conservation chambers, a nuclear reactor and housing for students and teachers. Seeds of fruit and nut trees, tropical forest species suitable for lumber, ornament, erosion control, shade and pulpwood are available by writing CATIE, Turrialba, Costa Rica. They also sell livestock well-adapted to the tropics. CATIE publishes a monthly newsletter in English. You can request it or arrange a visit to the Center by calling 56-64-31.

Birders will find the purple-crested gallinet and other rare waterfowl around the lagoon at CATIE. There is a trail from behind the administration building to the Río Reventazón, also a favorite with birders. You can catch a bus to CATIE where the main road crosses the tracks in Turrialba. Ask about schedules at the Almacén González.

The newly constructed **Hotel Wagelia,** at the entrance to Turrialba, 150 m west of the central park, offers an elegant menu with reasonable prices (C, hot water, no fans; B, a/c, TV, fridge; clean, small rooms, 56-1566, 56-1596). **Hotel Interamericano** (E, pb; F, sb, saggy mattresses but clean, friendly, cw, kitchen privileges, 56-0142) is near the railroad station.

Rancho Naturalista, high in the hills above Tuís, east of Turrialba, offers nature trails through virgin rainforest, habitat of four species of toucans, the snow-capped hummingbird and many other bird and butterfly species. Their comfortable lodge (hot water, good mattresses) overlooks the wide valley. Their creative cookery is a special attraction. $360 for a week's stay includes meals, lodging, transportation to and from San José and a free trip to another nearby birding site of your choice (Apdo. 364, 1002 San José, 39-8036).

Guayabo National Monument on the slopes of Volcán Turrialba is considered the most significant archaeological site in Costa Rica. It is a glimpse into the harmony between man and nature that existed in precolumbian times. Birds abound in the ruins, which are set in premontane rain forest and dotted with the guava trees that give the town its name. *Oropéndolas* (related to our orioles) hang their sack-like nests from tree branches. Water sings its song in ancient aqueducts.

Archaeologists have excavated only the central part of a 10,000-inhabitant city that existed from 1000 B.C. to about 1400 A.D. The exposed area is composed of circular mounds which were the floors of large buildings raised to keep them dry; paved sidewalks, some of whose stones are decorated with petroglyphs; a large stone carved with stylistic representations of two Indian gods: the jaguar, god of the forest, and the crocodile, god of the river; a system of covered and uncovered aqueducts which still functions well; and the oldest bridge in Costa Rica, a flat rock now broken in several places, which crosses one of the aqueducts. Several roads radiate out from the center of the town. Spot excavations verify that some go on at least 8 kilometers. It's theorized that the most important people--the chief, his family, and priests--lived in the center while common people lived outside.

oropendolas

Many mysteries remain about the civilization that inhabited Guayabo. No one knows why the people left (just before the *conquistadores* discovered Costa Rica), nor why Spanish explorers never found or never kept records of finding the site.

137

Yet the peace and beauty that reign in Guayabo echo a wise and gentle people.

From the *mirador* (lookout-point) you can see the green grassy mounds and stone sidewalks nestled within the rainforest. Hawks and vultures swoop and sail in front of the striking four-layered backdrop of mountains. Across the road from the site, behind the campground, a steep trail leads down to the fast-flowing Guayabo river where you can sit bathing your feet and looking for birds. You can also walk up the road past coffee and sugarcane fields for wide views into the green Guayabo valley.

In an effort to preserve the ruins, visitors are requested to tour Guayabo with a guide along specified routes only. Guides will meet you at the exhibition room. The park is open 8am-4pm, but because park personnel and volunteers are working full-time on restoration and protection of the ruins, it is requested that visitors come on weekends only. Camping is allowed. Bring raingear.

Hotel La Calzada, (E, 51-3677, cb, hw, 400m before the entrance to the Monument), is a very pleasant country inn, with comfy, light-filled rooms overlooking a large pond, a homey common area and great *campesino* food in their open-air restaurant. Whether you stop there during the rainy season to warm up with an *agua dulce con leche* or decide to spend a few tranquil days birding and writing in your journal, it's a nice place to be. There is no phone there, so you leave a message at 51-3677, and they contact the hotel by radio, then call back to confirm your reservations. La Calzada is a member of the youth hostel network. You can get discounts there with an IYHF card (see p. 65). Sometimes the Toruma (24-4085) in San José arranges inexpensive group trips to member hostels.

Getting there: San José-Turrialba buses leave every hour from c 13, a 6 ($.75, 2-hr trip). This bus stop is scheduled to change soon, so check with ICT, 22-1090, for new location. The Limón train leaves daily at 10am from the east side of Parque Nacional. By car, follow signs from Cartago to Turrialba, or take the above-mentioned back road from Cot, heading at first toward Volcán Irazú. Both are scenic and about equal in distance. The main road has more curves.

To get to Guayabo, take the Santa Teresita bus from the main bus stop in Turrialba at 10:30am or 1:30pm. It leaves you 4km from the entrance to Guayabo. José Miguel, the friendly owner of Hotel La Calzada, runs a once-a-day taxi service ($2) to meet the 10:30 Santa Teresita bus at the crossroads. Call the above number to let him know when you are coming. The 19km trip to Guayabo takes about 40 minutes by car from Turrialba, a bit longer by bus. The road is paved except for the last 4km.

Most people hike downhill to the crossroads to catch the 12:45pm Santa Teresita bus back to Turrialba. You can also hitch back with families returning by car.

On the way back to San José on the main road, there are a couple of interesting stops: **La Posada de la Luna,** west of the church in Cervantes, halfway between Cartago and Turrialba, serves *comida típica* and unusually delicious homemade desserts. Their dining room is surrounded by cases full of antique memorabilia: Spanish swords, precolumbian artefacts, Japanese *netsuke*--you name it, they've got it. At the entrance to Paraíso, on the right coming from Turrialba towards Cartago, you'll see the **Auto-vivero del Río,** a combination greenhouse and mini-zoo of native animals, including quail, *tepiscuintles, guatuzos,* ducks, turtles and a monkey. There is playground equipment for kids. Admission is free, but they ask for donations to support the animals. Besides plants, they sell rabbits and colored volcanic stones.

THE ATLANTIC COAST

Much of Limón province is a jungle-covered lowland. The coast is dotted with beautiful white and black sand beaches. A trip to Limón is a chance to enjoy the area's wild beauty and the distinct culture that characterizes it. Afro-Caribbean peoples migrated to the Atlantic coast before the turn of the century to work on the railroad, to fish and to farm *cacao* and coconut. Several kinds of English are spoken there, including an elegant Jamaican English and the patois that black people use with each other. "What happen" is the common greeting, but it is pronounced "Whoppen". Instead of saying *"Adios"* when they pass, people say "All right" or "Okay". For a fascinating history of the region, read Paula Palmer's *What Happen,* in which the elders of the black community tell their life stories.

Puerto Limón is Costa Rica's major Atlantic port. Its main attraction is the annual carnival that coincides with *El Día de la Raza,* October 12. Brightly costumed *Limonenses* parade to the rhythm of drums, tambourines, pots and pans, maracas and whistles. You're part of the parade too, drawn in by the irresistible Afro-Caribbean beat. The drinking, dancing and carousing last several days. Another annual event in Limón is the surfing championship that takes place on Playa Bonita, a touristy beach a few km north of town. Like Puntarenas, Limón is in transition from funky seaport to gateway to some of the country's most beautiful beaches. The streets are full of people, bicycles, dogs and an occasional vulture.

A few km to the north, in a more scenic area between Limón and the container port of Moín, is the **Hotel Matama,** with shady gardens, pool and international restaurant (Caribbean specialties served on Sundays only). It has recently been re-modeled, and the rooms are clean and tastefully decorated. There is no cross-ventilation, so you have to use air conditioning (L, a/c, hw, friendly staff 58-1123, 58-1919). **Hotel Maribú Caribe** (L, a/c, hw, pool, tel, 58-4010, 58-4543) is about 1km towards Limón from the Matama. Coming from the north you see its white, circular thatched cabinas on a hill like a tribal fort. It is perched on the only cliff in the area, so it has a great ocean view from its breezy restaurant. The rooms and pool are spotless, and the whole place has a sterility that makes it seem foreign to the Atlantic coast. The parking lot guards carry small sidearms. The restaurant is a bit overpriced, but the view makes it a worthwhile place to stop after the long drive to Limón. (See p. 109 for key to hotel codes). Just north of Limón is **Hotel Las Olas,** a large monolithic structure built on rocky coral at the ocean's edge (B, a/c or cf, hw, pool, rest, sauna, 58-1414). To get to these hotels you can avoid Limón altogether. Take the Moín turnoff to the left on the highway to Limón, then turn right just before the entrance to the port facility. You'll pass the beaches of **Portete** and **Playa Bonita** before you come to the hotels. We have heard that food is good at the big restaurant on Playa Bonita. Just as you enter Limón from the north, on the right, is **Restaurant Arrecife**, specializing in fresh seafood. A bit further on is **Springfield**, a favorite with locals for Caribbean cooking.

In Limón, the **Hotel Acón** (C, 50m. E of market, a/c, hw, TV, rest, 58-1010) is the best equipped. The **Park** (E, a/c and hw in some rooms, 58-3476), with a certain aging charm, is next to the sea wall, so receives the ocean breezes. The **Lincoln,** 200m N from the *mercado* is nothing special but reasonably clean (E, pb, tf, cw, 58-0074). The **International** next door has a/c in some rooms (D, pb, cw, 58-0434). There are lots of funky cheap hotels on the same street as the bus stop. One doesn't seem to be any better than another. You can stay just as cheaply in the more beautiful areas down the coast, so try not to get stuck in Limón for the night. If you do have to wait there, **Parque Vargas** is pleasant, with its huge palms, and you can take a refreshing walk along the sea wall. **Los Cuatro Mares** on the south side of the *mercado* is a nice, clean place to stop for a snack. Be careful in Limón after dark. Mugging is a danger. We were even stopped once by a uniformed person

141

who seemed to be trying to trump up something about our identification in order to get a bribe. This is very rare in Costa Rica. We just played dumb and walked away.

We recommend going south to the **Talamanca** region. When we first went to Talamanca in 1975, there was no road. We took a two-hour train ride from Limón to Penshurst on the Río Estrella, where we were met by a man in a dugout canoe who ferried us across the river to a rickety bus. Then it was another hour on a dirt road to Cahuita, a small village where horses grazed on the grassy paths between houses. That has all changed, now that the roads have come. Cahuita's grassy paths have become dusty streets, and the people of Talamanca find themselves thrust uneasily into the twentieth century. Independent farming and fishing are giving way to a tourist-based economy, with some related drug culture and theft. Tour buses lining the streets of this small town during the dry season make local people feel that their home is lost to them. During the rest of the year, Talamanca reverts to its relaxed pace. The beaches are uncrowded and the weather, in August and September especially, is beautiful in contrast to the afternoon rains in the rest of Costa Rica.

At the Pacific beaches, the local culture takes second place to a tourist milieu created by highland Ticos and foreigners of all nationalities. Talamanca, however, is still *tierra incognita* for most Ticos. The area was opened after a 1975 law was passed prohibiting construction within 150 meters of the shore. Then the point below Cahuita was declared a national park. Recently, the area south of Puerto Viejo has been made into a wildlife refuge. For these reasons the beaches retain their pristine beauty, and the people their unique way of life. "Laid back" is definitely the style on the Atlantic coast. If you require excellent service, air conditioning or hot water, it's best to stay on the Pacific. We hope that somehow the people of Talamanca can preserve their unique flavor without being run over by "tourism infrastructure".

Cahuita is now a 45-minute ride from Limón. One entrance to the National Park is along the white sand beach at the southern edge of town, but the park campsites are at the **Puerto Vargas** entrance on the other side of the point, 4 km south of Cahuita, and about 2 km to the left. There is water available

142

there, as well as outhouses and picnic tables. The Park Service charges a minimal fee. Signs indicate the sections of Puerto Vargas Beach that are dangerous for swimmers.

Cahuita National Park protects a coral reef that extends 500 meters out from Cahuita point. Take flippers and a mask to enjoy the underwater garden of 123 species of tropical fish, as well as crabs, lobsters, shrimp, sea anemones, sponges, black and red sea urchins and sea cucumbers. In order to snorkel, you must enter from the beach on the Puerto Vargas side and swim out to the reef. **Cahuita Tours** (ext. 232) can take you to the reef in a boat with a glass window in the bottom. From there you can get to the better snorkeling spots. The trip, which takes all morning, costs about $11. They also rent snorkeling equipment, bicycles, binoculars and scuba diving equipment. They're on Cahuita's main street, half a block from the Guardia Rural. Also ask around for José McCloud (ext. 256). He has been recommended as an excellent guide to the flora and fauna of the area and can tell you a lot about the community as well.

Biologists observe that the coral in the reef has stopped growing. They attribute this to silt washed down by the river from the banana plantations inland, which inhibits the coral's ability to reproduce--yet another instance of Costa Rica's struggle between economics and ecology.

There is a shady 7km nature trail between the beach and the jungle. It's 4km by trail from Cahuita to the point, another 3km to the Puerto Vargas camping area. You might see iguanas, sloths, and howler and white-faced monkeys along the trail. The freshwater rivers and estuaries are good places to spot caimans and herons. You can spend the day hiking and snorkeling, then come out on the highway at the Puerto Vargas entrance to the park and catch the 4pm bus back to Cahuita.

143

Hotels and restaurants: (See p. 109 for key to hotel codes.) There is only one telephone number for all Cahuita. Dial 58-1515 and ask for the extensions given below: **Hotel Cahuita** has cabinas (D, pb, tf, pool, ext. 201) and cheaper rooms (E, cb, nf) in the old hotel above their restaurant. **Cabinas Vaz,** across the street, are similar (E, pb, tf, rest, ext. 218). The **Sol y Mar Restaurant** next door offers local specialties and also has spacious, clean cabinas (E, pb, cw). The **Cahuita National Park Restaurant** features fresh seafood, fruit drinks and desserts. Open every day, 8am to 9pm. All the above places are at the park entrance. **Cabinas Palmer** (E, tf, communal fridge; D with kitchens, ext. 243) are very clean and homey, and have back doors that open onto a quiet yard with chairs to relax in. Owners are lovely, helpful people. Half a block from the bus stop. Down the street from Palmer's, and directly on the water, are **Cabinas Jenny,** dingy lower rooms (F, sb) and 2 rooms in a newly-built cabin with hammocks and mosquito nets (E, pb, nf but plenty of sea breezes). **Surfside Cabinas** are behind the school. They also have four rooms with fridges right on the water and a new restaurant, open every day 7am-9pm. Rice and beans served weekends only (E, pb, tf, ext. 246, 202, 218). **Cabinas Brisas del Mar** are near the sea, across from the school (ext. 267, clean, pb, cw, D).

You can have fresh coral crabs at **El Típico** near the entrance to town. Make sure you ask them how much their crab, lobster and fish costs. The price on the menu is for the smallest size. Our large crab, though delicious, was almost twice as expensive ($7.50) as the menu price. Near the Típico is a place to **rent surfboards and snorkels**. On the other side of town, one block to the right from the Guardia Rural, **Miss Edith** cooks up a storm, ladling out tasty, down-home Caribbean meals. In response to the requests of her loving customers, she also includes vegetarian fare in her menu, as well as native medicinal teas like bayrum, guanabana leaves, sorosi, and lemon grass. Good for what ails you. Closed Tuesday and only open for supper on Sunday; breakfast served 7am-9am. If you want her to make rondon, a native stew, let her know early in the day so she can get it started. You can also buy fresh lobster on the beach and bring it to her to cook. Miss Edith's sister is starting a laundry service; ask about it.

North of town is a long, beautiful black sand beach where the gentle waters are better for swimming than in the park.

About 1 km north, near the ballfield on Black Beach, are **Cabinas Atlántida,** diagonally across the field (E, safe parking, pb, cw, cf, screens, rest). Continuing north, **Cabinas Black Beach** are some of the nicest we've seen--charmingly designed 2-story stone and wood structures (E, pb, protected parking, ext. 251). One of the owners is Italian, so you'll find lasagne and other Italian dishes there. Next door, **Cabinas Brigitte** has cheap, dark rooms with mosquito nets (F, cb). She's Swiss, but cooks native-style for guests. **Cabinas Samuel** (F, pb, basic) don't have a sign, but are across from his refreshment stand. The dirt road becomes a trail about 100m beyond. At low tide you can walk north along the beach to **Cabinas Algebra**, which serves some of the best food we've had in Cahuita. If you have a car, you can reach them by going out onto the main highway, heading north, and turning right (east) at a small shed where you'll see their sign (D, pb, cw).

Club Campestre Cahuita is halfway between Limón and Cahuita. It has a large pool, a kids pool with slides and dark rooms with heavy-duty ceiling fans. Its generous but greasy restaurant is open all day, every day. Camping is allowed on the beach across the road from the hotel ($3). Rooms are only open to non-members during the off-season (C, pb, cw; D newer cabinas, pb, hw, 58-2861).

Puerto Viejo is 19km south of Cahuita, on paved road except for the last 6 km after the turnoff to Bribri. The town is smaller and less developed than Cahuita. **Stanford's Restaurant El Caribe** is famous for fresh seafood. His disco is jumping Thurs-Sun. You can cash traveler's checks there. Stanford's cabins are among the most secure and well-maintained in town (D, pb, tf). The **Soda Támara** is a popular place to eat (open 6:30am to 9pm, closed Tues). Try their *agua de sapo* (frog water), a refreshing drink with lemon and ginger (also very reasonable). Definitely the best breakfast in town is at the **Coral**, 200m toward the hills from the Soda Támara. Heated homemade wholewheat and French bread accompany the eggs and omelettes. The rest of the menu ranges from yogurt and granola to *gallo pinto* to hearty wholewheat buttermilk pancakes. Breakfast is served every day except Mon from 7 to noon. During the high season they sell homemade snacks until 5pm, then reopen at 7pm on Tues, Fri and Sat, for Margarita's famous and delicious pizzas. **Cabinas Recife** share the same building with the Coral (E, basic, cb, nf, mosquito nets). Miss Soyla is the best Caribbean cook in town. She used to run the **Bambú** restaurant next to Stanford's, but has not been cooking there recently. Ask around to see if she is back in business. Next to the Bambú are breezy, basic cabinas right on the beach (E, pb). The **Hotel Maritza** and its **Annex** (F, cb, nf, 58-3844), **Cabinas Ritz** (E, pb, nf) and **Manuel León's Cabinas** (F, pb, nf, a bit rundown, 58-0854), are also available. Make sure you have mosquito coils for these last 4 places. (See p. 109 for key to hotel codes.)

The **Hotel Puerto Viejo** caters to surfers. It has basic second-story rooms, most of which are well-ventilated (E, mosquito nets, nf, cb). They plan to feature one main dish each night-- Mexican, Italian, vegetarian, etc., with emphasis on natural ingredients. The area outside the reef in front of Stanford's has become famous in surfing lore as "La Salsa Brava". The area inside the reef is nice for those of us who like to paddle around and feel safe. Waves are world class from December to April. Another season opens up in June and July. In other months the sea is calmer, better for snorkeling. During the high season, surfers on their way out often sell their boards to new arrivals. This avoids the tremendous hassle of taking surfboards on the crowded Limón-Puerto Viejo bus. Some surfers hire a taxi or truck to haul their gear from Limón ($25-30). This is cheaper than renting a car in San José, and most of the good waves are an easy walk from Puerto Viejo. The dynamic Brazilian surfers who manage the hotel tell us that at least one surfboard per day breaks on the reef. La Salsa Brava is definitely not for neophytes. You can rent bicycles behind the hotel. **El Pizote Surf Lodge** preserves the natural wood style of most coastal cabinas, but is the only place on the coast with all the amenities--storage space, reading lamps by the beds, large comfortable mattresses, mirrors you can actually see yourself in, ceiling fans. Baths are shared, but there are 4 per group of 8 rooms. Bicycles, diving gear and horses are for rent, and there are nature trails back into the forest from the quiet grounds of the lodge, which also has guanabana and Hawaiian papaya plantations. The lodge is set back from the road about halfway down the black beach as you approach Puerto Viejo ($60 double, incl. breakfast and dinner, 29-1428).

Cabinas Chimuri are down a road to the right, 300m before you get to the black beach that leads to Puerto Viejo. The typical Bribri constructions of thatch over bamboo are set on a hill in the cool, shady forest.   A large, open-walled *palenque* serves as a common cooking area for the cabins (E, cb). Near the cabins are waterfalls with pools for a refreshing swim. Mauricio, the owner, is a member of the Bribri Indian Reserve. His nature tours on horseback are a favorite with visitors ($20/person). Longer treks through the Atlantic side of **Parque International La Amistad** are possible if people come prepared with good shoes, sleeping bags, etc. These 3-day camping trips require advance notice and payment so that supplies can be bought and preparations for the boat trip out can be made ($140/pers.) He also makes carved gourds and *jícaras,* drums, and bows and arrows in the traditional manner. Chimuri is a great place to stay for those who like simplicity, doing their own cooking, living in nature, and getting to know the Bribri way of life. The best way to secure a place there is to send a deposit to Mauricio Salazar, Puerto Viejo de Talamanca, Limón, Costa Rica, keeping in mind that it takes at least three weeks for letters to arrive, even within Costa Rica.

Cabinas Black Sands are located near where the road first turns right to go along the black beach. Get off at the Pulpería La Violeta and take the road to the left, parallel to the beach, following it when it veers to the right (about 400m).   This is the former Chimuri, one Indian-style thatch-roofed structure with three rooms and a shared kitchen (F, cb, cw; D to rent all 3 rooms).   It's right on the beach, private and tranquil, about a 20-minute walk to Puerto Viejo.

Communicating with Puerto Viejo in order to make reservations is not easy. You can leave messages for the hotel of your choice at either Manuel León's *pulpería* or the Hotel Maritza (numbers above), but having your call confirmed is another story.   The phones are often out of order or constantly busy because they are the only phones that residents and visitors can call out on.   You might just have to take your chances.   Do not go without reservations during Christmas or Easter.   Try to go on weekdays in the high season.

As we said before, August and September are good months to go because the weather is usually nice and nobody's there. The above hotels can give you information about the weather.

Fresh fruits and vegetables are delivered to town several days a week.   You can find them at **Johnnie's Discotheque and Chinese Seafood Restaurant** which serves cheap, hefty portions of greasy, salty "chinese" food. Local ladies, like Miss Dolly, make bread with coconut milk which is good with their homemade guava jam. They also pat unsweetened *cacao* into little rounds (available at the Soda Támara). Just the thing to take back for hot chocolate in town, which you can sip while you recall the misty beaches and reggae rhythms of the Talamanca coast.

The miles and miles of beaches, jungle and swamp south of Puerto Viejo have been declared a wildlife refuge all the way to the Panama border. Telephones, electricity and public transportation are nonexistent in this area. The people   live with nature by necessity.   Most locals ride horses or bicycles, or walk, because there are no buses.   Rustic accommodations are available in the beautiful Playa Chiquita and Punta Uva areas.

Cabinas Dasa rents two 2-story cabins on the beach south of Punta Uva with furnished kitchens ($210/wk, pb, cw, nf, 36-2631). To get info, keys and bedclothes, look for their yellow sign on the left, 4km south of Puerto Viejo. About 200m beyond the sign is **Maracú**, basic Indian-style cabins with kitchens (F, cb, cw, nf, 25-6215). The owners can take you horseback riding in the "bush", native vernacular for the beautiful hills full of orchids, bromeliads, howler monkeys, birds, butterflies, bugs and snakes. This area is definitely for those who want to live in nature with the local people, drink rainwater, deal with mosquitos, cook for themselves, and slow down long enough to harmonize with the tropical pace of life. About 2km farther south, also on the left, are **Restaurant Punta Uva**, the only place to eat in the area, and **Cabinas Selvyn** (F, basic, cb, nf, cw; larger separate cabin, D). There are also 2 houses for rent at the road leading to Punta Uva (turn left at the turquoise house).

Getting to Puerto Limón: Going by train to Limón is another way to enjoy the beauty of Costa Rica up close. The train takes a long time: 6-8 hours as opposed to 2.5 hours by bus or car. You see the tremendous differences in terrain as the train descends from the verdant central valley, to the banks of the roaring Reventazón river, to the jungly flatlands where bananas, ginger and *cacao* are grown. It passes between walls of tropical plants and flowers. Sit on the right side going down for the best view. People come aboard at every stop, selling fruit, drinks, *empanadas, patí, pan bon* and hard-boiled eggs. If you take the train from San José, you will get to Limón around dusk. Keep an eye on your possessions--there are no lights on the train and robberies have been known to occur. A word to the wise: bathroom facilities on the trains leave much to be desired. Always bring your own toilet paper anywhere you go.

The **Atlantic train station** in San José is on a 3, near the east end of the Parque Nacional. Trains leave San José at 10am and return from Limón at 6 am. Train tickets ($1.50), are not usually sold in advance, so arrive at least half an hour before departure to assure yourself a seat. If you want to go just as far as Siquirres and come back the same day, see p. 58.

The **Limón bus stop** is right across from the Limón train station. Buses leave almost every hour, but buy tickets in advance if it is a weekend or holiday ($1.25, 23-7811, 21-5917). If you are driving, the **Centro Turístico Pacuare,** just south of Siquirres, is a good place to stop for a snack and a swim.

Getting to Talamanca: The Sixaola bus leaves for Cahuita, Puerto Vargas and Puerto Viejo at 5am, 10am, 1pm and 4pm. The stop is one block north and half a block west of the Mercado Central in Limón. Get there early and be prepared for a struggle to get on board--these rickety buses are virtually the only means of transportation for most coastal dwellers, so they are crowded. If you catch the 7 am bus from San José, you should be able to make the 10 am bus down the Talamanca coast. You can be in Puerto Viejo by noon.

Buses leave Puerto Viejo for Limon at 6am, 1pm and 4pm. There is no 1pm bus on Sundays. They enter Cahuita too, about 30 min. later.

There is a **direct** San Jose-Sixaola bus that leaves from a 11, c 1/ctl each day at 6am, 2:30pm and 4:30pm (3-hr trip, $4, 21-0524, 58-1572). It can leave you either at the entrance to Cahuita or at the Bribri turnoff, about 6km from Puerto Viejo. It reaches the same Bribri-Puerto Viejo *cruce* around 6:30am, 9:30am and 3:30pm on its way back to San José from Sixaola and Bribri. There's not much to see in the town of Bribri. It is an administrative center more than anything. If you want to experience Indian culture, talk to Chimuri or Cahuita Tours for trips into the reserve.

Hitoy Cerere Biological Reserve is definitely off the beaten track and has hardly been developed for visitors. Trails are overgrown and unmarked and there are no camping facilities. Park guards have to spend most of their time cutting down ma-

rijuana that people plant within the reserve. But for hardy explorers, there are beautiful views, clear streams, waterfalls and
lots of birds to see. To get there you have to take a Valle de
la Estrella bus from Limón which winds into the banana plantations and get off at Finca Seis, the end of the line. Jeep-taxis
there will take you 10km farther in for around $4, and leave
you within 1km of the entrance. They will return to pick you
up at an agreed-upon time, and can take you back to Cahuita if
you want (1.5 hrs, $25).

green sea turtle

Tortuguero National Park: The area north of Limón, like
most of the Atlantic coast of Nicaragua, is a water-based society. All travel is by boat. Roads are planned for the future but
still do not exist. In 1974, a series of canals was built to connect the natural inland waterways between Limón and Barra del
Colorado, thus allowing coastal residents to get to Limón without the hazards of sea travel. In 1979 the government established a twice-weekly launch service up the inland waterway.
Tortuguero got its first electric generator in 1982.
   Tortuguero is the largest nesting area in the Caribbean for
the green sea turtle. The turtles mate offshore and the females
crawl onto the beach to lay their eggs from July through September each year. They return to Tortuguero every two to four
years to mate and dig their nests. Although their feeding
grounds can be as far away as Florida and Venezuela, none of
the 26,000 turtles tagged in Tortuguero has ever been found to
mate at any other beach. Long-term biological research on the
green turtle, started by the Caribbean Conservation Corp. in
1954, has helped greatly in the understanding and preservation
of this species. Interest aroused by Dr. Archie Carr's entertain-

ing and informative book about his wanderings in search of the green turtles' nesting ground (see Recommended Reading, p. 236) eventually led to the area being declared a National Park in 1970 by the Costa Rican government.

Sea turtles and tourists are not the only animals that benefit from the National Park. Fresh water turtles, crocodiles, sloths, howler, spider and colorado monkeys, toucans, *oropéndolas*, parrots, morpho butterflies, and many other animals abound in Tortuguero. It is also known as one of the world's richest fishing grounds for tarpon and snook.

Tortuguero has been famous for turtle shells, meat and eggs since the 1600's when the Spanish started *cacao* plantations on the Atlantic coast. Turtles were valued as a meat source on ships because they could be kept alive on board by keeping them out of the sun and sprinkling them with water. Turtle soup became a delicacy in England. Large-scale turtle export started in 1912. By the 1950's the green turtle faced near extinction.

From July through September you can see the nesting of the green turtles. Their flipper marks look like tractor treads, which show up as wide black lines on the beach at night. When observing nesting turtles at night, keep flashlight use to a minimum, as they are very sensitive to light.

When we were in Tortuguero in March, we saw two huge leatherback *(baúl)* females laboriously digging holes in the soft brown sand by the light of the full moon. The turtles lay about 100 eggs at each of several nestings per season. The eggs incubate for approximately 60 days, then the baby turtles bite through the rubbery shells and clamber up out of the nest, heading straight for the sea before dawn. Their instinctive navigational powers direct them into the open sea.

Dugouts: The best way to enjoy the exuberant vegetation and abundant wildlife of Tortuguero's canals is to rent a dugout canoe *(cayuca)*. Miss Rita, Juana Martínez, Juan Viñas, Mister Michek, Edgar López, Bill Sambola or Durham Rankin are some of the villagers who have been known to rent out boats. Ask about current rates. You can hire a guide for $10/day and up, plus the cost of the canoe. Paddle around for awhile to see if your dugout is the right size for you, and make sure it is of solid, one-piece construction and not caulked together. Cayucas are quite stable and easy to paddle. Ask for a plastic bailer for your boat.

The main waterway of the National Park is inland from the canal that comes from Moín. Paddle south. You will see smaller waterways branching off which you can explore.

The Tortuga Lodge and some private people rent motorboats to tour the canals of the National Park. This is okay for going places fast, but the noise disturbs the quiet beauty of the jungle streams.

To make your canoe trip more comfortable, make sure to bring the following:

Thick-soled running shoes and socks
Insect repellent
Suntan lotion and shield
Broad-rimmed hat or visor cap
Umbrella for sun or rain
Lightweight plastic poncho for rain or picnic cloth
Lightweight longsleeved and shortsleeved shirts
Towels
Lunch in waterproof bags
Water
Swiss army knife
Flashlight

Camping is allowed in the National Park, but remember that Tortuguero has one of the highest annual rainfalls in the world: over 200" a year. The beach at Tortuguero offers little shade, has rough unfriendly surf, and is frequented by sharks. Terciopelo *(fer-de-lance)* snakes are not uncommon on land, especially at night. There are nature trails on the narrow piece of land between the large canal and the sea.

Getting there: Because transportation to Tortuguero is a bit complicated, you might want to splurge on a tour for this part of your vacation. **Cotur** takes you by bus to Moín (2.5 hrs) and up the canals in their pleasant launches, the **Miss Caribe** and the **Miss America** (5 hrs). The 3-day trips include transport, meals and room at the **Jungle Lodge,** 1 km N of Tortuguero village on the left (A, incl. meals, pb, cf, rest., 33-0155, 33-6579, 33-0133, 33-0226). You can also go with them by plane and boat back the next day, or fly down for 2 nights and boat back. Prices range from $125 to $181. Bilingual guides take you hiking through the park and to the beach at night to watch the turtles. Cayuca tours on the canals are $5 extra. **Mawamba** has a larger, slower boat with showers and bar on board, that makes the same trip, staying at their new lodge across the river (B, pb, rest, 33-9964). They can also take you up and back from Moín in small 6-passenger speedboats (3 hrs each way), or give you a 2-day tour in the small boats. Prices range from $125 to $295. The **Hotel Matama** in Limón offers 2-day boat trips to Tortuguero (3 hrs each way) for $100. Guests stay in Parismina, just outside the southern boundary of the park (58-1123). **Costa Rica Expeditions** flies small 5-passenger planes directly to and from their comfortable **Tortuga Lodge** (L, pb, cf). The 1-day, 1-night tour includes boating through the canals of the park with a local naturalist guide. An optional night tour of the canals ($25) or turtle tour ($10) are available. They also offer 3-day bus and boat trips, a 2-day, 2-night train-boat-plane trip, and other boat-flight options (22-0333, fax: (506) 57-1665). Prices range from $130 to $249.

Depending on space, most the above tour companies will include non-tour passengers in their flights and cruises. If you do go on your own, call ahead and make reservations, since most hotels are booked with tour groups. The cheapest place to stay in Tortuguero is **Sabina's** in the village (E, cb, cw). More remote and pleasant is the **Tatané,** individual rustic cabins on the canal to Barra (E, cb, rest., owner will pick you up in the village in his boat). For both places, call 71-6716--that's a pay phone at the *pulpería*--and leave a message with Marco Zamora. The hotel owners should call back to confirm your reservation.

The cheapest way ($3) to get to Tortuguero from Moín is the **Gran Delta**, the main means of transportation for the people who live along the canals. This old, flat-bottomed boat is crowded and noisy, and the trip takes at least 7 hours. Because of frequent mechanical problems the Gran Delta is not functioning as of this writing. Call JAPDEVA, the Atlantic Port Authority, at 58-1106 for current information. Mr. Gabriel Taylor's big old launch leaves Moín on Sat at 10am when the Gran Delta isn't working.

SANSA has 1/2-hour flights to **Barra del Colorado,** N of Tortuguero near the Nicaraguan border (Tues, Thurs and Sat 6am, $10 one way, 21-9414, 33-0397, 33-3258). There are famous, well-equipped fishing lodges at Barra (see p. 74) and cheaper lodging at **Cabinas Tarponland** right on the airstrip (D, pb, tf, screens, 71-6917). They rent boats to Tortuguero ($50/boat). There are local coconut barges ($3.50) between Barra and Tortuguero that might have room for you.

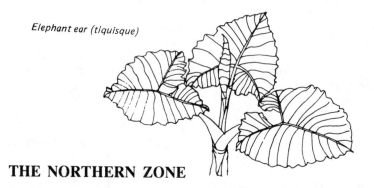

Elephant ear (tiquisque)

THE NORTHERN ZONE

The **Sarapiquí** region has become more accessible in the last few years and has several new projects of interest to visitors. **Puerto Viejo de Sarapiquí** was Costa Rica's main port in colonial times. Boats embarked down the wide Sarapiquí River north to the Río San Juan that forms Costa Rica's border with Nicaragua, and from there to the Atlantic. Now that *contra* activity has been stopped in Costa Rica, tourists can follow the same river route, then turn down the Rio Colorado to Barra del Colorado Wildlife Refuge and go from there to the canals of Tortuguero.

La Selva, the research station and biological reserve of the Organization for Tropical Studies, has brought fame to Sarapiquí. Biologists come from around the world to study the enormous variety of tropical plants and animals there. Recently, the 3500-acre research area was made part of a "protected zone" which connects it with Braulio Carrillo National Park to the south, in an effort to secure the large hunting territories needed by jaguars and pumas. 451 species of trees have been identified there so far, as well as 81 reptile species, 48 of amphibians and 113 of mammals. Over 400 species of birds either live in or migrate to La Selva from the highlands, including toucans, *oropéndolas*, tinamoos, and umbrella birds. Over 300 different species were observed in a single day in the "Birdathon", an annual event in which people pledge money for each different species observed by Audubon Society birdwatchers. The money goes to establish an endowment fund which will protect Braulio Carrillo on a permanent basis, and hopefully will serve as a model for funding conservation projects around the world.

One of the many courses offered at La Selva is not for biologists, but for "decision makers": government and business leaders from around the world who need to understand tropical ecology in order to guide their countries along the soundest path in the future.

Tourists can roam freely on the 50 km of well-kept nature trails, but the scientists there want visitors to understand that research and education are La Selva's top priorities. In order to assure this, all visitors, whether for a few hours or a few days, must make reservations through the OTS office in San José (36-6696). It is no longer possible to drop in. La Selva is expensive to visit, which makes it an attraction mostly for those with an interest in natural history. A day on the trails, three meals at the reserve's cafeteria, and a night in "rustic but comfortable" accommodations costs $70. There are special rates for card-carrying graduate students in tropical sciences. A less expensive way to visit is by spending just a day there, which includes lunch, for $15. A bus leaves the OTS for La Selva three times a week ($10).

Hotel La Selva Verde in **Chilamate**, 5 minutes by car west of Puerto Viejo, has one of the most beautifully designed lodges we've seen ($42.50/person, incl. meals, double occupancy; $37.50 in the older lodge near the road, $15 w/o meals). Their forest reserve along the river is great for birdwatching. They will arrange trips down the San Juan, or rafting, tubing and kayaking trips on local rivers for you. Make reservations in advance (71-6459).

El Rancho de Doña Rosa is a great place for *tico* food, and their prices can't be beat. Open every day 7am to 8pm, it's just a few meters towards Puerto Viejo from La Selva Verde.

Rancho Leona (71-6312), 12km southwest of Puerto Viejo in the village of La Virgen offers a varied menu from shrimp creole and eggplant parmesan to BLTs and cheeseburgers. They will also take you on an all-day kayaking trip down the Rio Puerto Viejo. No experience necessary. More challenging trips can be arranged for experienced kayakers. Included in the $65 fee are two nights free bunkbed lodging, if you so desire. While there, take a look at the beautiful necklaces and earrings they make, as well as Leona's lovely hand-painted T-shirts, depicting native birds and animals. They can also take you on hiking, camping and horseback riding trips, and know all the good swimming holes in the area.

A few km to the east of Puerto Viejo is **MUSA**, a cooperative of local ladies who grow and sell native medicinal herbs. They will give you a tour of their farm and explain the uses of the different plants. They also offer excellent rosemary *(romero)* and chamomile *(manzanilla)* shampoos and natural clay preparations. The farm is on the right as you approach Puerto Viejo from Horquetas.

Also to the east of Puerto Viejo is **El Gavilán**, a former cattle ranch which has been converted into a lodge. Tours of the rainforest and rivers by horseback and boat are offered. Arrangements must be made in San José because lodging, transportation, meals and tours are included in a package deal ($75/person, 53-6540, shared rooms and baths, hw, jacuzzi).

Getting there: The Río Frío bus leaves three times a day from c 12, a 7/9 in San José for Sarapiquí. The 6:30am and 12 noon buses go on the scenic route above Heredia that winds around the northeast side of Poás volcano to the northern plain and passes through La Virgen, Chilamate and Puerto Viejo before reaching La Selva. Don't go this route if you tend to get carsick. Otherwise, it is one of the most beautiful rides you can take, passing by the powerful La Paz waterfall on a hairpin turn, with vistas of the forests of Braulio Carrillo to the east. By bus it takes 4 hours, 2.5 hours by car, all on paved road.

The 4pm Río Frío bus goes on the Guápiles highway through Braulio Carrillo and turns north to pass through Horquetas, La Selva, Puerto Viejo and Chilamate, ending about 8pm in La Virgen. It is a good bus to take if you want to go kayaking at Rancho Leona.

If you are coming from Monteverde or Guanacaste and want to avoid going back to San José, you can take buses from Cañas to Tilarán and Tilarán to San Carlos. To do this, you will have to spend the night in San Carlos or La Fortuna (see p. 161). The San Carlos-Río Frío bus leaves at 6am, 9am and 3pm, taking about 2 hours to reach Puerto Viejo. By car, Cañas to La Fortuna takes about 2 hours, including 45 min on bad road on the north side of Lake Arenal. You can get from Volcán Arenal to Puerto Viejo in under 2 hours, avoiding San Carlos, if you turn left at El Tanque, a few km out of Fortuna, then take the turnoff to Muelle (route 4), following signs to Aguas Zarcas and always turning right. At Aguas Zarcas, 23 km W of San Carlos, turn left to San Miguel, and left again to La Virgen, Chilamate and Puerto Viejo, all on good road.

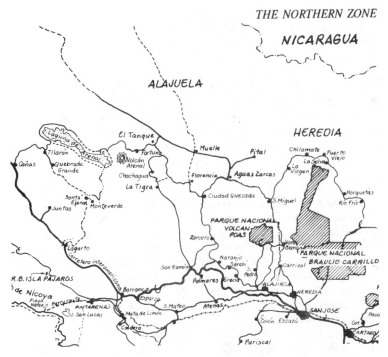

Many people are appalled at the destruction of vital rainforests, but few try to do something about it. Amos Bien, an ecologist and former manager of La Selva, decided that the best way to convince people not to cut down rainforests is to demonstrate that conservation through tourism and ecologically sound management is the best use of land from an economic standpoint. The result is **Rara Avis,** a 1500-acre forest reserve near Las Horquetas, southeast of La Selva. Rara Avis is the site of biologist Don Perry's research on the rainforest canopy, which he writes about in his fascinating book, *Life Above the Jungle Floor* (see p. 237). Brave visitors can observe the forest from the tramway from which he does his research, traveling 300m through the jungle and going as high as 50m off the ground. The ride involves the signing of a release and a $35 donation per hour to further canopy investigation. The new, 8-room Waterfall Lodge is 500 feet from a gorgeous 3-tiered waterfall, and is the most comfortable place to stay at Rara Avis ($65 double, pb, hw). El Plástico Lodge is more rustic but comfortable as well ($45 double, cb, hw). Both prices include 3 hearty meals, guides and transportation from Horquetas.

From Horquetas to El Plástico it takes about 3 hours to go 9 miles on very bad road. Once there, visitors must be willing to put up with muddy trails to experience the rainforest's pristine beauty. Experienced biologists accompany small groups to explain rainforest phenomena and point out wildlife.

Because of its isolated location, transportation must be arranged in advance by calling Rara Avis at 53-0844 (fax: (506) 32-6513). You can get substantial discounts at El Plástico with an IYHF card (see p. 65). Toruma in San José sometimes arranges low-cost group trips to member hostels (24-4085).

Ciudad Quesada (San Carlos) is located in the San Carlos plain of central Alajuela province, one of Costa Rica's most agriculturally productive zones. As is true in many areas, its forested hills and family farms are being bought up by large-scale cattle farmers, some of them expatriate North Americans. Although increasing export capacity, this contributes to Costa Rica's serious deforestation problem.

Ciudad Quesada is a midpoint for trips north to Volcán Arenal and Tabacón thermal spa. You can also go east to connect with highway 9 to La Virgen and Puerto Viejo de Sarapiquí. **Hotel La Central** (D, 46-0766, 46-0301) and **Hotel El Retiro** (F, 46-0463) are both clean and comfortable with private bath on Parque Central in San Carlos. There is a crafts cooperative on the northwest corner of the park. **Balneario San Carlos** has a large swimming pool, two kids' pools, a Ticostyle restaurant, roller skating twice a week, dances on Sundays, and a small lake for boating and fishing. Their somewhat rundown cabinas have fridges and hot water, no fans (E, 46-0747). You'll see signs for the Balneario 5 blocks northwest of Parque Central.

El Tucano, set back from the road in a shady forest, offers swimming pools, a sauna and a small, lukewarm, circular pool with jacuzzi, fed partially by a thermal spring. The grounds are beautifully kept, and an elegant restaurant offers an international menu including seafood and Italian specialties. Their new cabinas have bathtubs, a rarity here (A, pb, hw, 46-1822). Use of pools and sauna costs about $2 for non-guests. It's 20 minutes northeast of Ciudad Quesada on the road to Puerto Viejo. Take a Río Frío, San Miguel, Aguas Zarcas, Pital or Venecia bus from the terminal in San Carlos.

You can continue east from El Tucano 32 km to Highway 9. Go left to Puerto Viejo and La Selva, or right to San José via Heredia, one of the most beautiful drives in Costa Rica (see p. 156-7). The return trip takes about 3 hours.

San José-San Carlos buses leave almost every hour from 5am through 6pm from the Coca Cola (3 hours, $1.50). Try to get a Directo bus--it makes less stops.

Arenal fulfills the volcano stereotype. Its perfectly conical shape emerges from Alajuela's gentle green hills. From time to time, loud explosions are heard and a mushroom cloud of grey, brown, orange or blue smoke billows out of the top. Although the volcano is capable of inspiring intense fright and awe in visitors, inhabitants of nearby Fortuna de San Carlos and the dairy farms at its base seem to live with relative peace of mind. If you ask, they will tell you with surprising tranquility about the time it erupted.

Since Arenal was dormant until 1968, the only people who suspected it was a volcano were those who had scaled it and found a crater and steam vents at the top. But few listened to them, until an earthquake shook the area on July 29, 1968. Twelve hours later, Arenal blew, sending out shock waves that were recorded as far away as the Boulder, CO nuclear explosion monitoring center. All damage was 5 km west of the volcano, where people were knocked down by shock waves, poisoned by gases and struck by falling rocks. Three new craters formed during the eruption sending down lava flows which eradicated the town of Pueblo Nuevo. At the end, 78 people had died. Since then the volcano hasn't erupted; it just rumbles and explodes, and shoots out rocks, soot and smoke.

Arenal is the most impressive at night. In the dark you can see the bursts of fire and red-hot rocks hundreds of feet into the sky. In the day you only see smoke and hear the volcano's terrible roar. Incandescent material cascades down the sides, especially on the north. Explosions happen every few hours.

Although the volcano is not dangerous if you keep your distance, it is very dangerous to climb. One tourist was killed and another burned in July 1988 when they hiked too near the crater, foolishly trusting the volcano's placid appearance in between explosions. If they had seen it explode before climbing, they probably never would have attempted it. They also unwittingly risked the lives of 15 Costa Rican Rural Guards and

Red Cross workers who heroically searched the volcano to retrieve the body of its victim. Please do not climb this volcano.

It *is* wonderful to watch, though, and there are several places you can watch it from. You can camp out at **Tabacón**, the thermal pools 6 km east of Lake Arenal. There are showers and dressing rooms on the other side of the stream, as well as a ringside view of Arenal's performance.

Tabacón's thermal waters spring out of Volcán Arenal. They are channeled into a cement canal and sent down a tiled slide into a pool. The water splashes from the slide with such force that it creates a strong current that will take you all the way around the perimeter of the pool. There's a second, smaller and shallower pool that you can sit and soak in, and there are individual rooms where intensive showers massage your muscles.

The water feels good and is supposed to be especially healthful for people suffering from bad skin conditions. The caretaker swears it has cured him of skin discolorations, and he can give you accounts of other miracles. The whole complex is surrounded by the area's brilliant vegetation, and of course, smoking Arenal serves as a stunning backdrop. Open every day, morning to evening. It's most crowded weekends.

The **Arenal Volcano Observatory,** sometimes used by Smithsonian investigators in their vulcanological research, has recently been conditioned for guests. Located on a private macadamia farm, it offers a closeup view of the south side of the volcano and part of Lake Arenal. Accommodations are simple, with 3 bunkbeds per room, and a common dining area serving *campesino* food (pb, hw, $42.50/person incl. meals). A new cabin with kitchen, fireplace, and a great view of the lake is also available for up to 4 people. The climate at the observatory is cool and fresh, in contrast to that of La Fortuna, which can get a little muggy. Visitors must make reservations through Costa Rica Sun Tours (55-3518, 55-3418, fx: (506) 55-4410) although you do not have to be part of a tour to go there.

Beyond Tabacón is **Lake Arenal,** a large reservoir. The original Laguna Arenal was the source of a river whose waters flowed east to the Atlantic. But dams built for a hydroelectric energy plant enlarged the lake and diverted the waters. Now they flow out the NW side of the reservoir to irrigate the dry Pacific coast. Many people enjoy boating, fishing and windsurfing on the lake. The east side, near Tabacón, retains its original lush greenery, but as you travel west, you see the devastating effect of cattle ranching, as the exuberant vegetation gives way to grassy pastureland which, judging by the low water level in the lake, will soon go dry. A drive around Lake Arenal is a graphic lesson in ecology.

Arenal Lodge is partially owned by Peter Gorinsky, the famous fishing guide. It is a large, comfortable house with a library, billiard table, and a lovely view of Arenal in the distance ($100/pers. incl. meals, cb, hw, $265/day incl. fishing, 28-2588, 46-1881, fx: 28-2798). It's 4km up a gravel road near the northeastern tip of the lake. You can call them from a pay phone 100m W of the entrance.

Albergue Arenal is a new, inexpensive youth hostel overlooking the lake, 1km east of the town of Nuevo Arenal. Call the Youth Hostel Network at the Toruma (24-4085) for info on low cost group excursions for IYHF members.

Twelve km east of Tabacón is La Fortuna, the closest town to Arenal. **Cabinas San Bosco** are the nicest there (E, clean, pb, nf, 47-9050, 200m. N of the gas station). **Hotel La Central** is basic, fairly clean and friendly (F, cb, nf, 47-9004, 100m W of the gas station). **El Jardín,** across from the gas station, has good Tico-style food and playground equipment for kids. **La Vaca Muca,** 3 km W of La Fortuna, on the road to the volcano, offers generous *casados* and other local dishes. **El Coquito,** 2/3 of the way to Ciudad Quesada, is a good place to stop for a *refresco* and *ceviche*.

Getting there: The 5:45am San José-San Carlos bus (leaves from Coca Cola) continues on to Fortuna every day. You can also catch a Fortuna bus in San Carlos at 6, 9, 1, and 4:30. From Fortuna it's 13 km to Tabacón. Buses leave San Carlos at 6am and 3pm for Tilarán, passing through Fortuna and Tabacón around 8am and 4pm.

You can also come from the west, combining a trip to Guanacaste or Monteverde with a visit to Arenal by taking a half hour bus ride from Cañas to Tilarán, and catching the Tilarán-San Carlos bus at 12:30, which reaches Tabacón around 3:30pm. It takes a lovely route around the north side of Lake Arenal, paved except for one 8 km strip. By car, it's 1.5 hours from Tilarán to La Fortuna (see map, p.157).

A new road is opening up between San Ramón de Alajuela (1 hr W of San José) and San Carlos. The new road winds less than the Naranjo-Zarcero-San Carlos route, and borders a reserve which protects a beautiful stand of rainforest southeast of Monteverde and conserves the water supply for the town of San Ramón. The road should be paved by the beginning of 1990. Near the end of the road, after the town of La Tigra, is **Don Charlie's Ranch**, featuring horseback riding, birding, and Don Charlie's creative and delicious cooking. There are comfortable cabinas with kitchens ($50/pers. incl. meals, $35 w/o meals, pb, hw, kids' pool, bird zoo). Call Vesa Tours (28-9072) to arrange your visit. Once the road is paved, La Fortuna will be about a half hour from Don Charlie's.

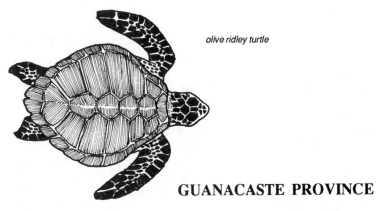

olive ridley turtle

GUANACASTE PROVINCE

Guanacaste was a totally autonomous province of Spain's Central American empire until 1787, when it was given to Nicaragua. It was taken away and given to Costa Rica in 1812, when Costa Rica's population was too small without it to be represented in the colonial government that ruled from Guatemala. After independence, both Costa Rica and Nicaragua claimed Guanacaste. *Guanacastecos* were divided too--Liberians, whose founders were Nicaraguan cattle farmers, wanted to join Nicaragua. Nicoyans were in favor of joining Costa Rica. Nicoya won in a vote, and an 1858 treaty declared Guanacaste part of Costa Rica.

Its long period of autonomy, the high indigenous population and its geographic isolation from the Meseta Central have contributed to make Guanacaste a unique part of Costa Rica. Many "Costa Rican" traditions originate in Guanacaste. The people, dark-skinned descendants of the Chorotega Indians, are possibly closer to their cultural and historical roots than other Costa Ricans. There is a special *campesino* richness in their friendly manner.

Most of Guanacaste has been converted into pasture land for beef production. The deforestation the region has suffered has altered its climate and ecosystems, causing occasional droughts. Brahma bulls lounge under the graceful, spreading shade trees that gave the province its name. The brilliant yellow blossoms of the *corteza amarilla* dot the plains in February, and in March the light red blossoms of the *carao* or carob tree brighten the landscape.

The clear, gentle waters of Guanacaste's beaches attract Ticos and foreigners alike. The dry climate helps keep mosquitos to a minimum.

163

Centro Ecológico La Pacífica, 4 km north of Cañas on the Interamerican Highway, is a shady, green oasis in the midst of Guanacaste's heat. It is a favorite with birders, as 225 different species have been observed in its woods and near the Río Corobicí, which flows through the ranch. Trees are labeled with their scientific and common names, and lists of the birds and mammals visible there are available to guests. Its tastefully designed cabinas (C, cf, hw, lovely pool, 69-0050) can be used as a base for trips to the beach, Lomas Barbudal Reserve, Santa Rosa National Park or Volcán Arenal. Swiss owned and managed, La Pacífica's restaurant offers a wide variety of excellent international cuisine.

Rincón Corobicí, right on the river just after the entrance to La Pacífica, is also a cool, pleasant place to stop for lunch or refreshments.

How can you set up a park or reserve so that the surrounding community benefits from it? Many campesinos feel that environmental concerns interfere with their livelihood rather than supporting it. This makes ecology and community development enemies, creating an impossible situation for both. By involving the community in the formation of its reserve, **Lomas Barbudal** is actively trying to bridge this gap. Rivers you can swim in, shaded by graceful trees and waterfalls you can hike to, are the main attractions at Lomas Barbudal. Local school children are helping plan the visitors' center and clearing trails. The dirt road to Lomas Barbudal is on the left, 20 minutes north of Cañas, right after Bagaces. The park entrance is about 6 km from the Interamerican Highway. Once you get there, reserve guardhouse is across a little stream, refreshments are about 200m to the right and the swimming hole is about 200m to the left. Camping is allowed. Bring insect repellent during the rainy season.

Palo Verde National Park and the adjoining **Rodríguez Caballero Wildlife Refuge** form one of Central America's last natural refuges for the thousands of birds that pass over this region on their annual migratory paths. North American ducks and egrets rest there during their migration. Birds from the Guanacaste plains touch down, too. In addition to the 260 species of birds that visit, Palo Verde is a habitat for mammals, amphibians and reptiles, many of which can be observed relatively easily. During the dry season, animals stay near the few permanent springs in the area, one of which is only a hundred meters from the park's administration building and campsite.

Palo Verde is on the east side of the mouth of the Tempisque River. The National Park occupies the southern part of the area and the Wildlife Refuge the northern part. Though both are open to the public, the National Park is better equipped for visitors.

Stretching along the banks of the river is a plain that floods during the rainy season and dries to a brown crisp in the dry season. Further from the river rise bluffs dotted with limestone cliff outcrops. The park administration is set in an old *hacienda* at the base of the bluffs; there are a couple trails that set out from there and climb to lookout points. The reserve also has several kilometers of trails.

You can sometimes join the park rangers on their daily horseback patrols around the park. Once a week they go to the **Isla de Pájaros,** a bird-filled island in the Tempisque. Because the park has relatively few visitors, the rangers are usually willing to take people along on their patrols ($25).

A permit is not required to visit Palo Verde National Park. If you plan to camp, though, it is necessary to notify the park administration beforehand. With advance notice they might also be able to offer meals or transportation for a fee.

To visit the Wildlife Refuge you do need a permit from the Dirección de Vida Silvestre in San José ($1.25, c 19, a ctl/2, 33-8112). You can camp at the Refuge. The Organization for Tropical Studies has a research station at the Refuge where you can stay if you call in advance (36-6696).

Getting to Palo Verde: Take the 7am Liberia bus from the Pulmitan station (c 14, a 1/3, 22-1650, $1.50) and get off at Cañas. Take the 11am Bebedero bus from the Cañas *mercado.* You'll have time for a good breakfast before the bus leaves. From Bebedero it's a very hot 3-hour hike to the Park. Park personnel might be able to pick you up in Bebedero if you call ahead by radio (33-5473), or you can hire a taxi in Bebedero ($9). By car, Bebedero is 15km W from the Cañas cemetery. Palo Verde is another 15km beyond that.

Getting to the Wildlife Refuge: Turn left at the gas station in Bagaces, N of Cañas. The Refuge is 32km from there.

During the dry season you can enter the area from the Nicoya Peninsula. Take a bus from Nicoya to Puerto Humo.

Check around to find Florentino Urrieta, who can take you across the Río Tempisque in his boat ($.75). From where you dock, the Refuge is a 1.5-hour hike to the left and the Park is about 3 hours to the right. Don't try this route in the rainy season--the whole plain is swamped.

Most bus transportation to Guanacaste is by way of **Liberia,** 45 minutes north of Cañas on the Interamerican. Even though it looks farther away on the map, a trip to Liberia from San José (4 hours) takes less time than a trip to Nicoya by way of the Tempisque ferry. You can take a circular route through Liberia, Santa Cruz and Nicoya, the gateways to the Guanacaste beaches, and come back on the ferry. Roads are paved along that circular route, making it a 2-hour trip by car from Liberia to the Tempisque. Due to the intricacies of Costa Rica's road system, it is much more difficult to make a tour of the beaches by going along the coast unless you have 4-wheel drive and it is the dry season.

About 2km before you get to Liberia, on the right, is **Hotel Las Espuelas** (C, 33-3169, 66-0144, hw, a/c, pool, rest.) the most pleasant and well-maintained in that area. Next to it is La Ronda, a pretty seedy place, but cheap (E, pb, pool, rest, 66-0417). There are three gas stations where the main road into Liberia intersects the Interamerican highway. They are the surest place to get gas on holidays. At this intersection are **Hotel Boyeros** (C, 66-0722, hw, a/c, pool, tel, rest.) and **Hotel Bramadero** (E with fans, D with a/c, a bit run down, quieter rooms in back away from pool, restaurant known for tender steak and tough chicken, 66-0371). **Hotel El Sitio** is about 100m to the west (B with a/c, C with fans, spacious grounds, pool, hw, rest, 57-0744, 66-1211). **Hotel La Siesta** is 5 blocks into Liberia and 2.5 blocks to the right from the Farmacia Lux (D, a/c, small pool, rest, clean, quiet, good value, 66-0678). Make sure you have reservations for all above hotels during the dry season.

There's a well-stocked ice cream store on the NE corner of the Parque Central in Liberia. **Las Tinajas** on the W side has tender deep-fried fish and chicken.

Rincón de la Vieja is one of Costa Rica's richest, most varied and little known parks. Volcanologists say that Rincón de la Vieja volcano, although active, is unlikely to erupt because the geysers and mudpots in the area help it "let off steam". It is a compound volcano made up of nine craters which melded together one million years ago. Rincón's most recent violent activity was in 1966-67. The volcano erupted frequently, destroying trees and grazing land. Some of the rivers that spring from the volcano's slopes were polluted by the poisonous gases.

Coatimundi (pizote)

The park is a watershed for 32 rivers, many of which empty into Guanacaste's major river, the Tempisque. Three hundred species of birds have been identified there, as well as deer, collared peccaries, pacas, agoutis, raccoons, jaguars, two-toed sloths, coatimundis and three species of monkeys. *Las Pailas* (The Cauldrons) is a 50-hectare wonderland of pits of boiling hot water, vapor geysers that stain the rocks around them red, green and yellow because of the iron, copper and sulphur in the steam, a mini-volcano that formed a couple of years ago, and the *Sala de Belleza* (Beauty Salon), seven bubbling pots of grey mud. You dip a stick in the smooth glop, let it cool, and make yourself a rejuvenating face mask. On the eastern side of the park are *Los Azufrales*, hot sulphur springs of perfect bathtub temperature, right next to a cold stream to splash in (don't let the sulphur water get in your eyes, and don't stay in longer than 5 minutes without alternating with the cold water).

The park is great for hiking because it is largely untouched, not too steep, and the trails are dry most of the year. Unlike the slippery, muddy cloud and rain forests, Rincón is a transitional area between dry and cloud forest. The trails get a bit muddy only at higher altitudes before the forest gives way to rocky, windblown volcanic terrain.

If you want to hike to the volcano craters and Laguna Jilgueros, a scenic lake where sometimes tapirs and *quetzales* can be seen, it's best to camp overnight. March and April are the best months for this, but it is always wise to bring rainsuits, warm clothes, several changes of clothing wrapped in plastic, good hiking boots, waterproof tents, and a compass. We saw a well-prepared group of campers who made the trip in July with no problem.

It is wise to hire a guide if you are going to the volcanoes, because paths are not clearly marked in the rocky terrain, and thick mists come up frequently. A guide is almost necessary also in Las Pailas because the dry, crusty earth around the mudpots is brittle and thin in some places. We know two cases of people who were severely burned when the ground under them gave way and they fell into boiling mud or water. The unsafe areas are not clearly marked.

One of the reasons that Rincón has been thought of as inaccessible is because the road to the park entrance is in bad condition, and lodging was unavailable. Now, Alvaro Wiessel, grandson of a German immigrant who named a crater of the volcano after himself when he "discovered" it in the 1850's, has made his country home into a warm and friendly hostel from which visitors can set out to explore the park. Las Pailas is 30 min. west of the hostel, Azufrales is an hour to the east, the campground from which to explore the craters and Jilgueros is a beautiful 2.5 hour hike through virgin forest to the north, with the craters 1.5 hours beyond. Horses and guides are also available. Room and board are $23/person, $14 with an IYHF card (see p. 65). Because **Albergue Rincon de la Vieja** is isolated, you must call for reservations so that they have time to buy provisions (66-0473, cw, cb, bunks, Apdo. 114, Liberia, Gte., CR).

To get to the Albergue, go 4.5km north of Liberia on the Interamerican till you see yellow bumps in the road which indicate a school zone. Turn right onto a lovely old gravel road which leads in about 10km to the small town of Curubandé. Continue 2km farther to the entrance to Hacienda Guachipelín, then through the gate 2km to where you see a sign saying "Albergue" to the left. If you have a regular car, go straight ahead and leave it inside the stone wall. You will have agreed on a time previously with the lodge, and they will have horses or a truck waiting for you. If you have a pick-up or jeep, turn left at the sign and go another half hour to the river, leave your vehicle, wade across, walk up the hill, and there you are. If you don't have a vehicle, the lodge will pick you up in Liberia for $25 divided by the number of passengers. Actually, it takes just about as long to get to the lodge as it takes to get to Monteverde, because even though the turnoff is an hour farther north, you spend more time on paved highway and less time on gravel roads.

You need 4-wheel drive and about 2 hours to get to the park administration building if you decide to go by the official access road. The park boundary is 25km N of Barrio Victoria in Liberia. Depending on time and space available, park guards might be able to help you with transportation, meals and lodging. Headquarters in Santa Rosa can make radio contact with them (69-5598).

While most of Costa Rica's parks aim to preserve virgin forest, **Santa Rosa National Park** not only protects the little remaining tropical dry forest, but tries to promote its regeneration. This park encompasses almost every ecosystem that occurs in Guanacaste. The most recent addition to the park is a large tract of pastureland, overgrazed and biologically bankrupt, where biologists are applying research findings about how forests propagate themselves. Seeds for forest regeneration are primarily carried by the wind, and by mammals and birds who eat seeds and then defecate in treeless pastures. Encouraging this kind of seed dispersal, and burning firelanes to control the spread of wildfires, will allow the dry forest to renew itself. Instead of making the park off-limits to *campesino* families who formerly eked out an existence as ranch hands, the park incorporates local people as caretakers, research assistants and guides. In addition to receiving a salary, they live and farm within the park, so that their social framework, as well as the environment, is preserved. The new addition, by the way, includes the area where the clandestine airstrip, which figured in the Iran-Contra fiasco, was located.

The three times that Costa Rica has been militarily invaded, the invaders were defeated at the Hacienda Santa Rosa's *Casona* (big house). These days the Casona is a museum with commemorative historical and environmental education exhibits. Near the museum is a trail you can follow for a short natural history jaunt.

There is camping in a central area with water, outhouses and nice big shady trees (for a minimal fee). The ranger will tell you which areas of the park are especially rich in wildlife at the moment.

A 13 km trail will take you to **Playa Naranjo,** a long stretch of white sand which you can usually have all to yourself. At *Argelia* house, right off the beach, there is a camping area, an outhouse and a windmill-pumped well. There is another camping area at *Estero Real,* which you can reach by bearing right at a fork in the trail to Playa Naranjo. It is shady, peaceful and close to the beach, and has water and latrines. Off Playa Naranjo is Witch Rock, famous with surfers the world over for creating the perfect wave.

Santa Rosa is home to a wide variety of easily observed animals. There are three types of monkeys. Howlers emit deafening growls through enlarged voice boxes. Spider monkeys owe their remarkable agility to a long tail with something like a fingerprint on its end which helps grip tree branches. White-faced monkeys, whose varied diet allows them to live in several ecosystems, are the most intelligent and inquisitive of the three.

Collared peccary (zahíno)

There are collared and whitelipped peccaries whose reputation for ferocity is misleading, a Santa Rosa biologist told us. Peccaries are actually scared of humans and flee when we are near. White-tailed deer wander in the savanna land and coatimundis prowl around forests. As in most areas of the Pacific coast, iguanas are everywhere. Caimans live in the estuaries of Playa Naranjo.

You'll see vultures, falcons and a blue and white jay with a feather on top of its head that looks like a curled ribbon on a

birthday present. This bird's beauty is contradicted by its ob-
noxious squawk. Twenty-two species of bats inhabit the park,
including two vampire varieties (they rarely attack humans--their
victims are almost always livestock). Pelicans, gulls, herons
and sandpipers are the most easily recognizable birds on the
beach. Cicadas buzz from tree branches, so loud that sometimes you have to shout to be heard.

One evening we came across a Pacific Ridley turtle digging
a hole to lay her eggs. 500,000 turtles supposedly nest on the
Pacific coast of Costa Rica, of which 200,000 choose **Playa
Nancite,** a two or three-hour hike from Playa Naranjo. Their
largest *arribada* usually takes place in October. After an approximately 60-day incubation period, the baby turtles hatch and
crawl into the sea. An estimated 2 percent survive all the
hazards of turtlehood and become adults.

Playa Nancite is covered with turtle eggshell fragments and
a few shells and skeletons of unfortunate mother turtles who
didn't make it. You can't stay at Nancite overnight without a
permit--it serves mainly as a biological research station. To
hike there from Argelia, walk north along the beach. At high
tide you must swim across a deep river that empties into the
ocean from an estuary. Currents are strong, so be careful.
During low tide, you can wade across. When you reach the
end of the beach, find the trail that traces behind the estuary
and you'll arrive at the Estero Real picnic and camping areas.
Inland from Estero Real, the trail turns off on the left and
climbs over a ridge to Nancite. Take water for the hike.

The formerly inaccessible **Murciélago** sector of Santa Rosa
is now easier to get to. Keep on the Interamerican 5-10 minutes beyond the Santa Rosa turnoff, and turn left on the road to
Cuajiniquil. About 15 min down the winding road to the park
is the **Restaurant Cuajiniquil**, where you can have a good
fresh fish lunch for about $3. Once you get to the administra-
tion buildings at Murciélago, there are swimming holes and a
camping area. In the dry season you can reach Playa Blanca, a
beautiful beach on the tip of the Santa Elena peninsula.
You can buy meals from the park cooks if you let them know
in advance that you're coming (69-5598).

Guanacaste National Park was opened on July 25, 1989.
It was created to protect the migratory paths of animals that

171

live in Santa Rosa, so it extends from the Interamerican high-way to Orosi and Cacao volcanoes to the east. Many moths procreate in the high mountains during the dry season, then fly down to spend the rainy season at a lower, warmer altitude. The *javali,* a wild pig, goes down from the volcanoes to the dry forest in January to search for seeds of the *encino* tree. Scientists studying wildlife in Santa Rosa found that it is impossible to protect these animals if the environments so necessary to their existence are not also protected.

Although Costa Rica has about .001 of the world's land-mass, it has 5% of the world's biodiversity. For instance, an estimated 3800 species of moths live in Santa Rosa alone. Studying all of them would take years. However, now, in an exciting new project, park employees have spent a year receiving intensive training in biological inventory techniques from some of the best scientists in the world. By all reports, the program is a tremendous success, due to the sharp powers of observation of the *campesinos*, their familiarity with the region and its wildlife, and their motivation to learn a new career that would never have been open to them a few years ago. Local people are now being brought to Guanacaste from parks all over the country, to be trained in the same techniques. All specimens will be turned over to the new **Biodiversity Institute** in Santo Domingo de Heredia, which hopes to be able to identify every plant and animal species in the country.

Three different biological stations exist in the new park to aid in this effort: one on **Volcán Cacao** has a rustic wooden lodge in cloud forest with a fantastic view. You go from Potrerillos on the Interamerican 7km to Quebrada Grande on dirt road. From there it's 10km to a place where you can leave a car. The station is an hour's climb from there. The **Maritza** station is a newly-built structure with dormitories, a lab and a dining room on the skirts of Volcán Orosi. It's an hour's drive (15km) on a fairly good dirt road which starts from the Inter-american opposite the turnoff to Cuajiniquil. You have to open and close about 6 barbed wire gates to get there. The **Pitilla** station is on the northeast side of Volcán Orosi at a lower elevation in rainforest similar to that found at La Selva in Sara-piquí. To get to Pitilla, you go right at a guard station about 5 minutes north of the Cuajiniquil turnoff, then about 25km on paved road to Santa Cecilia. The station is in Esperanza, 9km on dirt road from there.

All lodges accept visitors and can prepare meals if given enough advance notice. Guanacaste, Santa Rosa and Rincón de la Vieja parks are all administered from Santa Rosa headquarters (69-5598), so call there to make arrangements.

Getting there: Buses that go to Peñas Blancas on the Nicaragua border pass the entrance to Santa Rosa. They leave San José at 5am and 7:45am (c 16, a 3, 55-1932, tickets in advance, 4-hour trip, $2.50). Or catch a La Cruz (*not* Santa Cruz) bus from Liberia at 5:30am, 9:30am, or 2pm and ask to be let off at the "*entrada a Santa Rosa*". You must walk or hitch 7.2km to the Casona and camping area before you start your long hike to the beach. The trail to Estero Real is probably a creek in the rainy season. We made it down to the beach in a huge 4-wheel-drive jeep once, but the boulders made it a harrowing trip. A tank would be the appropriate vehicle.

By car, Santa Rosa is only 20 min north of Liberia on the Interamerican. The entrance to the Murciélago sector, thru Cuajiniquil, is about 5 min beyond, also on the left. The entrance to the Maritza station in Guanacaste National Park is to the right.

Los Inocentes is the large estate of the Víquez family near Volcán Orosi in northern Guanacaste. They have converted their old family *hacienda* into a lodge from which visitors can ride horses to the forests surrounding the volcano to observe birds, monkeys and other native animals. Trips to nearby beaches and Santa Rosa are also offered. Food and service are excellent, and one gets a sense of the graceful way of life of traditional Costa Rica (39-5484, 66-9190, $48/person incl. meals, shared baths, hw, pool; horses and guide $10/day). To get there, turn right at a security post about 5 minutes north of the turnoff to Cuajiniquil (the sign points to Upala and Santa Cecilia). After 14.5 km on paved road, you'll see a "Los Inocentes" sign, and a store to the right. The hacienda is the first gate after the store.

Beaches near Liberia (See p. 109 for hotel codes).

Playa del Coco is the most central of the beaches near Liberia. It has some of the least expensive cabinas in the area, most of the dancehalls, and its waters are full of small craft. It is not the place to go if you want solitude and relaxation. **Hotel Anexo Luna Tica** (E, 67-0127) has breezy second floor

173

rooms with fans. **Cabinas Luna Tica** (B, 67-0127, pb, cw, cf) are also a block to the left as you near the beach. **Cabinas El Coco** are right on the beach. The sound of the waves muffles the noise from the neighboring discotheque somewhat, but not completely (E, 67-0167, fans, relatively clean, cw, rest; cheaper, less breezy and noisier rooms in back, best to get front room on 2nd floor). The **Flor de Itabo** is about 1km from the beach as you enter town, in a very quiet area. It is a well-designed hotel with a lot of nice touches (A, 67-0011, fx: (506) 67-0003, hw, a/c, pool, rest, sportfishing, tours).

El Ocotal is the most elegant hotel in the area, perched high on a hill 4 km south of Coco (LL, 67-0230, 22-4259). Even if you can't afford its sport fishing, tennis and swimming facilities, you can visit its restaurant for breakfast ($3-5) or lunch and enjoy the beautiful view. A dirt road to lovely, shady Ocotal cove is to the right of the hotel gate, a 40-minute walk from Coco. **Bahía Pez Vela** (21-1586), right after Ocotal, has a small black-sand beach and comfortable cabinas for dedicated sportfishers. No children.

Playa Hermosa, 9km to the north, is quieter and cleaner, with gentle waves and clear water. The turnoff is to the right before you get to Coco. Follow signs to Condovac. **Cabinas Playa Hermosa** are quiet, fairly comfortable and right on the beach (C, 67-0136, fans, cw, good fish dinner for $5). Right next door are three campesino restaurants that offer a whole fish for $1.50. Halfway down the beach is **Aquasport,** where you can rent kayaks, board sails, sailboats, etc, or have an excellent seafood dinner (*paella* is their specialty). Posh **Condovac La Costa** overlooks Playa Hermosa from the north. If your beach experience requires a discotheque, there it is, plus sportfishing facilities, windsurfing, waterskiing and snorkeling rentals, tennis courts, and little golfcart-like vehicles that transport you up and down the hill (LL, hw, a/c, kitchens, pool, cable TV, rest., 67-0267, 67-0211, 21-8949, 33-1862).

Best for camping is **Playa Panamá,** 3km north of Hermosa. A wide bay makes for very gentle water, especially at low tide when tide pools form near the north end of the beach. Watch out for sea urchins! There are a couple of bars and *pulperías* on the south end, but the north end has beautiful shady trees. You'll have to bring your own water, or ask for it at the bars. You can hire a fisherman at any of the beaches to take you across Bahía Culebra to **Playa Nagascola,** where many Indian artefacts have been found. You can camp there, but there is no water.

Getting to Playa del Coco: A bus leaves San José (c 14, a 1/3) every day at 10am and returns at 9:15am ($2.10). Buses leave Liberia for El Coco (30 min trip, $.60) at 5:30am, 12:30pm and 4:30pm, returning at 7am, 1:30pm and 6pm.

Hermosa and Panamá: Buses leave Liberia for both beaches at 11:30am, returning at 4pm. You can also take a bus from Coco to the turnoff and walk or hitch 5 km to Hermosa or 8km to Panamá. A bus leaves San José (c 12, a 5/7) for Playas Hermosa and Panamá at 3:30pm and returns at 6am. Condovac also has a direct bus all year (21-8949). By car, Coco, Hermosa and Panamá are about a half hour from Liberia. There is a gas station on the road to Coco after the turnoff to the town of Sardinal.

If you want to continue south, take any of the above mentioned buses from the beaches and get off at Comunidad (also called Tamarindo Bar), where the road from Coco meets the road from Liberia. There you can intercept a Santa Cruz or Nicoya bus. In 15 minutes you'll be in Belén, where a bus passes around 10:30am and 2:30pm for Playas Brasilito and Potrero. You'll see the turnoff for the beaches about a block after you pass the plaza of Belén. A paved, winding road leads to the village of Huacas, where you turn off to the right. Turn right again after about 200 meters to go to Brasilito, Flamingo, Potrero and Pan de Azúcar. The road should be paved all the way to Potrero by the time you read this. The trip from Belén to Brasilito, the closest beach, takes about 1/2 hour by car, an hour by bus. There are a couple of gas stations in Filadelfia, about halfway between Comunidad and Belén.

The leatherback sea turtle is the largest reptile in the world, 5 feet long, some weighing over a ton. Around 80 leatherbacks come every night to nest in the beach at **Playa Grande** during November, December and January. Playa Grande is also becoming a favorite spot for surfers, because of its long waves. In a project called Friends of Playa Grande, Costa Rican boy and girl scouts are trained to count turtle eggs, to keep campers off the dunes where the turtles nest, and to warn tourists against the use of flashlights and flash attachments on cameras, which can scare the turtles and interfere with their nesting. The young conservationists have had a very positive impact on the visitors. The same scouts also protect turtle nesting sites on the Caribbean coast. To get to Playa Grande, go straight ahead on the road from Huacas instead of turning right for Playa Brasilito. There are no buses.

Brasilito is a small town on a grey-sand beach. Rooms at **Mi Posada** (D, cw, nf, 68-0953) are basic, clean and have private baths and a soda. Two second floor rooms catch the sea breezes, all others are ground floor. The ever-present juke box in the dance hall across the street might be a problem for some. To the left of Mi Posada on the beach are shady trees to camp or park under. To the right are restaurants and bars. El Rancho has a spigot you can get water from. The beach itself is no great shakes, but the people are very friendly. Half an hour south on foot is **Conchal,** a beach remarkable for its hill of shells. There is no touristic development as yet at Conchal, but camping is possible. A house on the beach gives out water at 6 pm. Leaving Brasilito you'll pass the entrance to **Hacienda Las Palmas,** fancy condominiums on a hill (XL, restaurant, pool, a/c, cable TV, access to sportsfishing facilities at nearby Flamingo Beach, 31-4343).

Five minutes down the road, you'll pass the entrance to **Playa Flamingo,** one of Costa Rica's most exclusive beaches, sporting its own marina and landing strip. The new **Flamingo Beach Resort Hotel** is huge, has a bar you can swim up to in its pool, boutiques, fancy restaurants, etc. The **Presidential Suites** next door offer one-and two-bedroom condos with maid and laundry service. Both have a/c, restaurants, and private terraces (XL, 39-1584, fx: 39-0257). They will arrange transport from the airport in Tamarindo if you don't have your own plane. Car rental is available from the hotel, as is windsurfing and scuba diving equipment. **Flamingo Bay Pacific Charters** offers well-equipped sportfishing. **Marie's Restaurant** nearby has good omelettes for breakfast. A Tralapa bus leaves San José every day at 10:30am for Flamingo (6 hrs, $3, c 20, a 3, 21-7202) and returns at 9:30am.

Across the bay from Flamingo, 6 km from Brasilito, is **Playa Potrero. Bahía Flamingo Beach Resort** offers spacious accommodations and a quiet, friendly atmosphere (L, kitchens, pb, hw, cf, restaurant, small pool, 68-0976). They rent a fishing boat, Hobi-cat sailboats, snorkeling equipment, horses and bicycles. American video movies are shown at night. A near-

Great blue heron
(garza azul)

by estuary offers a chance to see herons, caimans and monkeys. You can rent a campsite and use of their facilities for about $7 per person per day. Buses leave Santa Cruz for Brasilito and Potrero at 10am and 2pm.

Fifteen minutes by car farther north is **Playa Pan de Azúcar** and **Hotel Sugar Beach** (B, cw, a/c, 68-0959). It's a pretty beach with some shade, a rocky part for snorkeling and a sandy part for swimming. There's a great view from the open air restaurant and bar which is open every day. Pet monkeys, iguanas and a scarlet macaw entertain the guests. A charter boat is available for fishing and snorkeling trips. The hotel is 15 km from the turnoff at Huacas. There is no bus service beyond Potrero.

Getting there: See p. 175.

Beaches near Santa Cruz

The turnoff for **Playa Tamarindo** is 13 km S of Huacas on paved road. Tamarindo is a wide, white-sand beach with a large estuary--a favorite with surfers and windsurfers. The estuary has been made into a wildlife refuge. Leatherback (*baúl*) turtles nest on the beach, August to February. Many baby turtles have been crushed as they scramble to the ocean by inadvertent tourists because it is hard to distinguish them in the dry, loose sand high up on the beach. Be sure to walk near the water line, where it is easier to spot the baby turtles. These huge, ancient and impressive animals, who have lived on this planet for eons longer than we have, are in danger of extinction.

On the way to the beach, **Cabinas Pozo Azul** has a pool but not much atmosphere (C, pb, cw, a/c, fridges, 68-0147). **Pension Doly** (E, pb; F, cb) is the most basic of the Tamarindo hotels, but it's clean, friendly and right on the beach. Don't go swimming there though; that section of the beach is dangerous. Doly swears she makes the best fried fish in Costa Rica, and you can tell she does just by looking at her. Unfortunately we were full from a lackluster meal at the **Tamarindo Diriá,** where middle class Ticos go. It has lovely shady grounds and two pools, but can get crowded and hectic during tourist season (L, a/c, TV, hw, tennis, game room, 68-0652, 33-0530, fx: (506) 22-0568). **Cabinas Zully Mar** are in "downtown" Tamarindo, where the road ends in a clutch of bar-restaurants on the beach ($4 for a fresh fish dinner). The rooms are clean and the management friendly (E, pb, cf, 26-4732).

Getting there: SANSA flies to Tamarindo from San José Mon, Wed, and Fri at 1:10pm and continues to Playa Sámara at 2pm (check schedules at 33-0397, 33-3258, 21-9414). Hotels at all the beaches in the area arrange transport for guests from the Tamarindo airport. Empresa Alfaro buses to Tamarindo leave San José at 3:30pm from c 14, a 5, and return at 5:30 am (22-2750, tickets in advance). Tralapa buses leave at 4pm from a 3, c 20 and return at 7am (21-7202, tickets in advance). Buses leave Santa Cruz for Tamarindo daily at 3 pm, and at 10am also on weekends.

Tamarindo is about an hour from Liberia by car. There are gas stations in Filadelfia, between Liberia and Belén. If you have a flat tire, there's an outdoor tire repair shop on the left on the dirt road to Tamarindo, on a rise after a little bridge.

Playa Junquillal is a wide, almost deserted beach south of Tamarindo. It has two comfortably elegant and friendly hotels with nice pools, tennis courts and spacious two-unit bungalows. **Villa Serena,** (XL, 68-0737) is smaller, intimate, with three excellent meals included in its rates. Sauna and videocassettes are also available. **Hotel Antumalal,** farther down the beach, does not include meals in its rates (L, 68-0506). Hotel Junquillal, at the entrance to the beach, has a restaurant and three funky cabinas (D), and charges campers $3.75 per night for use of their facilities, such as they are.

Getting there: To reach Junquillal from Tamarindo, continue south 18 km to a crossing called "27 de Abril." Turn right onto an unpaved road and go another 12 km, through the town of Paraíso, where you turn left. The hotels are a short distance from there. If you are coming from Liberia, it is faster to take a turnoff to the right just before you reach Santa Cruz. From there it's 19 km to "27 de Abril." Turn left, and proceed as above.

A direct San José-Junquillal bus leaves from the Tralapa station at 2pm daily, arriving around 8pm and returning at 5am ($3, a 3, c 20, 21-7202). Daily Tralapa buses to Santa Cruz leave at 7:30am, 12, 4 and 6pm and return at 3am, 4:30, 6:30, 8:30 and 11:30am, and 1:30pm. Most San José-Nicoya buses also pass through Santa Cruz (c 14, a 5, 22-2750). If you need to spend a night in Santa Cruz, the **Diriá** (D, 68-0080) and the **Sharatoga** (D, 68-0011) both offer a/c and swimming pools, almost a necessity in the inland heat.

The old road to Nicoya goes to the left after you cross a bridge leaving Santa Cruz. It's a bumpy but interesting drive through the hills that are the heartland of the province. You'll pass through **Guaitil**, where local women have been reviving the art of pottery-making in the Chorotega style. Turn left on a street running into the central square. Pottery is displayed in front of peoples' houses. Stop for a chat with them and you'll feel the warmth and goodness of the Costa Rican *campesino*. Buses leave Santa Cruz for Guaitil every two hours between 7am and 5pm. The ride takes about 1/2 hour.

Beaches near Nicoya

While Liberia is the transportation and commercial capital of Guanacaste, **Nicoya** is the cultural capital. Its lovely colonial church, dedicated to San Blas, was built in 1644, and is presently undergoing restoration. It's open 8-12 and 2-6, closed Weds and Sun. Next to the church is a lovely, shady square abloom with flowers. **Hotel Jenny** (D, 68-5050, a/c, cw, TV) and **Las Tinajas** (F, 68-5081, cw, tf) are both pleasant places to stay in the center of town. The **Pensión Venecia** has no fans, but is clean and very cheap (F), across from the church. **Restaurante Jade,** 100m east and 75 north of the church, offers tasty Chinese food. **Hotel Curime,** south of town on the road to Playa Sámara has a pool, restaurant, and modern cabinas with fridges and the world's noisiest air conditioning (C, cw, 68-5238).

Nicoya is about 20 minutes from Santa Cruz on the paved road, an hour on the old road.

The **ferry** ride across the Tempisque is a pleasant 20 minutes. It crosses continuously, but if you get there when it is pulling away, you have to wait, which is why it sometimes takes as long to go by the ferry to or from Nicoya as it does through Liberia (5 hours). If you do not buy your ticket ($.20) quickly and jump on the ferry when it is there, your bus will leave without you. Buses that go to Nicoya by way of the ferry leave San José at 8am, returning at 4pm. Buses to Nicoya through Liberia leave San José at 6, 10, 1:30, 3 and 5pm (Empresa Alfaro, c 14, a 5, 22-2750, tickets in advance). The ferry also takes 12 cars at a time ($2.25).

Playas de Nosara is an international community with many North American and European residents. About half the land in this 12 square km development has been set aside as a wildlife reserve and park. The 200m maritime zone fronting 4km of beach is protected by the forest service. Because of these reserve areas, Nosara is generally much greener than the rest of Guanacaste. No hunting has been allowed there for 17 years, so birds and wildlife are plentiful. It is common to see coatimundis, armadillos, howler monkeys and even the jaguarundi, a cat with a grey diamond pattern on its fur which looks black from a distance. Parrots, toucans, cuckoos, trogons and pelicans are also easily observed. Humpback and grey whales can be seen offshore during the northern winter months. The beaches have community-maintained shelters for picnicking and camping. There are coral reefs and tidepools on Playa Guiones for snorkeling. Surfing is best there and at the Nosara River mouth. A small restaurant on **Playa Pelada** offers fresh fish and provides water for campers.

The views from the very pleasant **Hotel Playa Nosara** are magnificent (A, hw, cf, pool, rest., 68-0495). The hotel is high on a point, so you can see long Playa Guiones on one side and beautiful Playa Pelada on the other. The **Gilded Iguana** is famous for their Black Panther cocktail (named after the local jaguarundi), and serves soup and sandwiches Weds thru Sun, with a traditional bridge game on Sat. They rent furnished efficiency apartments (A, 68-0749). Some of the more than 80 homes of the Beaches of Nosara community are rentable by the week or month ($600-800/mo. incl. utils., maid service, 68-0747). The new **Condominio de las Flores** offers completely equipped apartments (A, 2 br, 2-bath, 68-0696). A few km to the north is the village of Nosara, where there is a gas station and a *pulpería*. **La Lechuza,** 2km N on the road to the village, is a favorite gathering place for residents, open for lunch Mon-Sat. **Cabinas Chorotega**, next to the gas station, are very clean, with fans and shared baths (F, 68-0836).

Getting there: SANSA flies Mon and Fri to Nosara at 6am (check schedules at 21-9414, 33-0397, 33-3258). Hotel Playa Nosara picks guests up at the plane. Regular buses leave Nicoya for Nosara at 12 noon and return at 6am. The trip takes about 2.5 hours by bus, and 1.5 by car on dusty, bumpy gravel roads.

Instead of going back to Nicoya, we explored the coastal road through Paraíso to Santa Cruz. The going was rough, with several river beds to cross, but it got a bit smoother after Marbella. The trip took 2 hours and wasn't that exciting.

Ostional Wildlife Refuge, just north of Nosara, is a good example of the new attitude in Costa Rican conservation. Ostional protects the breeding grounds of *lora* or olive ridley turtles, which arrive in great numbers between the third quarter and the new moon from April to December, with peak activity in August and September. The people of Ostional are allowed to harvest turtle eggs during the first 36 hours of the *arribada* since the eggs laid during that period are usually dug up and crushed by subsequent waves of mother turtles. The eggs are sold to bars across the country to be gulped raw as *bocas*. After the first 36 hours, community members guard the beach to make sure that the rest of the eggs are laid without disturbance. They will be glad to show you around and tell you about their cooperative. You can stay in new, simple cabinas there (F), and buy meals from local families. Call the village *pulperia* (68-0467) to reserve cabinas and find out if the turtles are active.

Getting there: During the dry season, you can ford the river between Nosara and Ostional, but the road is smoother going southwest from Santa Cruz via Marbella, at least through July. A bus leaves Santa Cruz at noon each day during the dry season and arrives at Ostional at 3:30.

Villaggio la Guaria Morada is a very elegant beachside hotel a few km south of Nosara, known for good food (LL, 68-0784, 33-2476, no fans, no screens on windows).

Playa Sámara, 1 hour S of Nosara, is the perfect long white sand beach with shallow, gentle waters. It's a favorite with swimmers and windsurfers. Many Ticos have summer homes there. **Hotel Las Brisas del Pacífico** is a lovely, quiet, well-designed hotel at the southern end of the beach (A, cf, hw, jacuzzi, pool, 68-0876, 55-2380, fx: (506) 33-5503). Its restaurant features the German gourmet cuisine of Wolf Antabi, which is worth a trip to the beach in itself. You'll have to do a lot of swimming and body surfing to work off Wolf's outrageous desserts, which he concocts each day according to his whim. When we were there, he served piping hot pineapple tempura in zabaglione sauce with a scoop of homemade chocolate ice cream. Not a place for the weak-willed.

A number of small cabinas and *hospedajes* are at the north end of the beach. **Hospedaje Yuri** (F, shared baths), seemed to be the nicest, with second-floor rooms to catch the breezes. Residents of the north end are good about letting visitors camp and use their facilities. **El Acuario,** 100m south of the soccer field, rents camping space and use of its toilets and shower for $.80. They have a good fish dinner for $3.

Getting there: A direct San José-Sámara bus leaves from Empresa Alfaro, a 5, c 14/16 at noon daily ($4, 6-hour trip, 22-2750, 23-8227, 23-8361, buy tickets several days in advance on 3-day weekends). Buses leave for Sámara from Nicoya at 3pm daily and also at 8am on weekends, returning from Sámara at 5:30am daily and again at 2pm weekends during the dry season. During the rainy season, there is one bus at noon only.

SANSA flies to Sámara as a continuation of its flights to Tamarindo on Mon, Weds and Fri for $18. Flights leave San José at 1:10pm, and take off from Tamarindo at 2:05pm. Check with SANSA about schedule changes and make reservations 2 weeks in advance during the dry season (21-9414, 33-0397, 33-3258). To drive to Sámara from Nosara, you have to ford an ankle-deep river about halfway there. The trip from Nicoya by car is about 1.5 hours.

About 5 minutes south of Sámara by car is **Playa Carrillo,** another beautiful white sand beach whose waters are kept calm by a reef at the entrance to the bay. There is not much shade for camping at Carrillo, nor are there facilities, but there is a large bar and restaurant with a great view at the entrance to the village, up on a cliff where it receives the sea breezes (good breakfasts for $1.50 and fish for $3). Next door are some rather unattractive cabinas (D, for up to 3 people). Carrillo also boasts an airstrip and an ice factory--the exclusive private fishing club Guanamar is located there.

If you travel south from Carrillo by car, you must ford the Río Ora at low tide. It's good to purchase a tide table if you plan to travel the unpaved coastal roads in Guanacaste (see p. 76).

About two hours south of Carrillo is **Playa Coyote.** It is long and deserted and was very windy when we were there. We were told that **Playa Caletas,** one beach to the south, has 15-foot waves. There are primitive showers and a bar at Coyote. It is most easily reached by gravel road from Jicaral, which is an hour northwest of Playa Naranjo, where the Puntarenas ferry lands. The trip takes 1.5 hours.

El Cerro **Barra Honda** is part of a flat-topped ridge that juts up out of the dry cattle-grazing land of the Nicoya Peninsula. People used to call the ridge a volcano because it's covered with large white limestone rocks piled around deep holes that look like craters. In the 1960's and 70's speleologists discovered that the holes were entrances to an intricate series of interconnected caves, some as deep as 200 meters, and the area was made into a National Park.

When the region was under the sea millions of years ago, marine animals deposited calcium carbonate that hardened and became limestone. Later, the land was pushed up out of the sea and rainfall started to corrode the limestone. Water combined with carbon dioxide and dissolved the limestone to hollow out the caves. In a process similar to how icicles grow, dripping water carrying calcium carbonate formed stalactites, stalagmites, curtains, organpipes, fried eggs, etc.

Within the caves a whole habitat flourishes--bats, insects, birds, blind salamanders and fish. In the *Nicoa* cave, speleologists discovered human skeletons. They had been there a long time; a stalagmite was growing on one skull. It is assumed that they were Indians from the region since some Indian artifacts were found near the skeletons.

Fortunately the caves have suffered almost no vandalism. The deep vertical drops at the entrances have discouraged all but the best-equipped from entering. The park rangers can take you down into *Terciopelo,* the cave with the most beautiful formations of all. A visit requires a week's notice to Parques Nacionales in San José; they won't take you down in the rainy season or during Holy Week.

Even if you can't get down into Terciopelo, a visit to Barra Honda is rewarding. You can explore the flat top of the ridge. The biggest trees are full of howler monkeys. Iguanas stand motionless. Lots of birds screech. The look-out point reached by following the *Sendero al Ojoche, la Trampa, la Terciopelo* affords wide views of the peninsula and the gulf of Nicoya. The *Sendero al Ceibo* leads to a waterfall decorated with lace-like calcium carbonate formations. It's about 6 km from the trailhead.

In the dry season it's very hot and dry, so bring water with you as you explore the ridge. The campsite is up the road to the right, on the left side of the trail. There are picnic tables and water.

Getting there: Barra Honda is a half hour from Nicoya by car. Take the main road east and make a left when you see signs for the village of Barra Honda. You can also come from the east via the Tempisque ferry and turn right at the Barra Honda turnoff. The road to the village is paved. Beyond that, the dirt road to the park gets narrower and bumpier, but National Park signs clearly mark the way. You can take a bus at noon from Nicoya to the village of San Ana (1.5-hour trip) and walk 2km to the park. Buses leave Nicoya for Barra Honda village at 10:30am and 3pm, leaving you 6km from the park.

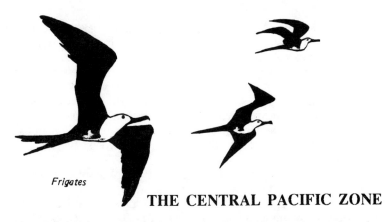

Frigates

THE CENTRAL PACIFIC ZONE

Puntarenas was Costa Rica's main port for most of the 1800's. The treacherous terrain between San José and the Atlantic Coast made an eastern port impossible, until the railway was completed in 1890. At first, oxcarts laden with coffee rumbled down to Puntarenas, where the precious beans were shipped to Chile, then re-exported to Europe. In 1843, English Captain William Le Lacheur landed in Puntarenas on the way back from a business failure in Seattle. Worried about the danger of sailing with an empty ship, the captain traveled five days by mule to San José, hoping to find some cargo for ballast. It turned out that coffee had been over-produced that year, and growers were desperate for new markets. Even though he was a stranger and had no money to give them, the growers entrusted him with a weighty shipment. He came back two years later with the payment, and a lively trade with England was established.

Puntarenas is no longer a commercial port, since the inauguration of Puerto Caldera a few years ago, but it is still the closest beach to San José. According to a recent study by the Ministry of Health, swimming is not recommended at the beaches in and near Puntarenas, but it is pleasant to stroll along the Paseo de Turistas, feel the sea breezes, and watch the sun set behind the mountains of the Nicoya Peninsula.

The town is only four blocks wide for most of its length, because it is built on a narrow spit. Fishing boats and ferries dock on the estuary side; a beach runs along the gulf side. The town is populated by people who always seem to be sitting on their front stoops placidly watching the traffic pass by. For visitors, Puntarenas has two distinct characters that the season determines: it is lively and full of people in the dry season, sleepy and tranquil in the rainy season.

In summer, people-watchers will enjoy the never-ending parade of tourists up and down the wide sidewalk next to the beach. Kiosks there serve snacks, *refrescos* and ice cream. There's a great, inexpensive series of concerts and plays at the Casa de la Cultura during the summer. We enjoy Puntarenas more in the rainy season when it is uncrowded, breezy and refreshed.

The loveliest hotel in Puntarenas is the **Portobello,** about three miles from downtown on the estuary. Its lush, colorful and beautifully-tended gardens create a sense of privacy and tranquility, and attract many birds (A, 61-1322, a/c, hw, pools, good restaurant). The Portobello and its nextdoor neighbor, Hotel Colonial, offer free mooring and use of facilities to sailboats passing through. **Hotel Colonial** (B, a/c, cf, cw. pools, swings, pingpong, etc.) appeals to a younger crowd. The **Yacht Club,** just before Portobello, also offers luxury accommodations (B, hw, a/c, pool, 23-4224, 61-0874). The green, residential San Isidro area, even farther out of town, near the hospital, has many cabinas with kitchens that can be rented by the day or week. **Cabinas Los Chalets** are the nicest (B, cw, pool, 63-0150). Frequent buses connect San Isidro with Puntarenas. See p. 109 for key to hotel codes.

Downtown, near the bus stop, are the **Cayuga** (D, hw, a/c, rest, 61-0344, c 4, a ctl) and **Las Hamacas** (D, cw, a/c, cf, pool, rest, 61-0398, a 4, c 5/7). The **Ayi Con** is probably the cleanest of the cheap hotels near the market (F, cb; E, pb, cw, a/c, 61-0164, c 2, a 1/3). The **Imperial** (E, tf, cw, 61-0579, fans) is a nice old building right across from the beach near c ctl. The upstairs rooms have more light. **Cabinas El Jorón** (C, hw, 61-0467, c 25, a 2) have fridges and a/c, but are dark and noisy. **Hotel Tioga** (B, 61-0271, a/c, indoor pool, cafeteria, breakfast included) is a favorite with visitors. A new hotel, **Las Brisas** (C, 61-2120, a/c, hw, small pool, 3 blocks west of ferry landing), is very clean, and offers unusually flavorful European cuisine. **Restaurante Miramare** on the ocean front specializes in Italian seafood.

Camping on the beach is safest near the public baths, to the right of the kiosks. The more deserted area to the left can be dangerous a night.

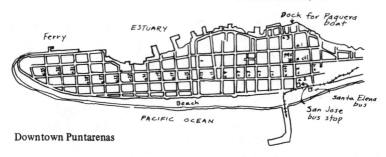

Downtown Puntarenas

A huge **ferryboat** leaves from the estuary at the far tip of town at 7am and 4pm every day with an 11am trip Thurs, Sat and Sun (61-1069, $.75/adult, $5/car). The hour-long trip takes you between verdant islands and makes you feel adventurous. If you have a car, you can continue south from Playa Naranjo, where the ferry lands, to Paquera, Tambor and Montezuma on the gulf side of the Nicoya Peninsula. There is no bus between Playa Naranjo and Paquera (see p.190). A Nicoya bus meets the ferry but it's a bumpy 3-hour trip. It's better to take the Tempisque Ferry to Nicoya (see p.179-80).

Hotel Oasis del Pacífico at Playa Naranjo (A, 61-1555, a/c, cf, pool, rest) offers sportfishing, horses, tennis. Playa Naranjo is not much for surf or swimming, but there are nice beaches within hiking, riding or sailing distance.

Calypso Tours takes you around the Gulf in their luxurious yacht, serves a gourmet seafood buffet on Tortuga Island where you can swim or snorkel, and provides fishing tackle for the trip back to Puntarenas. They pick you up at your hotel in San José ($65, discounts with OTEC card, 55-3022, 61-0585). Longer trips include visits to Carara Biological Reserve, Monteverde, or rafting down the Corobicí River.

Getting there: San José-Puntarenas buses leave from c 12, a 9 continuously from 6am to 7pm. Get there early on weekends and holidays. *Directo* buses take 2 hours ($1.50, 22-1867). The train ride takes a beautiful route through mountains, across gorges, over farmland ($1, 4 hrs, lots of stops). It leaves from the Pacific station on a 20, c 2 in San José at 7am and 3pm daily and returns from Puntarenas at 6am and 3pm, 26-0011).

San Lucas is Costa Rica's version of Alcatraz, much less formidable, on a large island in the Gulf of Nicoya. Prisoners run their own community; each works fishing, farming, cooking in the dining hall, etc. "Trustworthy" prisoners can construct and live relatively independently in their own houses. The island is an enlightening place to visit. The prisoners will tell you some extraordinary life stories and give some eye-opening philosophical reflections.

Sundays are visiting days--a boat leaves the dock behind the *mercado* in Puntarenas around 9am ($1.50 round trip). Get there around 7:30 since a lot of people try to crowd onto the small boat. Don't eat a lot of breakfast if you're susceptible to seasickness; the *lancha* gets batted around by the waves.

On their arrival visitors are flanked by prisoners trying to sell their handicrafts. The prisoners will shove things into your hands and ask for any money or gift you want to give. Besides the menial monthly salary they receive for their community work, this is the only money they can earn to pay for telephone calls, cigarettes, and purchases they need to make. So you might want to bring ¢10 or ¢20 coins. Cigarettes are also greatly appreciated. Don't bring radios, cameras, knives, or anything else that the guard could confiscate from you at the entrance.

Prisoners will give you a tour of the farm, or you can spend time at the Playa del Coco, a clean beach with polluted water across the island (from the dock it's up the hill and down to the left). You can buy food in the prisoner-run sodas. Chessplayers can ask around for Canfín, an interesting prisoner who claims to have beaten the University chess champion in a match.

Women should be aware that the prisoners are lonely and that unaccompanied women are likely targets for their affection. (Prisoners are allowed conjugal visits from wives or "official" girlfriends.)

Be back at the dock by 1:30 or 2. Better yet, before you get off the boat ask the captain what time the boat will leave.

A boat leaves the dock behind the market in Puntarenas at 6am and 3pm for **Paquera,** from which point you can continue by bus to Bahía Ballena and Montezuma.

Bahia Ballena is a deep, round bay on the southeast end of the Nicoya peninsula. Its waters are extremely gentle and warm, and true to its name, we sighted two whales the day we were there. **Hotel La Hacienda** (A, cw, cf, pool, rest, horses, 61-2980) is a beautiful, peaceful resort. Air transport can be arranged to their airstrip. In the village of Tambor on the southern rim of the bay is **Hotel Dos Lagartos** (E, pb, cheaper with cb, cw, nf, friendly, quiet, 61-1122, ext 236, 37-2470).

Bahía Ballena is about 2 hours south of Playa Naranjo by jeep and 1.5 hours from Paquera by bus. You can buy gas in Tambor.

Montezuma is a peaceful paradise. The beaches are full of beautiful shells of the most extraordinary colors and designs. The sun rises from behind the sea, which provides a challenging exercise in figuring out how the Pacific Ocean got to be east of you.

For a tour of the various beaches, walk north (left) along the coast. The first few rocky bays you pass have very strong currents, especially during high tide. Playa Grande, about 30 minutes away by foot, is calm and shallow, the best and safest place for bathing. There's fresh water in a shower in the park behind Chico's Bar, and a few fresh water streams near pleasant campsites that you'll see as you walk north along the beaches. Beware of hungry monkeys who will steal your food if you don't keep it in your tent. That ominous sound coming from under the dry leaves is probably just hermit crabs.

There's a gorgeous waterfall about 20 minutes away from town where you can swim, cliff-dive, and talk with local people. Walk along the road to Cabo Blanco for 300 meters. At the bridge, head upstream half a kilometer or so.

You can stay at the following hotels or camp (see p. 109 for key to hotel codes). If it's the dry season, call for reservations beforehand. As of this writing, the only phone in town is at **Chico's Bar** (61-2472). Their message service is not too reliable, so try to talk to people who run your preferred hotel. **Hotel Moctezuma** (E, pb; F, cb, fans) tends to be noisy because of Chico's bar next door, but has a good restaurant. In back of Chico's are **Cabinas Mar y Cielo** (E, pb, fans, right on the beach, quieter). **Cabinas Las Arenas** (F, cb, small rooms with natural breeze or fan, grill and firewood for guests) on the beach to the south are okay if you have quiet neighbors. **Cabinas Karen,** a white house near the entrance to town, offers simple rooms with cooking facilities, no fans (F). Next door to Karen's, Doña Marta Rodríguez also rents rooms in the **Casa Blanca** with kitchen and a balcony with hammocks. Doña Karen, who, with her late husband, was responsible for found-

189

ing the Cabo Blanco Reserve, also offers simple cabinas (F) with shared kitchens and baths set back in the forest on the fourth beach north of town.

There are peaceful cabins in the woods behind one of Montezuma's most beautiful beaches (B, kitchens, fans, write Iacono, Cóbano de Puntarenas, CR). It's the second beach to the left (north). They have a spigot of delicious spring water that campers can use. The owners make yummy fruit leather from apple-bananas and coconut, and run **El Sano Banano** in town which serves delicious vegetarian food and shows videos on a large screen 4 nights a week. They also prepare sack lunches and sell filtered water. **El Pargo Feliz**, 50m N of Chico's has good fish and lobster dinners ($4 and $10 respectively). You can camp on their front lawn with use of a shower and bathroom for $2.50/tent. **El Caracol**, along the Cabo Blanco road, serves seafood and *casados*.

South of town (250m along the road to Cabo Blanco) are **Hotel Lucy** (F) on a rocky beach with breezy rooms upstairs, fans downstairs, and access to a kitchen and clothes-washing area, and **Casa de Huéspedes Alfaro** (E), with large rooms for groups and families and a little soda.

Fresh fruits and vegetables are delivered to Montezuma on Wednesdays. If you come later in the week, it's best to bring your own. **Pulpería Manantial** will prepare fileted and seasoned fish for you to grill (be careful of gringo prices there).

Getting there: Take a bus to Puntarenas. From the dock behind the Mercado in Puntarenas take the *lancha* (boat) to Paquera--it leaves at 6am and 3pm ($1). The bus to Cóbano waits for the *lancha* at Paquera, and makes the trip down a bumpy road, through beautiful country, in about 3 hours ($1.50). From Cóbano take a taxi ($4) the 7 or 8km down to Montezuma. If you want to take the 6am boat you'll have to spend the night in Puntarenas. The boat returns to Puntarenas from Paquera at 8am and 5pm. If you ask around in Montezuma, you might find a local fisherman who will take you all the way to Puntarenas in his boat for $8-10.

If you have a car, take it on the big ferry from Puntarenas to Playa Naranjo (see p. 187) and follow the road south to Cóbano. The trip takes about 3 hours on gravel roads (dry season only, unless you have 4-wheel drive).

We explored the road going west to Río Negro and Manzanillo from Cóbano on our way to Playa Sámara in Guanacaste. You have to ford several rivers, and sometimes the road fades into little more than a trail, but we made it through. Just keep asking people if you're going the right way--there are no signs. We would have made it to Sámara in about 4 hours by jeep if we hadn't hit the Río Ora at high tide (see p. 183).

Howler monkey (mono congo)

A road continues south from Montezuma through Cabuya and on to **Cabo Blanco Wildlife Reserve.** You have to ford two streams; the 12km trip takes over an hour by jeep. Since it is an absolute reserve, visitors are not admitted without a permit from the Park Service in San José. You can take a fairly strenuous 2-hour hike up the *Sendero Sueco* and down to Playa Balsitas. Bring food and plenty of water. Hike left around the point to Playa Cabo Blanco for another 2-hour hike back. At high tide you won't be able to make it around the point, so ask the guards about tides before you leave. You'll see lots of howler monkeys. Don't stand directly underneath them--they like to pee on sightseers. There are pelican colonies on either side of the point, and beautiful pinkish coral sand in some places.

The road to **Monterverde** from the turnoff on the Interamerican highway is rough, steep and dusty. It's a two-hour climb through sadly deforested country until you reach the green pastures that lead to the famous cloud forest. Many Monteverdeans would like to keep the road that way: they not only want to preserve the cloud forest in its natural state, they also want to protect the simple, friendly lifestyle that has made their community such a special place. Many communities in Costa Rica have opened to tourism incredibly quickly over the last few years. The economy desperately needs the business that tourism brings, but things can be lost in the process. Monteverde, because it has always concerned itself with social issues, is perhaps more articulate about these problems than most rural villages that are being "invaded" by tourism.

A group of Alabama Quakers who felt that Costa Rica's disarmament policy was more in line with their pacifist tradition started dairy farming in Monteverde in the early 1950's. Visiting biologists found the cloud forest above their community rich in flora and fauna, and the Quakers, along with the Tropical Science Center, had the foresight to make it a biological reserve.

Monteverde is not a place you can visit in one day. You should make reservations at least two weeks in advance, especially during the dry season. You can spend whole days wandering along the trails in the reserve ($5 entrance fee, $10 after June 1990, closed Oct 6 and 7 each year). The forest stretches from the lush ferns and mosses that cover the ground to the dark canopy formed by the tallest trees. Vines and web-like moss hang down and swing slowly in the breeze. Some of the trees look top-heavy because their branches are so densely enveloped with epiphytes and moss.

The cloud forest is a bird and beast paradise. Bring binoculars to look for *quetzales*. Early morning is the best time to see them; they cluster where their favorite fruit grows on the trees near signposts 2 and 7 on the *Bosque Nuboso* trail. For the up-to-the-minute quetzal report ask at the field station. Beautiful and strange frogs also live in the cloud forest, but they're very difficult for the average inexperienced forest-wanderer to spot. The Golden Toad is remarkable for its color and the poison glands behind its ears. It has not been found anywhere else in the world outside the Monteverde area. They are easiest to see when they mate in the puddles left over from the first rains in April or May. You should look at the Golden Toad in the aquarium in the administration center: it's the bright orange one. There's also a transparent frog, and an army-camouflaged one, among others.

Guided tours: If you'd like to walk around with someone who knows what to look for, where to find it, and how to explain it all to you, several naturalists serve as guides: Gary Diller (61-0903), and Richard and Meg Laval (61-0952). Richard has put together a fascinating slide show about Monteverde's flora and fauna; Meg will take you touring on horseback. Reserve ecologists also take visitors on 4-hour natural history tours (61-2655). Ask at your hotel for other local guides.

The cheese factory offers tours 9-11am Mon-Sun and 1:30-3pm Mon-Sat. They sell delicious cheddar, jack, gouda and other cheeses there for less than San José prices. You can also buy great homemade wholewheat bread and rolls, fresh milk, and *cajeta* (scrumptious milk fudge) at the cheese factory. (Open 7:30am-12, 1-3:30pm Mon-Sat, 7:30am-12:30pm Sun.)

Watercolor paintings of Monterverde flora by resident artist Sarah Dowell are exhibited in local hotels. Visitors are welcome to tour her studio. Maps in the hotels give directions to her house.

Conservation: The **Monteverde Conservation League**, which for the last few years has been running a successful campaign to protect the rainforest on the Atlantic slope behind the reserve, is now devoting its efforts to reforestation. They also have an ambitious plan to link up remnant patches of forest (especially riverine strips) to make "green corridors" from coast to coast to ensure habitat for migratory birds and butterflies and to connect patches of cloud forest along the mountaintops. Call 61-2953 for more information.

Reserve ecologists present a spellbinding slideshow by world-famous photographers Michael and Patricia Fogden about rainforest wildlife from all over Costa Rica and Panamá. It is presented at local hotels for $50 plus donations. The Fogdens spend months at a time with sloths, frogs, snakes, insects and birds, trying to get just the right shot. You'll never see better wildlife photographs. Donations from

Rana vivicaria

the slideshow go to the Conservation League, or to the Reserve, which is presently trying to preserve and enlarge *quetzal* habitat on the Pacific slope. Future plans include 1- and 2-day workshops in which tourists can learn about rainforest ecology and even participate in research projects (61-2655).

Getting there: By bus there are three options:

1. There is a daily bus from Puntarenas to Santa Elena, a town 3 km from Monteverde. It leaves Puntarenas at 2:15pm, turns off the Interamerican highway at the Río Lagarto around 3:30, and arrives in Santa Elena around 5:30. You can leave San José on the 10am Puntarenas bus (c 12, a 9), arrive in Puntarenas around 12:30, have a leisurely lunch and catch the Santa Elena bus on the oceanfront, one block from the San José-Puntarenas bus station. The same bus returns from Santa Elena to Puntarenas each day at 6am.

2. A bus leaves San José (c 12, a 5/7, across from Maderas Los Rodriguez, $3.25) for Monteverde at 2:30pm Mon thru Thurs, and Sat at 6:30am. It returns to San José Tues thru Thurs at 6:30am and at 3pm Fri and Sun. It is a small bus, so get there early. There are bound to be more frequent buses during the dry season. For current schedules, call 61-2659 or 61-1152 (Spanish only) or check with your hotel when making reservations (all Monteverde hotels have English-speaking staff).

3. The 12:45 San José-Tilarán bus (c 12, a 9/11, 21-7865) connects with the Puntarenas-Santa Elena bus at the Lagarto turnoff around 3:15pm. Buy tickets 1/2 hour in advance.

If you don't mind gravel roads, you can also travel by car from Tilarán to Monteverde by way of Quebrada Grande, Cabeceras and Santa Elena. In Cabeceras you can choose to go straight, through Turín, or uphill to the left through Las Nubes. Both pass through beautiful scenery--the Las Nubes route is 2 km longer and gorgeous--both are equally bumpy. The trip takes 2.5 hours.

During the school year (March-November) a bus connects Santa Elena and Cabeceras. From there you can catch a bus to Tilarán. The bus trip takes 3 hours. Check at the Restaurant Imán in Santa Elena for current schedules (61-1255). If you stay overnight in Tilarán you can catch a bus to San Carlos which passes Volcán Arenal. (See Northern Zone section.) **Cabinas El Sueño** (E, hw, pb, 69-5347) are recommended in Tilarán, a clean, pleasant town a half hour uphill from Cañas and much cooler.

Hotels and restaurants: (See p. 109 for key to hotel codes.) After you've been chugging up the road for about 2 hours, you come to Santa Elena, a town about 3km from Monteverde. The bus from Puntarenas leaves you off there. Your hotel will send a taxi to meet you if you have made reservations. The bus from San José continues on to the cheese plant in Monteverde, stopping at various hotels along the way. In Santa Elena are 3 cheap Tico-style *pensiones,* the **Imán** (F, 61-1255), **Pensión Santa Elena** (F, 61-1151) and **Pensión González** (haven't checked this one out yet). All have restaurants, shared baths and cold water.

The **Sapo Dorado** (Golden Toad) is a nicely designed bar and restaurant in Cerro Plano, between Santa Elena and Monteverde. They serve elegant sunset suppers accompanied by classical music on their terrace overlooking the Gulf from 5pm to 7pm Weds-Fri. From 7pm on, Weds-Sun, the mood changes, light meals are served, and they play a variety of good taped music for dancing. You'll see their sign on the left heading towards Monteverde. It's about 300m up the hill.

In a few hundred meters you come to the new **Pensión Heliconia**, a Spanish-style building on the left with a comfortable, homey atmosphere (C, 61-1009, pb, hw, rest). A road to the right leads in about lkm to **Pensión Monteverde Inn** ($17 /pers. incl. 3 meals, pb and cb, hw, nice views, 61-2756, also have shared bunkbed rooms for about $10/pers. incl meals.; camping facilities also offered). About 100m farther along the main road is **Hotel de Montaña Monteverde** (A, 61-1846, pb, hw, rest) with views of the Gulf of Nicoya from its well-appointed rooms. The chalet-style **Belmar** (B, 61-1001, pb, hw) also has beautiful views, comfortable rooms, and a restaurant/bar. Its entrance is uphill from the gas station on the left, across from the office of the Conservation League.

You still have not arrived in Monteverde proper, and when you do you might not realize it, because Monteverde is not really a town. Most houses of community members are back in the woods where you don't see them, and are connected by footpaths. **Restaurant El Bosque**, on the right as you enter Monteverde, is a great place to go for lunch or dinner. A few meters down the road is a well-stocked food store and then **CASEM**, a crafts cooperative featuring beautiful embroidered and hand-painted clothing and souvenirs portraying quetzals, golden toads and other cloud forest flora and fauna.

The next entrance on the right is to **Pensión Quetzal**, the oldest lodge in Monteverde, with cozy, wood-panelled rooms ($22/person, cb, hw; $25 pb, hw; $30 at new cabins, all rates incl. 3 meals, 61-0955). The Conservation League's nature trail is about 100m from the Quetzal. Out on the road again, you'll see the cheese plant up ahead. There the road turns right and goes over a bridge. The **Pensión Flor-Mar** is about 200m beyond the bridge, where the road turns left to go to the Reserve ($20, cb, hw; $22, pb, hw, incl. 3 meals, friendly atmosphere, 61-0909). All above hotels will gladly make a bag breakfast or lunch for early birders; laundry services, horse and boot rental, and transportation to the Reserve are also available. The Reserve is a 45-minute uphill walk from the Flor-Mar.

Many Monteverde hotels are completely booked by tour companies from December through May, which is really the best time to go there. Most hotels require a deposit in order to secure a room, usually the cost of one night's stay. The Pensión Quetzal requires a deposit of $12/person for each night you want to be there. Your best bet would be to call the hotels directly before you leave home, confirm the availability of space, and send your deposit at least 6 weeks before you plan to arrive. Forget Christmas and Easter, which are booked months in advance. Write all hotels at Apdo. 10165, 1000 San José, CR.

Playa Doña Ana is a small beach which has been developed by the Tourism Institute, 2km south of Puntarenas. It has covered picnic tables, dressing rooms and showers, and a restaurant with blasting music which competes with the sound of the waves. Surfers say the waves at Doña Ana and Boca Barranca are great. Buses from Puntarenas to Mata Limón, Jacó, Orotina and Quepos pass by the entrance. The turnoff for Playa Doña Ana is right before the overpass on your way out of Puntarenas. The signs are not well placed. **Hotel Río Mar** (D, 63-0158, pb, rest) is to the left just before you get to Doña Ana.

Carara Biological Reserve is located near Orotina, southeast of Puntarenas, in a transition area between the dry climate of Guanacaste and the humid climate of the southern coast. It has wildlife common to both regions, like macaws, toucans, trogons, waterfowl, 3 kinds of monkeys, alligators and crocodiles, armadillos, sloths and peccaries. Jaguars, pumas, ocelots, jaguaroundis and margays are present, but hard to see. You can get there on any Jacó or Quepos bus. No camping is allowed in the reserve.

If you call in advance, reserve guards might be able to find time to guide you. Parques Nacionales can make radio contact with the reserve for you (33-5473). Unaccompanied tourists are only allowed on certain trails, but reserve personnel or professional guides can go with you into restricted areas. **Geotur**, in San José, specializes in guided nature tours to Carara (34-1867).

Playas Jacó and Herradura are the closest swimmable beaches to San José. **Playa Herradura** is right after the Río Caña Blanca, about 5 minutes north of Jacó, and 3km down a gravel road from the main highway. It is smaller than Jacó, the waves are gentler and there is more shade. Good trees for hammocks. Camping is allowed. There are sodas and a few cabinas on the beach.

Playa Jacó is long and wide, and much more developed than Herradura. The rip currents there can be dangerous, so don't swim alone (see p. 69-72). In a country full of tropical paradises, Jacó certainly does not stand out, but if you like sun and fun, surfing and beer-drinking contests, and you want to get to the beach and back as fast as possible, Jacó is for you. In fact, the ICT has created a "núcleo turístico" offering parking, locked closets, bathrooms and showers for $.60/person for those who want to visit for just the day. It's next to the **Pizzería Bribri,** to the right at the second entrance after Hotel Jacó Beach.

Surfers use Jacó as a base for trips to nearby beaches like Boca Barranca (very long left wave), Playas Tivives and Valor (rights and lefts), Escondida (accessible by boat from Jacó), Playa Hermosa (very strong beach break 3km south of Jacó, site of annual surfing contest) and Esterillos Este and Oeste, Bejuco and Boca Damas, all on the way to Quepos. Many hotels give surfers discounts from May to December.

There are plenty of hotels, cabinas and campsites (see p. 109 for key to hotel codes). Many have kitchenettes complete with utensils. They give substantial discounts during the off-season, and Jacó is often sunny when it's raining in San José. All the following establishments are off Jacó's main street, which runs parallel to the beach. We'll mention them in order of their appearance, north to south. **Cabinas Antonio** (D, 64-3043, pb, cw, fans), next to the main bus stop at the entrance to Jacó) are clean and relatively quiet. The Belgian-owned **Hotel El Jardín**, on the beach 100m from the bus stop, is clean, comfortable, quiet and includes breakfast in its reasonable rates. It's restaurant has the reputation of being the best in Jacó (C, pb, hw, cf, pool, 64-3050). Next is **Hotel Jacó Beach** (A, incl. breakfast, a/c, hw, large, circular pool, discotheque; cars, bikes, mopeds, surfboards, sailboats, kayaks, tennis equipment, etc. for rent, 64-3032, 64-3034). They are the center for most of the charter flights from Canada, so are very busy. **Tangerí Chalets** (L, 42-0977) have 3 bedrooms, kitchens, and pools for adults and kids. They prefer to rent by the week. The Dutch-owned **Villas Miramar** is one of the loveliest and most tranquil places in Jacó (B, 64-3003, kitchens, hw, cf, pools, gardens, down the fifth road to your right). **Cabinas Zabamar** have fridges (C, pb, cw, pool, 64-3174). **Hotel Cocal** is on the beach (B, clean, pb, hw, cf, pools, rest, 64-3067). **Las Gaviotas**, 250m from the beach, is new, clean and pretty. Rooms have patios and kitchenettes (B, hw, pool, 64-3092). **Cabinas Alice** (D, pb, cw, cf, 64-3061, 37-1412, toward the beach from the Red Cross) are dark and poorly ventilated. Doña Alice serves good food at shady outdoor tables. **Apartamentos El Mar** are secure, clean and spacious with kitchens and pool (B, cf, pb, hw, 25-7132, 64-3165). **Casas de Playa Mar Sol** are nice for families because each has a small wading pool in front of the house (A, 64-3008, cw, tf, kitchens).

Hotel Jacofiesta is new and probably the best in Jacó. Cheerfully painted on the outside with a broad blue strip at the base of white walls in the style of a *casa típica*, the rooms are light and airy, with efficiently-designed kitchenettes (L, a/c, hw, pool, rest, cable TV, 64-3147, fx: 64-3148). The **Marparaíso** (A, fans, cw, pb, rest, pools, jacuzzi, L with kitchens, 64-3025) is on the far end of the beach. It's very popular, but its design gives a crowded, closed-in feeling. Beyond it are **Cabinas Madrigal**, funky rooms (E, pb, cw, 64-3230), greasy restaurant, shady campsites with toilets, showers, makeshift tables and barbecue pits ($1/night). About 2 blocks inland from Madrigal's, where the street connects with the main highway from Quepos, is **El Bosque**, a nice place for breakfast.

Getting there: San José-Jacó buses leave the Coca Cola at 7:30am and 3:30pm, returning at 5am and 3pm (64-3074, 41-5890, 3.5 hrs). Get to the bus stop early on weekends because you'll be waiting with a big crowd of *josefinos*. A bus from Quepos to Puntarenas passes Jacó on the main road around 6am and 3pm. All Quepos and Manuel Antonio buses pass Jacó on their way to and from San José ($3.50-4). Look at schedule on p. 204 and add or subtract 1.5 hrs. for arrival times. Get off at Restaurant El Bosque, 2 blocks from the beach at the southern end. Get Puntarenas-Quepos buses to Jacó at 1:30 near the Puntarenas train station. Hotel Irazú has a comfortable mini-bus to and from Jacó every day (2.5 hrs, $11, 32-4811). Leaves Irazú 9:30am, returns 2pm.

By car, Herradura and Jacó are a 2-hour drive from San José on a winding road through beautiful countryside. Take the Atenas turnoff on the highway to Puntarenas. The road is in fairly good repair most of the way through the mountains, and offers some magnificent views. Near Orotina you can buy watermelon, mangos and sugar cane juice. After Orotina the road is excellent, with sea views on one side and green rice fields on the other. You also pass the entrance to Carara Biological Reserve (see above) about 20 minutes before Jacó. A new section of highway now connects Puntarenas and Jacó in an hour. You can continue on to Quepos (70km), Dominical and San Isidro de El General on the same road.

When you first glimpse the sea from the hills above **Manuel Antonio,** the word *paradise* might cross your mind. The lovely beaches were made into a national park before they could be turned into another Acapulco. So far, the hotels that have sprung up in the last few years have taken advantage of the beautiful views without calling too much attention to themselves. But as Manuel Antonio becomes more well known, the influx of tourism is taking its toll on the delicate environment.

Manuel Antonio is one of the few remaining habitats of the squirrel monkey, *mono tití.* Howler and white-faced monkeys, two-toed sloths, coatimundis and raccoons frequent the beaches, which are shaded by leafy trees. Iguanas pose like statues unless they are moving their heads up and down like pumps (a territorial sign made only by males).

There is a trail that takes you through the jungle to the top of Cathedral Point, where you can look down the vertical cliffs to the blue ocean 300 feet below. You start from Playa Espadilla Sur (the second beach) and take a circular route, about an hour from start to finish. At low tide you can also begin or end on Playa Manuel Antonio, the third beach. The trail is very steep in some parts and muddy and slippery in the rainy season, so don't go alone, and wear hiking boots if possible.

Manuel Antonio

The wedge-shaped piece of land that is now Cathedral Point used to be an island. As you can see from the illustration, a neck of land connects it to the beach. This rare phenomenon is known as a *tambalo*: a deposit of sand which builds up over thousands of years and finally connects an island to the mainland. Northern-flowing currents pushed water and sand through the opening between the island and the beach, and then flowed on to Punta Quepos, farther north, which forced the water back. The sand-bridge was formed after about 100,000 years of this action. Grass and shrubs gained a foothold on it, followed by the present-day trees that keep the formation from returning to the sea. The Manuel Antonio tambalo is one of the most perfect in the world.

The Indians who lived in Manuel Antonio 1000 years ago observed that while female green turtles were laying their eggs in the sand at high tide, the male turtles were waiting for them in the water. The Indians fashioned balsawood models of female turtles to attract the males into an area surrounded by rocks. The males would stay with the decoy females and be trapped by the rocks when the tide went out. You can see these precolumbian turtle traps on either end of Manuel Antonio Beach at low tide.

Snorkeling is rewarding at Manuel Antonio. In the dry season, when the water is clear, you'll see iridescent peacock-colored fish, conservative pin-striped fish, outrageous yellow fish with diaphanous capes, all going in and out of the coral rocks. Fins and a mask are all you need, and no snorkeling techniques are necessary. If you burn easily, watch out--you'll lose track of time staring at the fish while the sun is staring at your back. It's best to wear a T-shirt.

At the third beach, visit the screen-walled museum next to the guard's house. It contains informative diagrams explaining the geology, history, and biology of the park, and jars full of specimens that attest to the biological wealth of the park's land and water.

The entrance to the park is on the other side of a stream that changes width and depth with the tides. Try to go at low tide, because you have to wade across. Around high tide the water is waist-high.

Camping is no longer allowed within the park. Overcrowding was leading to pollution and destruction of the vegetation, threatening the wildlife. You can spend the day there, however.

Do not leave your belongings unattended on the beach. If anyone offers to guide you through remote areas of the park, they should have an official ID card, or be in park service uniform.

Manuel Antonio has many lovely places to stay, most of which are on the hill between Quepos and the park (see p. 109 for keys to hotel codes). The older, funkier cabinas are on the beach. If you're on a budget, low-cost lodging in Quepos is cleaner and more comfortable than the cheapest rooms near the beach. We cannot be lavish enough in our praise of the **Hotel Ceciliano**, about 50m west of the SANSA office in Quepos, for running an excellent low-cost hotel with light, airy rooms, immaculate tiled bathrooms, closets, and a tranquil, plant-filled atmosphere. After trudging in and out of so many makeshift cheapo hotels while researching this book, the Ceciliano is a real find (E, pb; less with cb, cf, cw, 77-0192). The **Hotel Quepos** (E, pb or cb, cf, cw, 77-0274) is also a good, clean place to stay. It's above the SANSA airline office, about 300m from the oceanfront. **Hotel Mar y Luna** (F, pb, less with cb, cw, tf, 77-0394) is cheap and fairly clean. Upper rooms have shared baths and windows. Lower rooms have private baths and no windows. **Hotel Malinche** (E, pb, tf, cw, 77-0093) has some nice touches in its decor and **Hotel Ramus** (E, pb, cw, tf, 77-0245) is okay too. The above three are located in the block west of the bus terminal. The market at the terminal is a good place to grab a quick bite to eat and to stock up on fruits and veggies.

La Buena Nota, a beachwear and gift shop, is the official information center for Manuel Antonio. It's on the oceanfront after the bridge at the entrance to Quepos. The **Soda Ana** and **Soda Isabel** in the next block on the waterfront have good, cheap *casados*, and the **Quepoa** on the south side of the market has tasty seafood. Our favorite place to stop for a *refresco* in Quepos is **El Kiosko,** on the oceanfront three blocks from La Buena Nota. If you like wild all-night fiestas with dancing in the streets, Quepos has its annual **Festival del Mar** around the end of January at the full moon.

We will mention hotels in order of their appearance on the road between Quepos and Manuel Antonio. **Cabinas Pedro Miguel** are funky rooms in a tranquil setting 6km from Quepos and 100m from the main road (E, small pool, pb, cw, cf, very hospitable, family-run operation, typical restaurant in high season, 77-0035). The European-owned **Hotel Plinio,** across the road, has comfortable, wood-panelled rooms off a wide veranda with hammocks, surrounded by lush foliage. It has one of the most popular dinner restaurants in Manuel Antonio, featuring delicious pasta, lasagne, eggplant parmigiana and pizza. Their homemade bread is worth a trip in itself. Open for breakfast and dinner only, closed Weds. Call for reservations. (C, including breakfast, pb, tf, cw, 77-0055). Farther down the road on your right is **Bahías,** a bar/restaurant featuring seafood, 46 varieties of tropical cocktails and wonderful music: tangos, vintage jazz, good stuff. Open evenings year round, all day during the high season. Next on the left is the entrance to **El Salto,** cabinas in a private biological reserve with a great view up and down the coast (LL, pb, tf, cw, pool, horses, bar/rest, 77-0130, Apdo. 119, Quepos, CR).

At the crest of the hill on the left is the brand new Canadian-owned **Hotel El Lirio,** spacious, well-designed rooms with a sea view (L, pb, hw, cf, breakfast incl, 77-0403, Apdo. 123 Quepos, CR). The **Divisamar** (L, pool, rest, hw, cf, a/c, friendly, helpful staff, 77-0371, fx: 77-0525) is across from the **Barba Roja,** a favorite with visitors because of its quality gringo-style lunches and dinners: burgers, nachos, BLT's, surf and turf, etc., and its varied and inexpensive breakfast menu. Open 7am-midnight, closed Mon. Above the Barba Roja is the **Mamaya Gallery,** with tasteful exhibits of local artisanry. Just before the road heads down toward Manuel Antonio are the elegant villas of the **Hotel Mariposa,** with pool, beautiful views from private balconies, and excellent service (XL, hw, cf, gourmet breakfast and dinner incl, no children under 15, 77-0355, 77-

0456, Apdo. 4, Quepos, CR). Next on the left is the French-owned **Hotel Byblos**, which rivals the Mariposa for excellent cuisine. Their spacious cabinas are set in a forest below the restaurant (LL, cf, a/c, hw, pool with jacuzzi, gym, 77-0411, Apdo. 15, Quepos, CR). The **Colibrí** (A, cf, hw, no children under 10, 77-0432, Apdo. 94, Quepos, CR) has charming cabinas with fully-equipped kitchenettes set back from the road in a lovely garden. **La Quinta** (B, pool, cf, hw, A with kitchens, 77-0434, Apdo. 76, Quepos, CR) is new and quiet, with spacious rooms and an ocean view. **Hotel Arboleda** (A, cf, rest, L, a/c, hw, 77-0414, telex: 2292 CONE CR) has rows of cabinas on a hill with ocean views, and others nearer the beach. They rent surfboards and catamarans. **Apartamentos Costa Verde** and **Condominios Costa Verde** have kitchens and views (B to LL, 23,7946, 77-0584, fx: 23-9446). The **Karahé** has lovely cabinas with beautiful views, but you have to walk up a lot of steps to get to them (A, pool, cf, hw, fridge, 77-0170, fx: 77-0152). Their restaurant specializes in Uruguayan-style beef and seafood.

Now we're down at the beach, where the less expensive cabinas are. The **Restaurant Mar y Sombra** is the traditional place to eat on Playa Espadilla, still about 1km from the park entrance. Espadilla is known for its dangerous rip currents (see p. 69-72). **Cabinas Ramirez** is nextdoor (D, pb, cw, tf, the more secure ones have metal bars and padlocks but are stuffy and dark, others have better ventilation, tend to be noisy, 77-0510). On the way to the park you'll see the **Del Mar Bar** on the beach. They rent surfing and snorkeling equipment. A road to the left goes to the following five places: **Cabinas Espadilla** (C, clean and light, tf, pb, cw, some with hotplates, 77-0416). Across the road is the **Costa Linda** "youth hostel" with small stuffy rooms. The ones in the back have more ventilation (E, cb, nf, shared cooking facilities; D with kitchens, pb, tf, 77-0304). The **Vela Bar** offers vegetarian specialties with a Spanish touch, as well as seafood and chicken. Cabinas in the back have locked wooden security boxes (C and B, tf, cw, some a/c, some balconies, L with kitchen, hw, 77-0413). The **Grano de Oro** has small, stuffy rooms adjacent to its restaurant (F, nf, cb, noisy, 77-0578). **Cabinas Los Almendros,** on the left at the end of the road, are clean and quiet (C, cf, cw, rest, 77-0225). Coming out again onto the road to the park are two more places: **Hotel Manuel Antonio** on the left (D, very clean, crowded rooms, cf, cw, rest, 77-0290) and **Cabinas Manuel Antonio,** right on Playa Espadilla (E, a bit run down, tf, cw, pb, 77-0212, 77-0255).

Almost all hotels offer a substantial discount from May through November. Make reservations 3 months in advance during Christmas or Easter, and at least 2 weeks in advance during the tourist season (December thru May).

If you have more time to spend, you might want to rent a house by the week or month. Accommodations range from a rustic cabina on a lovely private beach accessible only by foot or 4-wheel drive ($150/wk, no electricity, 28-1811) to a fully equipped, 2-bedroom house near a creek with a breathtaking view of Manuel Antonio ($350/wk during high season, 77-0292, 77-0345).

Getting there: Quepos buses leave from the western end of the Coca Cola at 7 and 10am, 2 and 4pm, returning at 5 and 8am, 2 and 4pm (4 hrs, $3.50, 23-5567, 77-0263). From Quepos, take a 20-minute bus ride 7 scenic kilometers to the entrance of the park ($.20, 5:45, 8 and 10:30am, 12:30, 3 and 5pm, returning 20-30 min later. Service is continuous on weekends during the dry season).

A **direct** San José-Manuel Antonio bus leaves the Coca Cola at 6am, 12 and 6pm, returning at 6am, 12 and 5pm ($4, tickets in advance on weekends and holidays, make return reservations and purchase tickets as soon as you arrive. Quepos ticket office is open 7-11 and 1-5; 7-11, 1-4 Sun). This bus will pick you up at your hotel on its way from Manuel Antonio to Quepos, but you must be out on the road to flag it down. Do not let anyone but the bus driver load or unload your baggage. Try to keep it with you if possible. Things have been stolen from the luggage compartment.

Quepos-Puntarenas buses leave at 4:30am and 1:30pm, returning at the same hours. All the above buses pass by Playa Jacó, 1.5 hrs from Quepos.

SANSA flies to Quepos Mon thru Sat at 9:30am returning at 10am ($8.50 one way, 20-min flight, buy tickets at least 2 weeks in advance during dry season, 33-0397, 33-3258, schedules change frequently). There are also 3:30pm flights, depending on the season. SANSA will transport you from their San José office (c 24, Paseo Colón) to the airport, deliver you to your hotel in Quepos or Manuel Antonio, and pick you up to get you to your return flight.

Sportfishing Costa Rica (see p. 75) has **charter flights** every day to Quepos during the tourist season for about $40 per person (38-2729, 38-2726, 37-5400, fax: (506) 38-4434).

By car, the trip takes about 3.5 hours if you take the Atenas turnoff and drive the narrow, winding road through the Aguacate mountains. This route gives you a glimpse of rural life and has some beautiful scenery. You can buy sugar cane juice and fruit along the way. If you feel more comfortable with better highways, go all the way to Puntarenas, follow signs to Jacó, and continue on to Quepos. It only takes a half hour longer even though it looks much farther on the map. The last 24 km before Quepos are in the process of being paved. Call La Buena Nota for the latest information (77-0345).

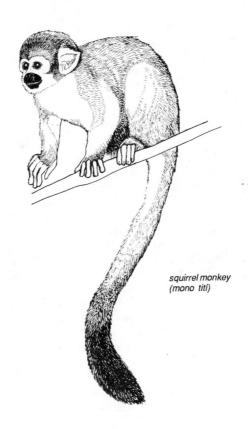

squirrel monkey
(mono tití)

king fisher

THE SOUTHERN ZONE

The Interamerican Highway becomes San José's Central Avenue, crossing the city from west to east, then turning right at Cartago to connect the Central Valley with the southern part of Costa Rica. The road winds into the mountains that surround fog-shrouded Cerro de la Muerte, the highest pass on the Interamerican. Since Don Pepe Figueres's farm, *La Lucha Sin Fin* (The Endless Struggle) is off this road, these mountains were the scene of the beginnings of the 1948 Civil War. There is a small monument to those who lost their lives in that conflict in Santa María de Dota, down a road to the right at Empalme.

Day hikers will enjoy a trip to **Copey**, a small town in the mountains above Santa María, about an hour south of Cartago. Its fresh, brisk climate at 7000 ft. makes for an exhilarating walk through hills of native oak. Treat yourself to a trout lunch at William Rodríguez' *soda* and buy tart, crispy local apples for dessert. You can visit Don Fernando Elizondo's well-developed trout farm and rent horses from Chema, his nextdoor neighbor. Take a San Isidro bus (c 16, a 1/3) to Cañón del Guarco, Km 58 on the Interamerican highway. You'll see the little yellow markers on the side of the road that tell you how many km you are from San José. From Cañón it's a 7km walk downhill on a dirt road to Copey. Santa María is another 7km downhill. It's customary in that region for drivers to offer rides to people on the road. Buses return to San José from the main square in Santa María at 6am, 9am, 2pm and 4pm. There are a couple of cheap hotels in Santa María, none so far in Copey. You can catch the bus to Santa María from San José at 6am, 9am and 12:30pm (c 21, a 16B, 27-3597).

In **San Gerardo de Dota,** Don Efraín Chacón and his family rent simple *cabinas* and provide delicious homemade meals for fishermen and nature lovers (C per person, including 3 meals, pb, hw, 71-1732). Trout abound in the chilly waters of the Río Savegre which passes the finca. At 1900 m (6300 feet), temperature averages 10°C (50-55°F) in this narrow mountain valley. Don Efraín takes advantage of the crisp weather to grow apples and peaches. *Quetzales* can be observed there, especially during their nesting season in April and May. Be sure to call ahead for reservations. To get there, take a San Isidro bus from San José and ask to be let off at the *"entrada a San Gerardo"*. The turnoff is at the 80-km mark on the Interamerican Highway. The Finca Chacón is a 9-km downhill hike from there. Don Efraín can pick you up if you call him ($12 round trip). If you travel by car, 4-wheel drive is recommended.

The Valle de El General is one of Costa Rica's jewels of nature. When the fog clears after Cerro de la Muerte, **San Isidro** and surrounding small towns offer beautiful flowers and a lovely climate. When driving to San Isidro, Copey or San Gerardo, dress in layers and try to go early in the day, before fog and rain reduce visibility to zero. This can happen even in the dry season. Landslides are a very real danger also during heavy rains.

San Isidro is the gateway to Chirripó National Park and Playa Dominical. The **Bar Chirripó** and **El Tenedor** on the Parque Central are good places to eat. There are several clean and inexpensive hotels in town, like **Hotel Chirripó** (E, pb; F, cb, hw, nf, 71-0529) and **Hotel Amaneli** (E, pb, hw, tf, 71-0352) Make sure your room is not facing the Interamerican highway as trucks and buses pass all night. Doña Ofelia Jiménez rents rooms and serves homemade food (25m south of Surtidor Boston in Barrio Boston). Six km S of San Isidro, on the left, is **Hotel del Sur,** with landscaped gardens, a large pool, tennis courts and shady retreats (D, pb, a/c, restaurant, 71-0233). See p. 109 for key to hotel codes.

Comfortable buses leave San José for San Isidro once an hour from three bus companies along the same block (c 16, a 1/3, 23-3577, 22-2422, 23-0686, tickets in advance, especially on weekends and holidays, 3-hr trip). Buses back to San José leave hourly.

Most people I talked with before venturing off to **Chirripó** told me about their own experiences on the mountain. Many Costa Ricans have climbed it once but won't ever go again. True, the trek can be painful, tiring, frustrating and freezing, but it's so satisfying to reach the summit, which as the highest peak in southern Central America, is really the top of this part of the world.

The bus ride to San Gerardo de Rivas from San Isidro follows a river. In the distance you can see the high mountains that you're about to climb. At San Gerardo, check in at the Park Headquarters, near the final bus stop. There you register and pay the nominal entrance and overnight sleeping fees. They give you two very basic maps. If you want to be able to know exactly where you are or if you're planning to explore any of the neighboring peaks or valleys, we recommend you buy a good, large-scale, topographical map (see p. 80).

When we were there, neither the employee at San Gerardo nor the ranger who lived in the station near the top knew much about hiking alternatives in the park. So don't depend on them for good information. The headquarters in San Gerardo can help you contact *campesinos* who use their horses to haul your pack up to the huts.

The park service people might let you sleep in their building, or on their front lawn. You can leave your tent with them while you're up in the mountains, since you sleep in huts up there. You can also sleep on the floor of the Salón Comunal in San Gerardo for a few colones. Luis Hernández, who collects for the Salón Comunal, also rents out rooms (F) in Soda and Cabinas Chirripó.

The first day is long and grueling. Hikers make the 14 straight uphill kilometers to the huts in anywhere from seven hours to two days. It took us 11 hours. We left at 4:30am, while it was still dark. We took the Thermometre short cut, which is supposed to shorten the trip by an hour. You walk up the road from San Gerardo, veering right at the forks passing over two bridges. It's about 500 meters to a sign that says *Sendero al Cerro Chirripó* and points up--you climb over the fence and head straight up through the steep pasture. Stay to the left of the forest, pass through an opening in the fence at the top of one false summit, and continue along a ridge until you get to the next fence. The whole climb should take half an hour or 45 minutes.

*Black-faced solitaire
(jilguero)*

There you are on the trail. It's well-marked. Signs every 2km give you the altitude and distance to the summit. Subtract 4km for your distance to the huts. You will be slapping flies, sweating and slipping on your long haul, but if you can take your mind off the strain, you'll really enjoy where you are. The trail climbs through a dense cloud forest where *jilgueros* sing their amazing song which sounds like blowing through a flute made from glass. The song is simple, but very fine. Since the bird likes to stay up in the highest treetops, it's difficult to spot. The jilguero's natural habitat is the cloud forest. Sadly, as people are destroying cloud forests in Costa Rica, they destroy the jilguero too.

The first opportunity to get water is at a stream off the trail from a point 15 minutes past Llano Bonito. Since this is four or five hours into the hike, be sure to bring plenty of water. After the water comes *La Cuesta del Agua* which is the longest haul of them all--it took us three hours to climb. It ends at *Monte Sin Fé* (Faithless Mountain), where you walk into a new kind of forest. It's drier and the trees are shorter with less green foliage. Green, orange, and yellow moss hangs from the grey lichen-covered branches and wags in the wind like furry beards.

The next major landmark is the *refugio natural*--a big cave where five people could sleep if it's raining, up to ten if it's not. A stream next to the cave was dry when we were there in February. This cave is only 1.5 hours from the huts, so try to make it. You have to climb *La Cuesta de los Arrepentidos* (Repentants' Hill), then the trail traces around the side of a mountain. When the view opens up you can see *Los Crestones* on the top of a ridge straight ahead. These are huge sharp rocks that look like they were folded accordion-style. The huts are in the valley just below them.

Arriving at the huts is a relief. The third, the yellow one, is where you should try to stay. There's a wood floor and a good wood stove. If you're lucky, someone will have a pot of water boiling and will offer you a hot cup of tea.

Mornings are clear in the summer until 9 or so, then the valley fills with fog. Wisps of fog drift in until they crowd together and form dense clouds. Visibility minimizes, and at 2 or 3 it rains for about 45 minutes, so be on the trail by dawn. Besides avoiding the rain, it's a pretty hour to be outside. As the sun touches the frost-covered leaves and grasses, the ice melts, the plants stretch and whole meadows squeak softly.

There are many places to explore. Of course you should go to the summit of Chirripó, an hour and a half up the same trail. You pass through the *Valle de los Conejos,* where no rabbit has lived since a destructive fire in 1976. *Lagartijas,* little lizards, have occupied the valley. Each lizard has a different sheen that perfectly matches the rock it suns itself on. On the top of Chirripó you can see both oceans if the clouds haven't rolled in by the time you get there. There's a register to sign in a metal container wedged between the rocks in the summit cairn. Right below Chirripó is the *Lago San Juan.* You can swing by it on your way down. It's fun to take a quick swim and there are ideal sunning rocks on the lake's banks.

The lake-filled *Valle de las Morenas* is on the other side of the peak, with a hut where you can stay. Ask for its key at the San Gerardo park station. If you want to continue hiking in that direction, you can pass over *Cerro Urán* and continue along the *Camino de los Indios,* a trail known and used almost solely by the local Indians. Talk to Parques Nacionales in San José and hire a guide for this hike. You can also climb Urán and take the Camino de los Indios back through another valley to San Gerardo. Talk to Parques Nacionales and take a good map.

Other day-hike possibilities are *Cerro Ventisqueres,* the second highest mountain in Southern Central America, whose trail takes off from the main trail a bit below the Valle de los Conejos. It is supposed to be a relatively easy hike. You can also hike from the huts to Los Crestones. From there you can see the black acres of charcoal trees that burned in a massive fire in April 1985. The top of the ridge is reached by going up to the left of Los Crestones. Follow the ridge left to *Cerro Terbi,* a mild half hour. There's a register in the cairn stones up there, too. To make it a round trip, continue on the ridge a few hundred meters and descend on a trail that goes through a steep chimney and ends up in Valle de los Conejos. You can also continue walking along Terbi's curving ridge, ascending and descending the peaks it includes, going down into Valle de los Conejos when you get tired. When you go on your day hikes take a map and compass, a sweater, a rainjacket and water. Since the whole area is above timberline, you can always see where you are as long as inclement weather and fog do not envelop you. Watch out for lightning. Some people have gotten lost and died there, so be careful. Be sure to bring:

1) warm clothes and a warm sleeping bag. It is very cold up there. If the ranger is around he can lend you blankets. I slept in a polarguard sleeping bag with one blanket inside it, another on top, another underneath, all my clothes on, and a friend beside me. I was almost warm.

2) binoculars to look for birds and to look out into the distance from the top of mountains and ridges.

3) munchies for the hikes. Dried bananas and peanuts are good for energy when you're climbing. Carrots proved to be our lifesaver on the Cuesta de Agua. They quench your thirst and give you something to do slowly and steadily as you climb that never-ending hill.

4) a poncho to keep you dry during the multiple rainshowers that occur daily.

5) a water bottle, at least one liter per person, to replenish all the liquid you'll lose sweating.

Getting there: From the market in San Isidro, buses leave for San Gerardo de Rivas at 5am and 2pm. The trip takes 1.5 hours ($.60). When asking which of the many buses to take, specify San Gerardo de *Rivas,* because there's another San Gerardo. To be able to start your hike before dawn, arrive a day early and spend the night there. The 10:30am bus from San José will get you to San Isidro in time to catch the 2pm bus to San Gerardo.

The scenery along the unfinished Costanera Sur Highway south of **Playa Dominical** is reminiscent of California's Big Sur coast--with lush tropical vegetation, of course. Someday the highway will connect Dominical with Palmar Norte near the Osa Península. Swimming at the long beach at the village of Dominical is quite dangerous. **Cabinas Costa Brava** (E, funky, pb, tf, pb, rest.) are about 1 km S of the village.

About 4km S are **Cabinas Punta Dominical**, on a rocky point overlooking the ocean   (D, screens, hammocks, hw, pb, cf, fanned by ocean breezes, restaurant, horses, 25-5328). We want to give special kudos to these cabinas for maintenance, design, privacy, comfort, tranquility, views, good food and friendly, trustworthy staff. If you have the time and can get reservations in advance, it is really worth the trip (about 4 hours from San José including rest stops). Swimming is best at low tide when coral rocks give way to sandy-bottomed beaches. Camping is allowed on the beach north of the point. If you are camping, bring fresh fruits and vegetables from the plentiful market in San Isidro, as they are usually not available on the coast. About 3 km south of Punta Dominical are **Cabinas Abavacú** (D, cooking facilities, pb, nice ocean views, Apdo. 364, San Isidro de El General, CR).

Buses leave San Isidro de El General at 3pm daily for Uvita, south of Dominical, leaving you off at the entrance to Cabinas Punta Dominical (800m to the right). A bus returns from Uvita at 8am. You can also take a 7am or 1:30pm bus from San Isidro through Dominical and up the coast to Quepos. Buses leave Quepos for San Isidro at 5am and 1:30pm. Check local bus schedules by calling Memo's Restaurant in Dominical (71-0866). By car, Dominical is about 45min from San Isidro on newly paved road. The Costanera Sur is still unpaved but in good condition. Roads between Quepos and Dominical are not so good.

Boruca is a small indigenous town cradled in a green valley in the southwestern part of Costa Rica. The countryside is beautiful--you can walk up the red dirt trails for views across mountains, valleys and rivers.

The Borucas traditionally celebrate the new year with the *Fiesta de los Diablitos,* a dramatic reenactment of the war between the Spanish *conquistadores* and the Indians in which the Indians win. Indians throughout America share the Diablitos tradition, though usually their drama represents a war between the Spanish and the Moors. In Boruca the Diablitos are men disguised as devils. One man is the bull. Costumes are fashioned from burlap sacks and the balsa wood masks that Borucan artisans carve. The Diablitos taunt the bull with sticks and he prances around and chases them.

The group, accompanied by a drummer and a flute player, meets on a hill the night of the 30th of December. At midnight, a conch shell sounds and they run down the hill into town. They spend the whole night going from house to house, giving a short performance at each house and then relaxing to enjoy the *chicha* and *tamales* they are offered. The group visits most houses in town that night and during the next three days. The third day of the fiesta the Diablitos symbolically kill the bull. A huge bonfire reduces the bull to ashes.

Except for the occasional traditional fiestas, the pace of life in Boruca is slow and steady. Men leave town early in the morning to work small *fincas* in the nearby hills. Women usually stay at home. They weave naturally-dyed cotton yarn on simple looms they tie around their waists, making belts, purses, and little table cloths. Men carve expressive masks out of balsa wood. Both men and women carve elaborate scenes into the shells of large *jícaras* (gourds).

It's good to plan to visit for at least three or four days to get to know the people and the area. A family who usually has room for visitors is headed by doña Dolores Morales. They live directly below the blue *pulpería*. You should pay the family for food and the bed, and you might want to bring some things from the city that are expensive or not available there: powdered milk, children's clothes (shirts, shorts, underwear), barrettes, pens and paper, candy.

Getting there: It takes a whole day to get to Boruca from San José. Take the 8:30am bus from the Zona Sur station (a 18, c 4, 21-4214) to Buenos Aires or to the *bomba* (gas station) along the Interamericana, 1 km out of town. A school-bus leaves Buenos Aires at 1:30 (March to November only), stops at the bomba soon after, and arrives in Boruca (18 km up and down a mountainous dirt road) at 3:30 or so. Or you can get off the Zona Sur bus at the *Entrada de Boruca* about 30 min past the bomba, and walk 8 km up the path that takes off to the right of the highway. The hike takes about 2 hours.

The **Península de Osa** reaches out of southwestern Costa Rica into the Pacific Ocean. Its large virgin rainforests receive 4000 milimeters of precipitation per year. For years its incredible wealth of tropical flora and fauna was protected from human destruction by the peninsula's isolation from the rest of the country. Then a lumber company moved in, more settlers came, and sports hunters began killing endangered animals in large numbers. Scientists urged the creation of a national park to protect the peninsula: in 1975, 108,022 acres in the western corner of the Osa were declared **Corcovado National Park.**

213

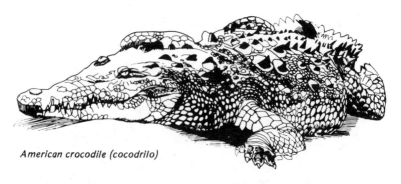

American crocodile (cocodrilo)

Corcovado contains eight unique habitats that range from mountain forests to marshes and swamps. So far, scientists have identified 500 species of trees, 285 birds, 139 mammals, 116 amphibians and reptiles, and 16 kinds of fresh-water fish.

Corcovado used to harbor another kind of inhabitant: *oreros* (gold panners), who lived in the jungle and sifted for their fortunes in the park's rivers. Few struck it rich, but most at least made a living. The Banco Central set up a special office in Puerto Jiménez to buy the gold, which the country used to help pay the interest on its huge foreign debt. But the gold panners' numbers grew so disproportionately that their activity started causing real destruction. The silt from their panning was filling up the lake in the park's basin. So in February and March 1986, the Park Service and the Costa Rican Civil Guard removed all the gold panners, promising them a certain amount of money for potential income lost. After a year without payment, the *oreros* came to San José and camped out in protest in the city's parks until the government came through with the checks they had promised. Now, panning activity has started again, this time in the forest reserve bordering Corcovado. Even though it is destructive, the Park Service has decided to let it go on instead of risking more harm to Corcovado itself.

A surge in human settlers is threatening the delicate ecological balance of the unprotected forests in the Osa. An expanding national population, a shortage of land available elsewhere for cultivation, and the new road that connects Osa by land to the rest of Costa Rica have been factors encouraging settlement. *Campesinos* have moved in and started burning and cutting back the jungle to build their houses and cultivate small plots of land.

Here is where the situation takes on its sad irony. The shortage of available land is so serious that clearing land (destroying jungle) seems like the only alternative to many people. But rainforest soil is very poor when there's no forest covering it. Its self-fertilization by dead leaves, plants and animals stops, rendering it infertile. The ground is clay, which compacts and becomes rock hard.

The jungle provides a habitat for thousands of animals which die without it. Its trees produce chemicals that are extracted for use in medicines like morphine, codeine, quinine. Oxygen is a byproduct of their photosynthesis. The jungle conserves the humidity of the land and protects its water-sheds.

Visiting the Península de Osa is a good way to learn firsthand about the conflict between conservation of natural resources that will help humanity in the long-term, and the short-term possibilities that many people consider their only option for survival.

Now, thanks to international support for Costa Rica's conservation efforts, the Fundación Neotrópica (see p. 35) is starting to address this problem through its BOSCOSA project. In-depth studies are being done of the needs of *precarista* (squatter) communities in the Osa, and strong relationships are being formed with the people. Through studies of animal and plant species that grow in forest reserves, new crops and livestock projects are being experimented with to provide solutions for both human and environmental problems. Costa Rican conservationists are realizing that they must create their own models for sustained development, rather than relying on techniques developed in countries with different cultural and economic patterns. They are forging a new understanding of human and environmental issues as one and the same.

Puerto Jiménez is a small, pleasant town, with friendly people. There are good white sand beaches south of town, beyond the second point that juts out into the gulf. The town is the gateway to Corcovado; the **Park's administration office** is at the south end of the town's main street. In order to visit Corcovado, you must obtain a permit from this office. If you are planning to fly into Corcovado, you must call the office (78-5036) to tell them who you are and how many days you plan to stay. Camping is allowed in the park, but if you arrange with the administration beforehand, you might be able to stay at the research station at Sirena ($1/night). Bring your own food. If you plan to camp, bring mosquito nets, repellent, long socks, several changes of cotton clothing, swimsuits, a flashlight and two pairs of hiking or running shoes, or rubber boots.

There are several ways to get to the park:

Hiking: A bus leaves Puerto Jiménez at 5:30am for La Palma (hour trip). From La Palma it's a 3-hour walk to the park's northeastern entrance at Los Patos. A well-marked trail takes you from Los Patos to Sirena on the west coast in 4-6 hours. From there you can circle back through Playa Madrigal, a 4-hour hike from Sirena, and camp at the La Leona station. From La Leona it's an 8-hour hike down a dirt road back to Puerto Jiménez.

On Mon and Sat, a 4-wheel-drive taxi goes from Puerto Jiménez south along the coast to Carate, a short hike from the La Leona station ($3.50/person). You can also arrange for the taxi on other days ($45-60/taxi) through the park office. From La Leona you can circle back to Los Patos.

By plane: You can rent a small plane in Golfito that will fly you directly to Sirena (Aeronaves de Costa Rica, 75-0278, $100/planeload). To get to Golfito, take a 7-hour bus ride from San José (21-4214, $3) or fly Mon thru Sat at 8:45am on SANSA (33-3258, 33-0397, 21-9414, $12). Be sure to call the park administration first. Aeronaves will also fly you in from San José for about $250/planeload (32-1176). Many of the nature tour companies listed on pp. 45-6 have guided tours to Corcovado.

Getting to Puerto Jiménez: Buses leave San Isidro de El General at 5:30am and 12 noon for Puerto Jiménez (5 hrs). You can also intercept the Villa Neilly-Puerto Jiménez bus at 7am or 3pm at Chacarita (Piedras Blancas) on the Interamerican highway, by taking any Zona Sur bus from San José.

An old **launch** leaves the municipal dock (*muelle*) in Golfito for Puerto Jiménez every day at noon. The ride across the gulf takes an hour and a half. The launch returns to Golfito from the dock below the bus station on the northern part of Puerto Jiménez's beach at 6am. You can buy coffee from the cook and watch the early birds diving for their fish breakfasts.

Aeronaves de Costa Rica might renew its flights to Puerto Jiménez from Golfito (75-0278).

In Puerto Jiménez, **Cabinas Manglares** (E, a/c, pb, shared kitchen facilities, 78-5002) is at the bridge on the road to the

216

airport and the outer beach. **Cabinas Marcelina** (F) and **Brisas del Mar** (F) are right in town (see p. 109 for hotel codes).

Marenco Biological Station, about 5km north of Corcovado on the Pacific, is dedicated to "conservation, education, tourism and adventure". One of Costa Rica's leading families has made their private rainforest into a reserve, and has resident biologists to help visitors understand the intricate ecological relationships there. Their cabinas, not luxurious, but simple and well-designed (4 beds to a room, shared baths), overlook the Pacific and the Isla del Caño. Meals are delicious and wholesome, served family-style. Naturalists enjoy Marenco because they have a chance to see rainforest, river and sea wildlife all in the same area. Some of them even take off their binoculars long enough to enjoy snorkeling around Marenco's coral reefs. A half-hour hike through a series of lovely rocky coves ends at the Río Claro where a deep natural pool lends itself to a refreshing fresh-water swim. Marenco offers tours to the formerly inaccessible northern part of Corcovado National Park, hiking to La Llorona, where a waterfall cascades onto the beach.

Because of Marenco's isolated location, transportation is coordinated through their office in San José (21-1594, Apdo. 4025, 1000 San José, fx: 55-4513). A 3-night tour costs around $515, including food, lodging, air and boat transport from San José and guides (min. 4 pers.). Guided day trips are extra: $15 to Río Claro, $65 to Isla del Caño and $75 to Corcovado.

Drake Bay, purported to be the landing spot of Sir Francis Drake in Costa Rica, is about 10 minutes north of Marenco by boat. **Drake Bay Wilderness Camp** is right on the beach with a nice lodge, good food, and free snorkeling equipment and canoes. They offer a number of guided tours for visitors to choose from, including hiking or camping in Corcovado, trips to Isla del Caño, and ocean fishing ($45/person incl. 3 meals, pb, hw, cf, trips and transportation extra but reasonably priced, shady campground, charter flights available, 71-2436, 20-2121, fx: (506) 32-3321).

There are two other lodges at Drake Bay, but they were closed at the time we were doing our research. Call (713) 489-9156 for info on **Phantom Isle Lodge**, which specializes in scuba diving and sportfishing, and (506) 39-2801 for info on **La Paloma Lodge**. As with Marenco, it is best that you arrange transport with them beforehand. Otherwise, you take a bus or a SANSA plane to Palmar, then a bus to Sierpe, a village on the Sierpe River. You have to go down the river a couple of hours and out into the ocean to get to Drake Bay. The crossing from the wide river mouth into the ocean is dangerous and must be done according to the tides by an experienced skipper. The lodges will send one to pick you up in Sierpe. There are dugouts that take local people in and out for cheap, but they are usually overloaded and have been known to capsize at the river mouth.

The port of **Golfito** has a gorgeous setting, with lush, forested hills surrounding a deep bay on the Golfo Dulce, the misty outline of the Península de Osa in the distance.

The United Fruit Company moved to the Golfito region in 1938 after banana diseases, depletion of good soil, and massive labor strikes led it to abandon its plantations in Limón. Golfito became the company's headquarters and main port. The company constructed houses and barracks for its employees, schools, a hospital, stores, a dairy farm, etc. They built a huge loading dock that could handle 4000 bunches of bananas per hour and a 246-km railway from the plantations in the nearby Diquis and Coto valleys. About 15,000 people migrated from Guanacaste and other provinces to work for United. The company gave workers small plots of land along the railroad track for houses and gardens. In its heyday, Golfito was a crowded, steamy banana port.

But no more. United stopped production a few years ago and finally moved out in 1985 after deciding that their profit-making potential was exhausted. Production costs were high, there were some violent labor conflicts in the early 80's, the Costa Rican government raised its export tax on bananas, and the Pacific banana market of California and Japan was too small. Most of the facilities they had constructed were left to the state. They made a large grant to the University of Costa Rica and the University of Kansas to study the effects of their departure on the local people.

Banana lands have been converted to African palm plantations. The clustered palm fruits are pressed to produce the oil used in lard and margarine. Since African palm cultivation doesn't require much human labor, it has not relieved the unemployment caused by United's departure. The former use of

218

copper sulfides in pesticides in the banana plantations has made it impossible to grow rice and other food crops in the area, due to the high levels of chemicals that persist in the soil.

Many people migrated to other parts of the country to find work; some have settled in the Osa. If you can get them started, people will talk to you about the *Yunai,* as they call United, with nostalgia or resentment, sometimes in the English they learned from their former employers.

Golfito is about to undergo a renaissance as a duty-free port. A special facility will allow Ticos to buy $400 worth of merchandise every 6 months if they stay in the area 72 hours or longer. So there should be an increase in hotel and transport facilities in the area. The imported items will still be sold with a 65% tax, which will not make them of much interest to foreigners, but does make them cheaper than imported goods in San José.

The town is stretched along one main road squeezed between the Gulf and a steep jungle-covered cliff. The northern part was the Zona Americana, where the administrators lived. It's a quiet neighborhood with big wooden houses set up on stilts, surrounded by large lawns and gardens. The farthest area north is the airport, built within a golfcourse that is planted with exotic trees and bushes that United imported from Africa and Asia, now completely overgrown.

The south part of town is the Pueblo Civil, full of bars, restaurants, brothels and hotels. It feels much more like a crowded, active port town that the tranquil, distinguished Zona Americana; it's hard to imagine that the two sectors form the same town.

Food is good at **El Uno** near the municipal dock. In town near the gas station are the **Delfina** (F, cb; E, pb, tf, cw, some with a/c, 75-0043) and **El Puente** (E, tf, D, a/c, cw, pb, 75-0034). **Cabinas Las Gaviotas** at the entrance to town is probably the most pleasant place to stay (D, tf; C, a/c, some with kitchens, 75-0062). See p. 109 for key to hotel codes.

The forested hills surrounding Golfito have been made into a wildlife refuge to protect the town's water supply. The adventurous can take a 15-minute boat-taxi out to **Captain Tom's Place**, eat Jungle Burgers, and stay in his hotel, a converted 62-foot trawler on a beach across the bay from Golfito.

Getting there: Golfito buses leave San José (c 4, a 18, 21-4214, $3, 7 hours) at 6:30 and 11am, or take any Zona Sur bus to Río Claro, where the road to Golfito leaves the Interamerican. Villa Neilly-Golfito buses pass through Río Claro hourly (1/2 hour trip).

SANSA flies to Golfito Mon thru Sat at 8:45am and returns at 9:45am ($12 one way, make reservations and buy tickets in advance, schedules change often, 33-0397, 33-3258, 21-9414).

Tiskita Lodge (L per person, double, incl. 3 meals, pb), 2.5 hours south of Golfito, offers rustic but comfortable cabins with kitchens, sea breezes and great views of the coast. Agronomist Peter Aspinall has planted 100 varieties of tropical fruits there from around the world which attract many birds and monkeys. Pet toucans, scarlet macaws and parrots wander among the trees. Packages including charter flights and guided nature walks are available through Costa Rica Sun Tours, 55-3518, 55-3418, fx: 55-4410.

The Villa Neilly-San Vito road was built in 1945 before the end of World War II by the USA as a strategic protection point since the area is due west of the Panama Canal. The gravel road rises so sharply that in 20 minutes, Villa Neilly's heat is forgotten in the cool, misty mountains that lead to **San Vito** (3150 feet above sea level). The trip takes 2 1/2 hours in a crowded, aging bus, but the countryside is lush and not as deforested as in other areas. Immigrants from post-war Italy founded San Vito in the early 50's. In the last few years its population has doubled to 37,000. It's a clean, modern town nestled in a high mountain valley.

The **Wilson Botanical Gardens,** 6km uphill from San Vito on the Villa Neilly road, were started in 1962. The main collections in the 30-acre gardens are of tropical palms, araceae, bromeliads and heliconias, though many other plants are also featured in the lush design of the gardens, inspired in part by the great Brazilian horticulturist, Burle-Marx. Some 210 species of birds inhabit the 270-acre forest reserve that surrounds the gardens, traversed by 4 miles of paths. The gardens, which had been deteriorating for several years, are now undergoing a renaissance under the direction of Dr. Luis Diego Gómez of the Organization for Tropical Studies (see Bibliography).

The administration building contains dormitory-style accommodations ($40/day incl. meals). No children under 12. Reservations must be made in advance through the Organization for Tropical Studies (36-6696, Apdo. 676, 2050 San José, CR).

You can take the San Vito-Villa Neilly bus to the gardens at 7am and 1:30pm, or take the Villa Neilly-San Vito bus at 6am, 1pm or 3pm. A taxi from San Vito is about $2.50.

Direct buses to San Vito leave San José at 7am and 2pm from a 18, c 13 near Plaza Víquez (23-4975, $4.80, 6 hours, tickets in advance). This route is paved all the way, and crosses the Rio Térraba on a ferry (5 min.) at Paso Real, east of Palmar Norte. The ferry should be replaced by a bridge by the time you read this. These buses also pass the Botanical Gardens after a stop in San Vito.

The nicest place to stay in San Vito is **Cabinas Las Mirlas,** next to the Ministry of Agriculture office (E, hw, 77-3054). The individual cabins are perched among fruit trees overlooking a creek. **Hotel Pitier** (E, pb, hw) and **El Ceibo** (E, pb, hw, nice diningroom, $5 for fish dinner, 77-3025) are also clean and inexpensive. All of them are too close to the local disco on weekends. For peace and quiet, stay at the Botanical Gardens.

Parque Internacional La Amistad extends over the Talamanca mountains from the southern border of Parque Nacional Chirripó down into Panamá. It is the largest park in the country (192,000 hectares). Composed of eight life zones, La Amistad is one of the richest ecological biospheres in Central America.

Margay

221

Preliminary surveys indicate that two thirds of the country's vertebrate species are found in the park. Some animals are not protected anywhere else in Costa Rica. The park is an important refuge for animals that require large areas for hunting, foraging and reproduction, like the jaguar, margay and puma.

Facilities in the park are still being developed, but camping is allowed near the park entrances at Las Mellizas, Aguas Calientes and Helechales. The Las Mellizas area is the best for hiking and the easiest to get to. Take a San Vito-La Lucha bus at 9:30am and walk 6km. A regular car can drive all the way to the park station. There you can get information on trails. Taxis can drive you in from San Vito for about $80 round trip per taxi. Meals can be arranged through the cooks at Las Mellizas farm. Water in the streams is good. Trout fishing is possible, with a permit from the Servicio de Vida Silvestre (c 19, a ctl/2, No. 66, 33-8112 in San José).

Hiking deeper into the park should only be undertaken by experienced tropical trekkers. There are wild animals, few paths, and the topography is abrupt. North Americans have been known to suffer from hypothermia there. But hiking in the Las Tablas forest reserve at the entrance to the park is safe and rewarding. Horses and guides can be arranged for at Las Mellizas. For current conditions, call Parques Nacionales (33-5284, 33-8841).

Isla del Coco (Coco Island), 500km off the Pacific coast, boasts 200 dramatic waterfalls, many of which fall directly into the sea. Because the island is uninhabited, animals there are not afraid of humans. The fairy terns find humans so interesting that they hover about them curiously.

Although its geological origin remains a mystery, scientists believe Isla del Coco is a volcanic "hot spot" at the center of the Cocos tectonic plates. The Coco Island finch is a sub-species of the finch endemic to the Galapagos Islands which prompted Darwin's questions about evolution. Several species of birds, lizards and fresh water fish are endemic to the island, that is, they are found nowhere else on earth. Whereas on mainland Costa Rica there are so many species that the behavior of each is highly specialized, on Isla del Coco individual birds of the same species will have different feeding habits-- very interesting from an evolutionary standpoint. Some 77 non-endemic species, mainly sea-birds, can also be observed there.

European sailors probably first discovered the island in the 1500's. Many early visitors were pirates who rested and restocked fresh water there during their expeditions. They named the island after its numerous coconut palms, but apparently enjoyed the coconuts so much that there are almost none left today. Passing boats landed pigs, deer and goats on the island to provide meat for return voyages. Having had no predators, these animals now constitute the majority of the wildlife there.

There are two main tales of buried treasure on the island. The Portuguese Benito Bonito, "The One of the Bloody Sword", is said to have buried his fabulous treasure there. At the time of Peru's wars of independence from Spain, the aristocracy and clergy entrusted their gold and jewels to Captain James Thompson, who promised to transport their riches to a safe port. Thompson disappeared with the loot and is supposed to have hidden it on Isla del Coco. Although many treasure hunters have searched the island, no one has found anything yet.

Hunting for gold doubloons might not be rewarding at Isla del Coco, but scuba divers find it rich in natural treasures. A sailboat can be contracted from Puntarenas to take people to the island. Contact Parques Nacionales for current information (33-8841, 33-5284).

Fairy tern

TIQUISMOS--HAVING FUN WITH COSTA RICAN SPANISH

Ticos are amused and delighted when foreigners try to speak Spanish, especially when they include *tiquismos*, expressions that are peculiar to Costa Rican or Central American culture.

Not only the vocabulary, but the way of using words is important. Spanish speakers use a lot of *muletillas* (fillers, literally "crutches") in their speech. They "address" the person with whom they are speaking more often than is done in English, and they do it in a way that English speakers might consider slightly offensive. It is common that women will be called *mamita, madre, mi hijita,* (little mother, mother, my little daughter, all roughly corresponding to "honey"). Latins love to use salient physical characteristics as nicknames. Common ones are *gordo* (fatty), *flaco* (skinny), *macho* or *macha* (Costa Rican for fair-skinned or fair haired), *negro* (dark-skinned), *chino* (it doesn't matter if you're Asian or just have slightly slanting eyes, your name is Chino), *gato* (blue or green eyes). You just have to be slightly *gordo* or *flaco* to merit those names. If you're really *gordo* or *flaco,* and people really like you, you get a special name like *repollito* (little cabbage) or *palito* (little stick). *Gordo* and *negro* are commonly used as terms of endearment, regardless of appearance.

Anyone under thirty is usually called *maje* by his or her friends. This is a special Costa Rican measure of friendship, which literally means "dummy" but figuratively is more like pal or buddy. It is used widely as a *muletilla. Majes* have various expressions of approval such as the famous *pura vida* (great, terrific), or *tuanis* (cool), *buena nota* (groovy). *Mala nota* is ungroovy, *furris* is uncool and *salado* means "too bad for you". Expressions of extreme approval are *qué bruto, qué bárbaro,* and disapproval, *qué horror,* or *fatal, maje.*

The above are the slang expressions of urban youth. However, all Ticos are aware of polite, courteous and respectful forms of speech. They make their world more pleasant by using little expressions of appreciation. For example, if someone helps you in a store or on the street, you say "*Muchas gracias, muy amable*" (Thank you very much, you are very kind), and they will say "*Con mucho gusto*" (With much pleasure).

It is customary in the morning to ask "*Como amaneció?*" (How did you wake up?) "*Muy bién, por dicha, y usted?*" (Very well, luckily, and you?) "*Muy bién, gracias a Dios.*" (Very well, thank God.)

When talking about a future event or plan, Ticos will often include *si Dios quiere* (if God wants, God willing): "*Nos vemos el martes, si Dios quiere.*" (We'll see each other Tuesday, God willing.)

If you are in the city and see someone on the other side of the street that you know, you call "*Adios!*" In the countryside, when you pass someone on the road, it is customary to say *adios* even if you don't know them. In these situations, *adios* means hello. It is only used to mean goodbye when you're going away for good. Everyday goodbyes are *hasta luego* (until then, until later), and the other person might add "*Que Dios le acompañe*" (May God acompany you).

Giving a coin to a beggar in the street often earns you a special blessing: he or she will say "*Dios se lo pague*" (May God repay you).

Vos is a form of second person singular address used throughout Central America instead of *tu.* Small children, however, are usually addressed as *usted*, probably in order to teach them to use this more respectful form with their elders, until they know how to make the differentiation themselves. The fact that the archaic *vos* is used even now in Costa Rica shows how isolated it was during colonial times. The verb form used with *vos* is made by changing the *r* on the end of an infinitive to *s*. Thus with the verb poder, "*tu puedes*" becomes "*vos podés*", and with sentirse, "*tú te sientes*" becomes "*vos te sentís*".

Other fillers that are used commonly in Spanish are terms like *fijate, imaginate,* and *vieras que,* for which there are no real equivalents in English. Roughly, they could be translated as "would you believe" or "just think!" These expressions are used to give emphasis to what the speaker is saying. For example:

"Fíjate vos que no me dejaron entrar!" (Would you believe it--they wouldn't let me in!)

"Imagínese cómo me dió pena verla así" (Imagine how bad I felt to see her like that.)

Vieras is often used to give the equivalent of the way we use *"sure"* in English:

"Vieras qué susto me dió!" (I sure was scared, or, you should have seen how it scared me.)

Achará is another particularly *tico* expression which indicates regret at a loss:

"Fíjese que el perro comió mis begonias.   Achará mis florecitas." (Would you believe it--the dog ate my begonias. My poor little flowers!)

When you come to someone's house, especially in the country, it is customary to stand on the ground near the porch and *say "Upe!"* as a way of letting them know you're there. When they ask you to come in, as you enter the house you say *"Con permiso"* (with your permission). If they offer you something to eat, it is much more polite to accept than not to accept. Giving makes people happy, and if you don't let them give to you, it hurts them. People will ask you about your family, whether you're married, how many children you have. Most can't quite grasp the idea of people not being married or not having children.   When you're sitting and talking and finally no one can think of anything else to say, you say, *"Pues, sí"* (Well, yes).

Learn some of these expressions and practice them until you don't make any *metidas de pata* (literally, "putting your foot in it", or mistakes). Ticos will be glad to help you. If you do make a mistake, there is a word which is instant absolution: just say, *"Diay?"* That means, "Well, what can you expect?" or "What can be done about it?"   As you get to know the Ticos, you'll find out that this little word comes in very handy.

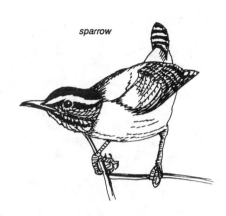

sparrow

STAYING LONGER

Options for Residency

Securing permanent residency here is a complicated and increasingly difficult process. Temporary residency can be obtained by students in registered university or language school programs, or by volunteers with US Peace Corps (or its Canadian, Swedish, French and Japanese equivalents) or Caritas, Catholic Relief Services and many other church-affiliated groups.

Retired businessmen can join the International Excecutive Service Corps, a private, non-profit firm sponsored in part by AID. They have a skills bank in Stamford, Conn. which matches volunteers with third-world companies needing consultants. Volunteers are paid living expenses only. Eight other "developed" countries in addition to the US have similar organizations (IESC, Apdo. 70 Centro Colón, 1007 San José, CR (506) 33-9855).

To live here on a permanent basis you must either have a lot of money to invest in starting your own company (*inversionista* status), or apply for *pensionado* or *rentista* status. Pensionados are retired persons who receive at least $600/month from a qualified pension or retirement plan, or from Social Security. Rentistas must purchase a Certificate of Deposit in a Costa Rican bank for $75,000, which is enough to guarantee them a $600/month income for 5 years. They must renew the CD in order to maintain their status. Rentistas can also prove that they have investments outside Costa Rica which will guarantee them an income of $1000/month, thus eliminating the necessity of buying the CD.

You must apply for these residencies through the nearest Costa Rican consulate in your home country. You must supply the following documents: birth certificates for you and your dependents; all marriage and divorce certificates; naturalization certificates (if applicable); and a letter from you home police department certifying that you have no criminal record. Pensionados must obtain a letter from their pension or retirement plan company or Social Security stating that the pension is for life and that the stated monthly amount will be paid in Costa Rica. The pension company must have existed for at least 20 years, and must provide a statement of incorporation and economic solvency, certified by a CPA, which in turn must be authenticated by a Costa Rican consul. References from two banks with which the company deals must also be provided.

Rentistas must submit a letter from a bank or recognized investment company stating that the amount of monthly income the candidate receives is stable, permanent and irrevocable and that it will be paid in Costa Rica for no less than five years. The company providing the income must have existed for over three years and must supply statements of incorporation, economic solvency and bank references, as above.

All documents must be authenticated by the Costa Rican consul nearest to the place where they were issued. This costs $40 per document. All documents must be translated into Spanish by a translator approved by the Costa Rican Ministry of Foreign Relations.

In addition, the candidate must submit two copies of his passport, one copy for each dependent and four passport-size photos for each person involved. He must sign a sworn statement that he will live in Costa Rica at least four months a year, and must submit to a chest X-ray for TB, and blood tests for syphilis and AIDS.

Pensionados must provide fingerprints and photos before they receive residency permits, so that their identities can be checked by Interpol, in an effort to eliminate criminals who present falsified police documents.

Both pensionados and rentistas can set up their own businesses, but they cannot be employed by someone else. There are 7000 pensionados and rentistas living in Costa Rica, half of whom are from the U.S. and Canada. For more information, send a $5 US money order to:

> **Asociación de Pensionados y Rentistas**
> Apdo. 700-1011
> San José, Costa Rica
> Tel: (506) 23-1733, ext. 261 or 211 or 33-8068

The Costa Rican government doesn't want foreigners to take jobs from Costa Ricans. Therefore, most foreigners are not allowed to work unless they are performing a task that Ticos cannot do. But with some thought, you might be able to discover a skill you have which will help you establish residency. Qualified teachers are needed at the English, French, and German-speaking schools in San José. English teachers are often needed by the various language institutes. The National Symphony needs musicians, The *Tico Times* needs reporters. Doctors, lawyers, architects and engineers are plentiful here, and are protected by powerful professional associations which make entry difficult for foreigners.

Legal Advice

Do not plan to do your residency yourself unless you have plenty of patience to deal with the lines, the national holidays, the lunch-breaks, the misunderstandings, the offices that have moved from where they were a month ago, the impossible-to-find phone numbers, etc. If you've got comfortable shoes and love to meditate or catch up on your reading while waiting in line, you'll find *trámites* (bureaucratic machinations) just your cup of tea. If you are nervous and impatient or have fallen arches, you will suffer.

Obtaining residency can take anywhere from a couple of months to a couple of years, depending on how well-prepared you are and how efficient your legal help is. Here are our guidelines for choosing a lawyer in Costa Rica:

1. Shop around. There is usually no charge for meeting and consulting with a lawyer. Find someone you respect and can communicate with easily. Actually, your residency will probably be handled by law students working in the lawyer's office, and they will be the ones you end up having to communicate with, so meet them too. Probably the most important person to have a trusting relationship with is the secretary. Some lawyers are always "not there" or "in a meeting" according to their secretaries. You can call for *weeks* and never get a chance to talk to them.

2. Talk with other residents about whom they would recommend. Find a lawyer with whom people have had positive experiences in the field you are interested in. *Licenciado X* may be a terrific international lawyer, but you can bet his specialty isn't residencies, so don't expect him to be good at it.

229

3. Don't go to someone because he's a "nice guy" or somebody's friend. "Honest and efficient" is better than nice. Costa Ricans are always nice, even if they are irresponsible and slow.

4. Legal fees vary greatly. Some very good lawyers charge more because they know that what they do is far superior to the run of the mill. If you have the money, it is worth every penny to have a good lawyer here. Of course the mere fact that a lawyer charges more does not mean he is good. Some very reliable lawyers are not all that expensive. Guidelines have been established to govern legal fees. They were published in the *Gaceta* (the legal government newspaper). You can make a copy from the archives of the Biblioteca Nacional.

5. Most legal work does not get done unless you keep tabs on what your lawyer is doing. It is best if you educate yourself on rules and regulations, etc. Do not sit back and expect that every thing is humming along now that *Licenciado X* has your affairs in his capable hands. Check and double check, ask to see receipts, ask to see your *expediente* (file). Watch out if the lawyer tells you *"Tranquilo. No hay problema. No se preocupe."* (Relax. No problem. Don't worry.) This is Costa Rican for "Don't make me think about it".

6. Whether you have a good lawyer or a mediocre one, things still take a long time to get done here. So, as long as you know that things are *en trámite,* enjoy the relaxed pace and go on a couple of long weekends yourself.

Real Estate and Investments:
"...the potential investor in Costa Rica should beware of ALL glib, fact-filled English-speaking promoters flogging ANYTHING, whether it's gold mines, beach property, condos, agribusiness, or mutual funds. Unfortunately, Costa Rica has long been a haven for con men, whose favorite targets are trusting newcomers. This doesn't mean, however, that legitimate investment opportunities don't exist, in agribusiness as well as in other areas. They do, and it's unfair to tar all projects with the same brush. Would-be investors here, like everywhere else, are advised simply to move cautiously, ask lots of questions, and check with well-established, reputable companies before parting with any money. That way, they can be confident of making a good choice."
--*The Tico Times*, Apdo. 4632, 1000 San José, CR; weekly, 32pg., $45/year.

Contact the **American Chamber of Commerce of Costa Rica,** Apdo. 4946, 1000 San José, CR, (506) 32-2133.

Renting

Houses and apartments in San José rent from about $200/mo. and up. Suburban and country houses can rent for as little as $100/mo. "Unfurnished" usually means without stove or refrigerator as well as without furniture.

SCHOOLS

English-language schools are excellent. They follow the U.S. academic year and prepare students for acceptance in U.S. as well as Costa Rican universities.

Costa Rica Academy. Kinder through grade 12. West of Cariari Country Club. Apdo 4941, San José, 39-0376.

Country Day School. Kinder through grade 12. Escazú. Apdo 8-6170, San José, 28-0873.

The Marian Baker School. Prekinder through grade 12. Apdo. 4269, SJ. San Ramón de Tres Ríos, east of San José, 34-3426, 34-4609.

International Christian School. Kinder through grade 12. Apdo. 3512, San José, Barrio Escalante, 25-1474.

Bilingual private schools are usually less expensive and also prepare students for U.S. college acceptance. They follow the Costa Rican academic year which begins in March and ends in November.

Anglo-American School. Primary. Apdo 3180, San José, 25-1729.

Colegio Humbolt. Classes in German. Rohrmoser, 32-0093.

Colegio Metodista. Kinder through high school. Apdo 931, San José, 25-0655

Escuela Británica. Primary. Located in Pavas. Apdo 8184, San José, 22-0719.

Lincoln School. Kinder through grade 12, junior college. Moravia. Apdo 1919, San José, 35-7733.

Saint Anthony School. Primary. Moravia. Apdo 29, Moravia, 35-1017

Saint Clare. Junior high, high school. Moravia, Apdo 2910, San José. 35-7244.

Saint Francis. Kinder through grade 12. Moravia. Apdo 4405, San José, 35-9161.

Saint Joseph's Primary. Apdo 132, Moravia, 35-7214.

Saint Mary's School. Kinder through third grade. Escazú, 28-0329.

RELIGIOUS SERVICES

Baha'i: Prayer breakfast every Saturday at 8am, 800mts. S of the first entrance to Bello Horizonte, Escazu. Info center on c 22, a 4, 22-5335.

Baptist: English services Sundays at 9am, followed by fellowship and Sunday school. 150m N of Banco Anglo in San Pedro, 25-4885.

Catholic: Saint Mary's Chapel. English mass Sundays at 4pm. Adjacent to Sheraton Herradura Hotel, 39-0033.
Mass in English Saturdays at 5pm at San Rafael de Escazú Church.

Christian Science: Sundays at 11am, a 8 c 21, 21-0840.

Episcopal: Services in English Sundays at 8:30am at the Church of the Good Shepherd, a 4, c 3-5, 22-1560.

Hare Krishna: Centro Cultural Govinda, 235m N Banco Anglo, San Pedro, 34-1218, Finca Nueva Goloka Vrindavana, Cartago-Paraíso Road, 51-6752.

Jewish (reformed): Services Fridays at 8pm at Congregation B'Nei Israel, 600m W of Pop's La Sabana (old road to Escazú), 57-1785.

Hebrew school, pre-school for children, teen study and social programs, 24-3482.

Methodist: El Redentor. Sundays at 10:30, Sunday school 9:30. Women's Aglow Fellowship meets on Wednesdays, a ctl, c 9/11, 22-0360.

Mormon: Sacrament meetings 9am, English adult Sunday school, 9:30am Sundays, 100m S, 100m E of Pulpería La Luz, Barrio Los Yoses, 25-0208.

Protestant: Escazú Christian Fellowship, Sundays at 6-7pm, annex to Country Day School, 28-2754.

Quaker: Bilingual worship service at 11am Sundays at the Friends Peace Center, a 6 Bis, c 15, 33-6168, 24-4376.

Theosophical Society: nightly lodges, a 1, c 11-15, 21-7246.

Union Church: Free bus service from hotels Irazú, Ambassador, Gran, Amstel, and from Escazú. Sunday school at 9am, fellowship at 10, services at 10:25; Moravia, 26-3670.

Unitarians: Sundays at 5:30 at members' homes, 40-4424, 26-3691, 23-2617.

Victory Christian Center: Sundays at 10am, 125m W of Tennis Club in Sabana Sur, 20-1771, 82-7720, 28-9934.

Yoga: Gran Fraternidad Universal, a 7 (B), c 15, 57-0928.

LABOR REGULATIONS FOR DOMESTIC HELP

All domestic employees have the right to social security benefits from the *Caja Costarricense de Seguro Social*, maternity benefits set by the Ministry of Labor, the Christmas bonus, and severance pay.

Whether live-in or not, the employee is entitled to the minimum wage set by the Ministry of Labor (23-7166). Live-in help can be required to work no more than 12 hours a day and other employees eight hours. The employee has one half day off each week, a 15-day paid vacation after 50 weeks of continual service, and half-days on January 1, Holy Thursday, Good Friday, May 1, September 15 and December 25. If they work these days, then an additional half-day salary must be paid. Days off should be previously scheduled.

The new employee must be registered with the Caja, in the fifth floor Department of Inspections (23-9890). The employer must bring identification such as a passport or residency *cédula,* the employee's *cédula* and the facts about the job and wages. The employer then receives a computer form which s/he uses to make the monthly payments to the *Caja* (19.5 percent of the monthly wages). The employee receives a paper giving him/her the right to the *Caja's* services (health care, maternity care, pensions). The monthly payment does not require a personal trip and may be made by a messenger. If you lack a messenger, lines at the *Caja* seem shortest between 10:45 and 11:15.

An employee/mother-to-be is entitled to one month off before the birth and three months afterwards, with half of her monthly wage. The *Caja* will also pay her half the monthly wage in maternity benefits. Pregnancy is not a legal reason for dismissal.

The Christmas bonus (*aguinaldo*) is paid to employees who have worked from December 1 through November 30. The bonus, in the case of non-profit organizations like households, is equivalent to two weeks' salary, or an average two-week salary if the wages have varied over the year. For regular employees, the *aguinaldo* is equivalent to one month's salary. Most employers pay the *aguinaldo* early in December; others wait until Christmas and combine it with a personal gift.

If the employer has cause to dismiss an employee, s/he must pay unused vacation time, the proportionate *aguinaldo* and all wages due. S/he must also document the dismissal with the *Caja.*

If the employer must lay off help for reasons other than performance, such as leaving the country, s/he must give the employee prior notice, severance pay, unused vacation pay, the *aguinaldo* and wages due.

Should the employee decide to leave, the employer is not obligated to pay severance pay.

TRAVELING CATS AND DOGS

People wishing to bring their cats and dogs into Costa Rica must write to the *Jefe del Departamento de Zoonosis* and ask for a *Permiso de Importación* (import permit): Departamento de Zoonosis, Apdo. 10123, 1000 San José, CR (23-0333, ext. 331). In your letter, include the animal's name, breed, size, color, age and sex, your planned arrival date, the address where you'll be living in Costa Rica, $1 to cover processing costs, and your return address. Allow at least 6 weeks for the permit to return to you before you leave.

The cat or dog must then be certified by a registered veterinarian to be free of internal and external parasites, which document must then be certified by a Costa Rican consul. The pet must also be up-to-date and certified in its rabies, distemper, hepatitis, parvovirus and leptospirosis vaccinations. The rabies shot must be not less than 30 days old and no older than three years.

If the animal arrives in Costa Rica without these documents, it could be quarantined, refused entry or destroyed. A month's grace period is allowed if the departure or arrival dates on the *Permiso de Importación* don't correspond with your trip's dates for some reason. Information on requirements for other animals is available from the above address or the Ministerio de Agricultura (tel: 31-2341).

People wishing to take cats and dogs out of Costa Rica must present a certificate from a registered Costa Rican veterinarian of a health examination and the animal's vaccination records to the Ministerio de Salud, where they will be stamped. They then go to the Banco Central for a *Permiso de Exportación* (export permit). This can be done up to 15 days before leaving the country.

Dogs are not regarded with the same affection as they are in North America and Europe, and are used as guards rather than as pets. If there is any scare of a rabies epidemic or the like, government agents go around feeding poisoned meat to dogs, especially in the countryside. Several friends have lost beloved pets in this way.

RECOMMENDED READING

Abrams, Harry. *Between Continents, Between Seas: Precolumbian Art of Costa Rica.* New York, Harry Abrams, Inc., 1981.

Bell, John. *Crisis in Costa Rica: The Revolution of 48.* Austin, The University of Texas Press, 1971.

Biesanz, Mavis, Richard and Karen. *The Costa Ricans.* Englewood Cliffs, NJ, Prentice-Hall, Inc. 1987.

Bonilla, Alexander. *La Situación Ambiental de Costa Rica.* San José, Ministerio de Cultura, Juventud y Deportes, 1985.

Boza, Mario. *The National Parks of Costa Rica.* San José, Editorial Heliconia, 1987, softbound, 112 pages, bilingual text, beautiful photographs.

Boza, Mario. *Costa Rica National Parks.* San José, Editorial Heliconia, 1988, hardbound, 271 pages, bilingual text, beautiful photographs.

Bradt, Hilary. *Backpacking in Mexico and Central America.* Cambridge, MA, Bradt Enterprises, 1982.

Carr, Archie. *The Windward Road.* Gainesville Florida State University Press, 1979.

Cornelius, Stephen E. *The Sea Turtles of Santa Rosa National Park.* San José, Fundación de Parques Nacionales, 1985.

DeVries, Philip, *The Butterflies of Costa Rica*, Princeton University Press, 1987, 327 pp., 50 color plates.

Gallo and Mayfield, *The Rivers of Costa Rica*, color photos, maps, hydrographic tables, 1988.

Glassman, Paul. *Costa Rica.* Passport Press, Box 596, Moscow, Vt. 19890.

Golcher Valverde, Federico et al. *Investors Guide to Costa Rica.* San José, Costa Rican-American Chamber of Commerce, 1985.

Gómez, Luis Diego. *Vegetación y Clima en Costa Rica,* San José, UNED. 2 volumes, 21 maps, 1987.

Janzen, Daniel, Editor, *Costa Rican Natural History.* Chicago, University of Chicago Press, 1983.

Mena, Ramón, *Costa Rica*, 130 photos, San José, 1988.

Moser, Don. *Central American Jungles.* Time-Life Books, Inc., 1975.

Palmer, Paula. *What Happen, A Folk History of Costa Rica's Talamanca Coast.* San José, Ecodesarrollos, 1977.

Palmer, Paula. *Wa'apin Man.* Editorial Costa Rica, 1986.

Perry, Donald. *Life Above the Jungle Floor,* New York, Simon and Schuster, 1986. 170 pages, index, 52 color photos.

Searby, Ellen, *The Costa Rica Traveler.* Windham Bay Press, Box 34283, Juneau, AK 99803, 1987.

Skutch, Alexander F., University Press of Texas: *Parent Birds and their Young; Birds of Tropical America; Life Ascending* University of California Press: *A Naturalist on a Tropical Farm; Nature through Tropical Windows* University Presses of Florida: *The Imperative Call* University of Iowa Press: *Helpers at Birds' Nests*, 1987 Ibis Publishing Co, Santa Monica, CA, *Life of the Woodpecker* Crown Publishers: *The Life of the Hummingbird*

Stiles, Gary. *Field Guide to the Birds of Costa Rica,* Cornell University Press, Ithaca, NY, 1988.

Young, Allan. *Costa Rica: Nature, Peace and Prosperity on the Rich Coast.* Milwaukee, WI, Interamerican Research Corp., 1984.

Young, Allan. *Field Guide to the Natural History of Costa Rica.* Trejos Hermanos, San José, 1983.

Periodicals:

The Costa Rica Report. Published monthly. Apdo. 6283, 1000 San José, CR.

Mesoamérica. Published monthly by the Institute for Central American Studies, Apdo. 300, 1002 San José, Costa Rica.

The Tico Times. Published weekly. Apdo 4632, San José. (22-8952, 22-0040).

Video:

1 hour color VHS videotape about CR, $30. Cota International, PO Box 5042, New York, NY 10185.

INDEX

242

MAP OF DOWNTOWN SAN JOSE

Bus Terminals

HORIZONTES
Nature Adventures

Explore

Costa Rica's famous National Parks and Reserves. Visit Cloud and Rainforests at Monteverde and Corcovado National Park.

Discover

Manuel Antonio's spectacular beaches or take a scenic boat ride on the canals of Tortuguero.

Experience

one of our nature tours including whitewater rafting, bicycle tours and day trips to nearby parks and reserves. Call: 22-20-22 or visit us at Edificio Cristal 2nd floor, Ave. 1, Calles 1 and 3.

HORIZONTES NATURE ADVENTURES
P.O. Box 1780-1002, P. Estudiantes, San José, Costa Rica.
Télex 3534 HORI CR. Fax (506) 55-4513

248